THE DIVE SITES OF
THE MALDIVES

**SAM HARWOOD
AND ROB BRYNING**

Series Consultant: Nick Hanna

PASSPORT BOOKS
NTC/Contemporary Publishing Company

Sam Harwood and Rob Bryning co-own Maldives Scuba Tours and have spent the last ten years running live-aboard dive boats in the Maldives. They have extensive experience of diving the region.

This edition published in 1998 by
Passport Books
An imprint of NTC/Contemporary Publishing Company
4255 West Touhy Avenue, Lincolnwood (Chicago), Illinois, 60646-1975
U.S.A.

Copyright © 1998 in text: Sam Harwood
Copyright © 1998 in Underwater Photography (by Jack Jackson): New Holland Publishers (UK) Ltd
Copyright © 1998 in The Marine Environment: New Holland Publishers (UK) Ltd
Copyright © 1998 in Health and Safety: New Holland Publishers (UK) Ltd
Copyright © 1998 in photographs: Sam Harwood and Rob Bryning (except individual photographers as credited below)
Copyright © 1998 in artwork and cartography: New Holland Publishers (UK) Ltd
Copyright © 1998: New Holland Publishers (UK) Ltd

All rights reserved. No part of this publication may be reproduced, stored in a retrieval system, or transmitted, in any form or by any means, electronic, mechanical, photocopying, recording, or otherwise, without the prior written permission of NTC/Contemporary Publishing Company.

International Standard Book Number: 0-8442-4848-7
Library of Congress Catalog Card Number: 97-75810

First published in the UK in 1998 by
New Holland Publishers (UK) Ltd
London • Cape Town • Sydney • Singapore

Project development: Charlotte Parry-Crooke
Series editor: Pete Duncan
Copy editor: Paul Barnett
Design concept: Philip Mann, ACE Ltd
Design/cartography: William Smuts
Cover design: ML Design

Reproduction by Hirt and Carter, South Africa
Printed and bound in Singapore by Tien Wah Press (Pte) Ltd

Photographic Acknowledgements:
All photographs by Sam Harwood and Rob Bryning except: Phil Barthropp 41, 55 top, 61, 67 bottom, 71, 89, 123 bottom, 129, 137 bottom, 142 top right, 145, 149, 160c, 161e; Nick Hanna 31 top, 73, 74, 139; James Jackson 19, 92.

Front cover: *Author Sam Harwood with squirrelfish, anthias and corals.*
Front cover inset: *South Malé Atoll seen from the northwest.*
Spine: *Honeycomb moray eel.*
Back cover: *Swirling school of blue-lined snapper.*
Title page: *Feeding* Tubastrea *at night.*
Contents page: *Gantry of the* Skipjack *in Faadhippolhu Atoll.*

The author and publisher have made every effort to ensure that the information in this book was correct when the book went to press; they accept no responsibility for any loss, injury, or inconvenience sustained by any person using this book.

AUTHORS' ACKNOWLEDGEMENTS

Over the years of running Maldives Scuba Tours and the MV *Keema* we have met many people from around the world who have, in their own way, helped us to learn more about the Maldives. We cannot begin to mention them all but special thanks should go to:

- Gilla Harwood who is the backbone of our office and Rod Heath who has provided hours of technical support
- Midge and Ray for all their loving support and encouragement
- The crew of the MV *Keema* old and new
- Chas Anderson, Sue Butress and Liz Wood who, between them, have great enthusiasm and knowledge of the Maldivian marine environment
- Rainer Schaetz who has diligently and patiently supported us in Malé
- Elaine Brodie who has always helped us and welcomed us to the Brodie Guest House
- Our team of dive guides Carl Nicholls, Nizaaru and Rahman
- Phil Barthropp for his sense of humour and loyalty
- Our customers and agents and especially Gordon Taylor and May Leng who are our greatest ambassadors
- Robert, Hyke, Axel and Marc from Subaqua Reisen
- Abjee, Athif and Ibre from Eslire Maldives
- John and Elizabeth Allen and their fish curries
- Jose from Eurodivers
- Helmut and Barbara, Stefan, Kimmo, Herwarth, Eric and Rosie
- Shaheen and Shaheeda for being good friends
- Mohammed Ali for his smile
- Leuro and his perfect spaghetti
- Ismail Waheed for his hard work in the workshop

PUBLISHERS' ACKNOWLEDGEMENTS

The publishers gratefully acknowledge the generous assistance during the compilation of this book of the following: Nick Hanna for his involvement in developing the series and consulting throughout and Dr Elizabeth M Wood for acting as Marine Biological Consultant and contributing to The Marine Environment. Special thanks also go to Ocean Leisure, London.

CONTENTS

HOW TO USE THIS BOOK *6*
INTRODUCTION TO
    THE MALDIVES *9*
TRAVELLING TO AND IN
    THE MALDIVES *17*
DIVING AND SNORKELLING
    IN THE MALDIVES *25*

NORTH MALÉ (KAAFU) *35*
    Northern Area *38*
    Southern Area *46*

SOUTH MALÉ (KAAFU) *61*

FELIDHOO (VAAVU) AND
MULAKU (MEEMU) *75*
    Felidhoo (Vaavu) *77*
    Mulaku (Meemu) *88*

ADDU (SEENU) *93*

SOUTH AND NORTH NILANDHOO
(DHAALU AND FAAFU) *99*

ARI (ALIFU) *105*
    Southern Area *107*
    Northern Area *118*

SOUTH AND NORTH
MAALHOSMADULU
(BAA AND RAA) *131*
    South Maalhosmadulu (Baa) *133*
    North Maalhosmadulu (Raa) *140*

FAADHIPPOLHU (LHAVIYANI) *145*

THE MARINE ENVIRONMENT *155*
UNDERWATER PHOTOGRAPHY *162*
HEALTH AND SAFETY FOR
    DIVERS *165*

BIBLIOGRAPHY *172*
INDEX *173*

FEATURES
Manta Rays *52*
Colour on the Reef *71*
Sharks of the Maldives *86*
Anemones and Clownfish *102*
Night Diving *128*
Traditional Fishing *150*

How to Use this Book

THE REGIONS
The dive sites included in this book are arranged within eight atoll regions: North and South Malé, Felidhoo and Mulaku, Addu, South and North Nilandhoo, Ari, South and North Maalhosmadulu, and Faadhippolhu. Regional introductions describe the key characteristics and features of these areas and provide background information on climate, the environment, points of interest, and advantages and disadvantages of diving in the locality.

THE MAPS
A map is included near the front of each regional or subregional section, to identify the location of the dive sites described and to provide other useful information for divers and snorkellers. Although certain reefs are indicated, the maps do not set out to provide detailed nautical information, such as exact reef contours. In general the maps show: the locations of the dive sites, indicated by white numbers in red boxes corresponding to those placed at the start of each dive site description; the locations of key access points to the sites (ports, beach resorts and so on); reefs and wrecks. Each site description gives details of how to access the dive site. (Note: the border round the maps is not a scale bar.)

MAP LEGEND

THE DIVE SITE DESCRIPTIONS
Within the geographical sections are the descriptions of each region's premier dive sites. Each site description starts with a number (to enable the site to be located on the corresponding map), a star-rating and a selection of key symbols, as shown opposite. (Note that the anchor symbol used for live-aboards is merely symbolic: no boat should ever drop anchor over a reef.)

Crucial practical details (on location, access, conditions, typical visibility and minimum and maximum depths) precede the description of the site, its marine life, and special points of interest. In these entries, 'typical visibility' assumes good conditions.

THE STAR-RATING SYSTEM

Each site has been awarded a star-rating, with a maximum of five red stars for diving and five blue stars for snorkelling.

Diving			*Snorkelling*	
★★★★★	first class		☆☆☆☆☆ first class	
★★★★	highly recommended		☆☆☆☆ highly recommended	
★★★	good		☆☆☆ good	
★★	average		☆☆ average	
★	poor		☆ poor	

THE SYMBOLS

The symbols placed at the start of each site description provide a quick reference to crucial information pertinent to individual sites.

Can be done by diving	Best dived in the southwest monsoon (May–November)
Can be reached by resort dive boat	Best dived in the northeast monsoon (December–April)
Can be reached by live-aboard boat	Good in all seasons
	Can be done by snorkelling
Shore dive	Suitable for all levels of diver

THE REGIONAL DIRECTORIES

A regional directory, which will help you plan and make the most of your trip, is included at the end of each regional section. Here you will find, where relevant, practical information on how to get to an area, where to stay and eat, and available dive facilities. Local non-diving highlights are also described, with suggestions for excursions.

OTHER FEATURES

At the start of the book you will find practical details and tips about travelling to and in the area, as well as a general introduction to the region. Also provided is a wealth of information about the general principles and conditions of diving in the area. Throughout the book there are features and small fact, panels on topics of interest to divers and snorkellers. At the end of the book are sections on the marine environment (including coverage of marine life, conservation and codes of practice) and underwater photography and video. Also to be found here is information on health, safety and first aid, and a guide to marine creatures to look out for when diving in the Maldives.

INTRODUCTION TO THE MALDIVES

Through the centuries, seafarers plying the Indian Ocean have regarded the reefs of the Maldives as a treacherous area to be avoided at all costs. The early references made to the Maldives passed on the same clear message that, despite the islands' natural beauty, there was great risk involved in navigating through and even near the archipelago. Still, today, ships stay well clear of Maldivian waters, and this is one reason why the Maldives remain unspoiled. The irony is that the very reefs which kept the invaders at bay have become the jewels in the Maldivian crown. There is no doubt that the diving in the Maldives is among the best on the planet.

THE COUNTRY

The Republic of the Maldives is a magnificent chain of tiny islands stretching 868km (539 miles) across the Indian Ocean, with the northernmost island at 7°06'30"N and the southernmost island just crossing the equator at 0°42'30"S. At its widest point the country is 130km (79 miles) from west to east. Set amidst a huge expanse of ocean, islands come and go as the winds, waves and currents build and erode them, and the exact number varies according to the season and method of classification.

The islands are geographically grouped into ring-shaped reefs called atolls. An atoll encloses a central lagoon with a flat, sandy bottom at a relatively shallow depth of 35–85m (115–280ft). Around its perimeter runs an outer reef, intermittently broken by deep channels that allow oceanic water to flow in and out of the central lagoon. Many of the islands are in fact emergent portions of the outer reefs, although inside the atoll there are also numerous smaller ring-shaped reefs and islands. The atolls vary in size and in the number of islands they contain. One of the smallest, Thoddoo, has just one island and is about 2km (1 mile) in diameter. The largest, Huvadhoo in the south, is a giant 74km (45 miles) by 65km (40 miles) and contains about 250 islands.

The 26 atolls of the Maldives comprise approximately 1200 islands. Of these only some 200 are officially classed as locally inhabited islands, though this figure does not take into

---

Opposite: *Lily Beach on the outer rim of Ari Atoll is a typically idyllic Maldivian resort island.*
Above: *Maldivians are devout Sunni Muslims and learn to read the Koran at an early age.*

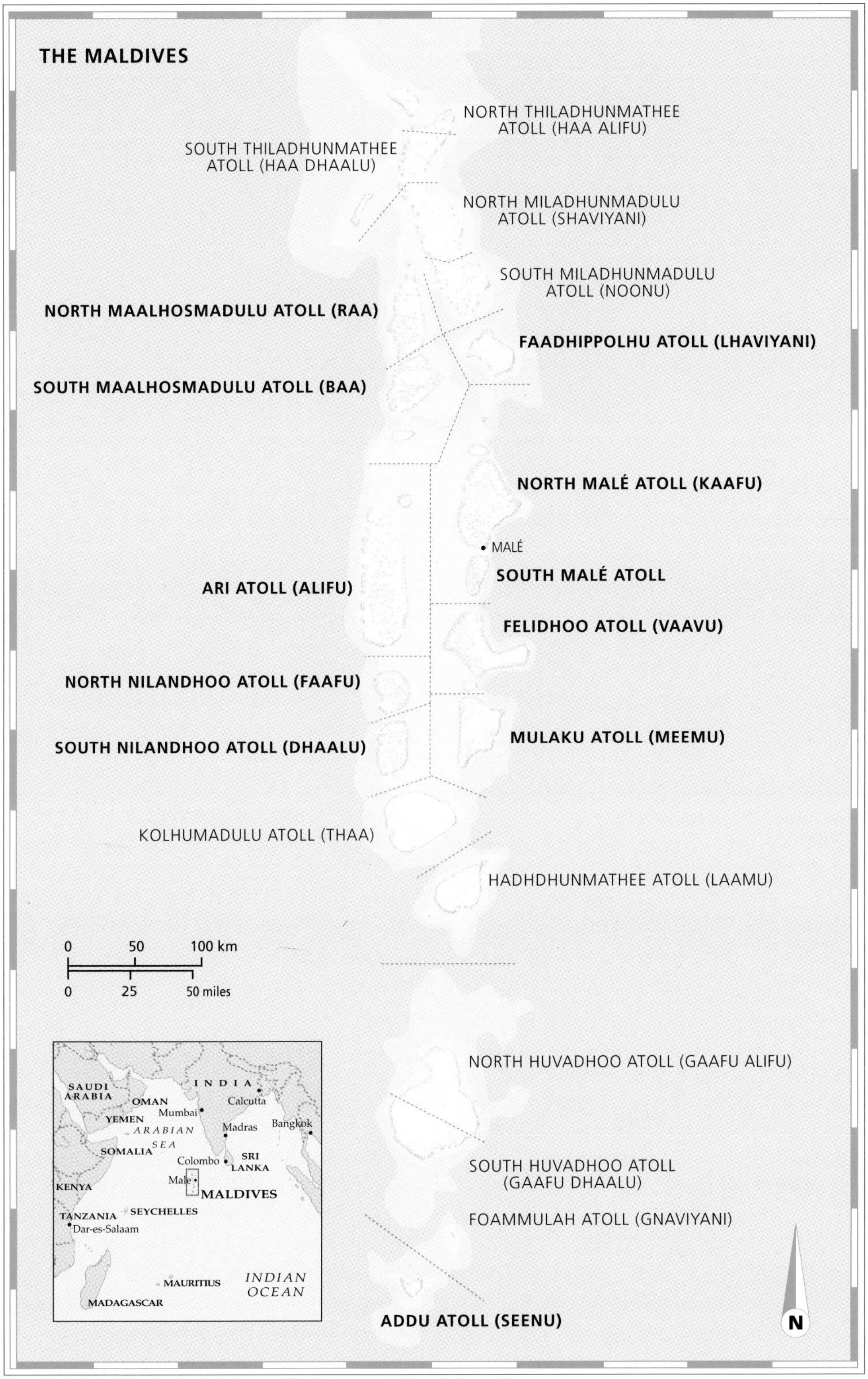

THE MALDIVES

NORTH THILADHUNMATHEE ATOLL (HAA ALIFU)

SOUTH THILADHUNMATHEE ATOLL (HAA DHAALU)

NORTH MILADHUNMADULU ATOLL (SHAVIYANI)

SOUTH MILADHUNMADULU ATOLL (NOONU)

NORTH MAALHOSMADULU ATOLL (RAA)

FAADHIPPOLHU ATOLL (LHAVIYANI)

SOUTH MAALHOSMADULU ATOLL (BAA)

NORTH MALÉ ATOLL (KAAFU)

• MALÉ

SOUTH MALÉ ATOLL

ARI ATOLL (ALIFU)

FELIDHOO ATOLL (VAAVU)

NORTH NILANDHOO ATOLL (FAAFU)

SOUTH NILANDHOO ATOLL (DHAALU)

MULAKU ATOLL (MEEMU)

KOLHUMADULU ATOLL (THAA)

HADHDHUNMATHEE ATOLL (LAAMU)

```
0        50      100 km
|----|----|----|
0       25       50 miles
```

SAUDI ARABIA
INDIA
OMAN
Calcutta
YEMEN
Mumbai
ARABIAN SEA
Madras
Bangkok
SOMALIA
Colombo
SRI LANKA
KENYA
Malé
MALDIVES
TANZANIA
SEYCHELLES
Dar-es-Salaam
MAURITIUS
INDIAN OCEAN
MADAGASCAR

NORTH HUVADHOO ATOLL (GAAFU ALIFU)

SOUTH HUVADHOO ATOLL (GAAFU DHAALU)

FOAMMULAH ATOLL (GNAVIYANI)

ADDU ATOLL (SEENU)

N

account islands which have been developed as tourist resorts. Some 80 islands have been turned into resorts since 1972, and more are in the process of construction.

The distinction between locally inhabited islands and resort islands is an important one. Maldivian inhabited islands are partly closed to visitors, as a measure to safeguard the islanders' devout Muslim lifestyle from foreign influence; the government is determined to restrict the impact of tourism on the country's resources.

CLIMATE

The Maldives is in the monsoon belt of the northern Indian Ocean, and experiences a fairly complex weather pattern. Many people think of monsoons as periods of high rainfall, but in fact the wind is the key factor. There are two seasons in the Maldives: a dry northeast monsoon (called *iruvai* by the Maldivians) and a wet southwest monsoon (*hulhagu*). From May to November the prevailing winds are from the southwest and bring an average of 215mm (8.5in) of rainfall and 208 hours of sunshine per month. Around mid-December the winds veer to the northeast and, with the change in direction, bring a much drier climate. Rainfall averages 75mm (3in) per month in this season, and the average monthly sunshine is 256 hours.

Maldivian days are hot and humid throughout the year, with temperatures of about 25–30°C (72–80°F) and humidities of 60–80%. There is not much of a difference in terms of sunshine between the seasons but a huge difference in the amount of rainfall – just as in any tropical country. When it rains in the Maldives it rains hard, usually for just a short time.

The Maldives is sometimes affected by cyclones passing through the Bay of Bengal; the most likely times for these are April/May and again in October/November. However, these storms seldom pass close to the Maldives and, when they do, the effects are generally short-lived. The area either side of the equator is well known to mariners as the Doldrums on account of its weak winds.

The weather pattern has a strong influence on the currents. During the northeast monsoon, ocean currents are driven through the atoll channels from the northeast; conversely, during the southwest monsoon, they flow into the atolls from the southwest. These patterns have enormous significance for diving (see page 26).

TOURISM

White sandy beaches, beautiful turquoise lagoons and stunning diving inspired the opening of the first resort, Kurumba Village in North Malé Atoll, in 1972. Numerous other resorts were subsequently opened in the atolls of South Maalhosmadulu, Faadhippolhu, North Malé, South Malé, Felidhoo, Ari and Addu, making tourism one of the most important trade sectors of the Maldivian economy. In 1995 some 325,000 tourists visited the Maldives. In 1997 the government announced the proposed development of 14 new resort islands, bringing the atolls of North Maalhosmadulu, South and North Nilandhoo and Mulaku into the tourist frame.

ATOLL NAMES

Location names in the Maldives can be bewildering. To complicate matters, two systems apply for the main atolls: a geographical atoll name and an administrative grouping. North and South Malé, for instance, are separate geographical atolls, but combine to form one administrative district (Kaafu). In this book geographical atoll names have been used foremost, with the administrative name following in brackets where appropriate:

• North Malé (Kaafu)
• South Malé (Kaafu)
• Felidhoo (Vaavu)
• Mulaku (Meemu)
• Addu (Seenu)
• South Nilandhoo (Dhaalu)
• North Nilandhoo (Faafu)
• Ari (Alifu)
• South Maalhosmadulu (Baa)
• North Maalhosmadulu (Raa)
• Faadhippolhu (Lhaviyani)

FACT FILE

Area: 90,000 sq km (34,750 sq miles)
Population: 249,280
Language: Dhivehi
Religion: 100% Islam
Total no. of islands: approx. 1200
Locally inhabited islands: 202
Designated resort islands: 89

Tourism has brought with it a strengthening of the country's infrastructure, the growth of support industries and the revival of traditional handicrafts. On the other hand it has also added to the pressure on the environment. Since the late 1980s the government has been aware of the need to minimize both the environmental and cultural impact of tourism, and has tried to ensure that both elements are managed as effectively as possible. Tourists must be accommodated only on registered tourist islands or on safari boats, and regulations govern visits to uninhabited islands and locally inhabited fishing islands. The outer islands are still relatively unaffected by the tourist industry, however, and life there continues as it has done for hundreds of years.

THE PEOPLE AND THEIR HISTORY

The Maldives has been a crossroads for sea traders for many centuries, and nothing reflects this more than the faces of the Maldivian people. Not much is known of the early history of this island people, as no records are available until about the 12th century. However, the language and some archaeological finds indicate that the first settlers in the Maldives were Dravidians from southern India and Buddhist Sinhalese from Sri Lanka. In the 12th century Arab traders making their way to and from Malacca and China were among early travellers to land on the islands, either intentionally – to take food and water from the locals – or unintentionally, when shipwrecked on the reefs.

Contact with Arabs led to the conversion of the Maldivian people from Buddhism to Islam. The earliest records date from this time and show that from 1153 the country was ruled by 89 sultans and two sultanas. By the 16th century the Maldives was a significant trading nation, and had become the target of numerous pirate attacks by the Malabars of India.

In 1558 the Portuguese successfully fought to occupy the northern islands, including the capital, Malé. They remained for 15 years until three Maldivian brothers combined their armies and eventually, in 1573, forced them out. This is the only sustained length of time that the archipelago has found itself occupied by a foreign power.

As supremacy over the Indian Ocean passed from the Dutch to the British, trade between Britain and her colonies increased. Safe navigation of the Indian Ocean became of paramount importance, and in 1829 Commander Robert Moresby was commissioned to survey both the Maldives and the Laccadives, further to the north. His work was not published until 1837, but the Admiralty charts which Moresby drew up have remained in use ever since – they are still the main source of hydrographic data for yachtsmen and navigators. In 1887 the sultan signed a treaty with the British Governor of Ceylon (Sri Lanka) conferring upon the Maldives the status of British Protectorate – on condition that the British refrained from interfering in local affairs and administration.

At the start of World War II the British built an airstrip on the island of Gan in Addu Atoll. An RAF base was established on the island, which became the main staging post for troop movements on the Indian subcontinent and in

BODU BERU AND BANDIYAA JEHUN

Folk music is an important part of Maldivian island life and all the islands have their own *bodu beru* performers who come together for special island festivals. *Bodu beru*, which means 'big drum', is performed by 15 men including at least three drummers and a lead singer. The songs, usually of heroism or romance, always begin with a slow beat, building up to a wild crescendo. *Bandiyaa jehun* is performed by young girls and is said to be an adaptation of the Indian Pot Dance. The girls sing to the rhythm of their rings beating on the pots; the songs are about love or tell stories of island life.

the Far East. The base remained operational until 1965, when the Maldives became fully independent.

Today, the Maldives is a democratic republic, with President Maumoon Abdul Gayoom at the helm. There is no party political system in the Maldives: the citizens' Majlis (Parliament) comprises 48 members, two elected from each atoll and eight nominated by the president. The president himself is nominated by the citizens' Majlis and elected by public referendum for a renewable five-year period; the president then appoints his own cabinet.

The people of the Maldives are devout Sunni Muslims and the Islamic faith is fundamental to their everyday lives. Islam is practised in a relatively liberal form; women are allowed to work and are not forced to conceal their faces as in many Middle Eastern countries. Nevertheless, all Maldivians are taught to read and recite the Koran, and prayers are held five times a day. At prayer time all shops and offices close for fifteen minutes, as Maldivians follow the call of the *mudeem*, or muezzin, to the mosque for prayer. During Ramadan, the ninth month of the Islamic calendar, people fast from sunrise to sunset, and all cafés and restaurants are closed during the day.

MALDIVIAN DIVORCE

If a Maldivian husband wishes to divorce his wife he need only say "I divorce you" three times and write a short note to the island's administrative office to let them know. They say that the Maldives has the highest rate of divorce in the world and eight out of ten people have been divorced at least once. At one stage the government had to introduce a law allowing the same couple to remarry only three times. It is much more difficult for a woman to instigate divorce; she must take her case to court and prove adultery or cruelty by her husband.

Below: *Fishermen jockey for position at the edge of Malé harbour, the colourful centre of commerce of the Maldives.*

BETEL NUTS

A favourite pastime of many Maldivians, both young and old, is to chew betel nut and gossip about their day. The nut is carefully sliced and wrapped in the large, green betel leaf together with a clove and a small portion of coral lime. The whole package is popped into the mouth and chewed intently. The betel nut has a deep red juice that can stain teeth and mouths if it is chewed too much, but is said to aid digestion and act as a mild narcotic.

LOCAL BIRD NAMES

Grey heron	Maakanaa
Indian house crow	Kaalhu
Koel bird (male)	Kaalhu koveli
Koel bird (female)	Dindin koveli
Fairy tern	Kandhu wallu dooni
White-tailed tropic bird	Dandhifulhi dooni

Below: *Migratory birds rise from an uninhabited island.*

FLORA, FAUNA AND AGRICULTURE

Although there is little moisture-holding capacity in the coral-sand-based soil of these small islands, the terrestrial flora and fauna are not as sparse as one might expect.

The most important species in the economy of the Maldives is the coconut palm, the principal agricultural product of the country and an important contributor to the Maldivian diet. The leaves provide material for thatching and basket-making, the coir is used for rope-making, the oil has many uses, and the wood is used for boat-building.

Breadfruit, bananas, mangoes, papayas and lime trees are also commonly cultivated. Vegetables grown include eggplants, chillies, pumpkins, water melons, cucumbers and sweet potatoes, though none of these vegetables is produced commercially, farming being done entirely on a subsistence basis. Some of these plants were deliberately introduced by the government to support the island farmers, but most came to the Maldives as seeds carried in the ocean currents from India and Sri Lanka.

To visitors the most noticeable plants are the brightly flowering species of purple bougainvillaea and the scented frangipanni and jasmine.

Many of the insects remain to be formally identified, but it is known that there are at least 67 species of butterfly. The armoured rhinoceros beetle is common, and has been

Above: *Papayas grow readily enough to be cultivated by islanders on a commercial basis.*

responsible for so much damage to crops, particularly coconut palms, that the government has resorted to infecting some beetles with a virus as a form of biological control.

The reptile life is interesting and includes many geckoes and lizards, which are welcomed by the islanders, as they control the insect population. Two non-poisonous species of snakes, *Typhlops braminus* and *Lycodon aulicus capucinus*, are found fairly frequently, as is a short-headed species of frog.

About 115 bird species frequent the Maldives, most of which are migratory visitors. Of the small number permanently resident the most noticeable is the Indian house crow (which is viewed as a pest) and the koel bird. There are 13 species of heron, two of which – the Maldivian pond heron (*Ardeola grayii phillipsi*) and the Maldivian little heron (*Butorides striatus didii*) – are thought to be indigenous. The commonest heron seen in the Maldives is the grey heron, which you can often spot fishing in the lagoons and on the shallower coral reefs. The fairy tern, among the prettiest terns, is found only in the southern atolls. If you find yourself being dive-bombed on an uninhabited island by a white-tailed bird, then you are lucky enough to be seeing a tropic bird. This is an oceanic species which comes to the islands only to nest and can be quite aggressive.

As the sun sets you may see flying foxes, which come out to feed at dusk; they hang in colonies during the daylight hours. This is one of two bat species found in the Maldives – the other, *Pteropus hypomelanus maris*, is very rare.

LANDFINDERS

It is thought that the house crow was introduced to the Maldives by early seafarers who carried the birds to check the proximity and direction of the nearest land. The crows would be released, and if they circled and returned to the ship the mariners might assume there was no land nearby. If the bird flew off in one direction, that was to be the direction of their landfall. The crows have become a pest on the fishing islands as they steal crops and drying fish stocks. Islanders have tried to control them by poisoning and shooting, with some success.

TRAVELLING
TO AND IN
THE MALDIVES

Most passengers come to the Maldives by air. Malé International Airport, on Hulhule Island, is served by a small number of international scheduled and charter airlines. The main scheduled carriers are Air Lanka (UL), Indian Airlines (IC), Singapore Airlines (SQ), Emirate Airways (EK), Pakistan International Airlines (PIA) and the national carrier, Air Maldives (MH). International charter flights arrive from Italy, Switzerland, the UK, Germany, South Africa, Finland and the Far East, but it is not always possible to book these on a seat-only basis. Flight times are about 45 minutes from Colombo, Sri Lanka, four hours from Singapore and 13 hours from London. There are no direct services from North America. The airport island is a ten-minute boat-ride from the capital, Malé.

Although there are no official international sea routes into the Maldives, some cruise ships call in at North Malé Atoll. Yachtsmen can clear themselves into the country at Malé, and will then be given permits to sail in North and South Malé atolls. The crews of yachts entering the country for the first time should contact the customs office (tel 323413/fax 322633) three days before arrival; the requisite paperwork with the Maldives Port Health Authority and the Department of Immigration and Emigration can be dealt with after arrival.

Tourists with pre-booked accommodation are usually asked on arrival to give their flight tickets to the representative of the relevant resort island so their return flight can be reconfirmed for them in Malé. The tickets are returned on the day of departure. There is a US$15 airport departure tax, payable outside the departure building prior to check-in.

HEALTH
Recommended vaccinations are against cholera and typhoid; a fresh tetanus shot is also advisable. Vaccinations are not required unless you are travelling from an area infected by yellow fever (in which case you need a vaccination certificate). Malaria is not much of a problem in the Maldives: a few cases have been recorded in the outer atolls, but none in the

Opposite: *A lengthy jetty extending across the lagoon is a necessity on many atoll islands.*
Above: *The Maldivian crew of a live-aboard boat prepare to ship anchor.*

CONSULATES AND HIGH
COMMISSIONS

- British Consular Correspondent
  tel 311205
- Royal Danish Consulate
  tel 315175
- Honorary Consulate of Germany
  tel 317515
- Royal Norwegian Consulate
  tel 315176
- Swedish Consulate
  tel 315174

AIRLINE REPRESENTATIVES

Air Maldives is the ground handling
agent for all airlines arriving into Malé.
Ticket enquiries and reconfirmations
should be made by phoning these
numbers:

Air Lanka	tel 328456
Air Maldives	tel 314808
Emirates	tel 314805
Indian Airlines	tel 314807
Pakistan International	tel 314809
Singapore Airlines	tel 314803

tourist atolls. There are, nevertheless, plenty of mosquitoes, and some can give a big bite – make sure you pack plenty of insect repellent.

Generally the Maldives is a healthy country to visit. Your most likely cause of illness is drinking untreated water. If you are visiting a locally inhabited island, do not drink tap water; bottled water is available from all the islands you are likely to visit. If you can't get hold of bottled water, ask your hosts for *bo feng*, which is drinking water collected from rainfall. Beware of the tropical sun; sunstroke and sunburn are the most common tourist ailments.

Most importantly, make sure you carry a good travel-insurance policy. Medical standards in the Maldives are generally quite poor, and the private clinics available in Malé are expensive.

If you do fall ill, tell the resort management; they will either organize a visit to an island where there is a doctor or have you evacuated back to Malé, where there are medical facilities. A few resort islands have resident doctors.

For diving-related incidents there is the Hyperbaric Treatment Centre on Bandos Island Resort, North Malé Atoll, 8km (5 miles) from the airport (tel 440088). For more details on diving-related health problems, check the information in 'Health and Safety for Divers' at the end of the book.

VISAS AND IMMIGRATION

Visas are issued on arrival. Most travellers are given a 30-day visa; Italians are given 90 days. A special application must be made if you need an extension of your visa: you must fill in an extension form and supply two passport-style photographs, making your submission well before the expiry of your first visa. With luck, your island or boat representative can organize this for you. All tourists must have a valid passport, onward or return airline ticket, or funds to purchase such a ticket, as well as sufficient funds to cover their expenses during their stay.

CUSTOMS FORMALITIES

Customs formalities are usually quick and trouble-free. There are strict laws forbidding the import of pornography, alcohol, pork (and all products containing pork), narcotics, poisons and hazardous chemicals, firearms and explosives. There are also firm regulations concerning alcohol in the Maldives and, though available for consumption on resort islands, alcohol cannot be privately imported. If you are carrying alcohol in your luggage the customs officials will confiscate it and issue a receipt; on production of the receipt you can get your alcohol back when you check through customs on the way home.

If you bring in any electrical goods, the customs officer may want to write the serial number and details into your passport. You will be required to show the item as you clear through customs on your departure, failing which you must pay duty. Divers carrying a large amount of photographic equipment should make a packing list of serial numbers and details before arrival.

When leaving the Maldives, note that the export of black coral and black-coral products, triton and trochus shells, pearl oysters, turtle shells and products and all stony corals is strictly forbidden.

MONEY

The Maldivian unit of currency is the Rufiyaa (divided into 100 laari), but it is rarely used in resorts. Most tourist transactions in the resorts, locally inhabited islands and Malé take place in US dollars, and many resorts actually refuse to take Rufiyaa. Avoid converting money into the local currency, as you will not be allowed to convert it all back if you fail to use it. The best currency to have is the US dollar, but resorts will also accept Sterling and the Deutschmark, which are usually converted to US dollars first to calculate a rate of exchange. Most resorts cash travellers' cheques and accept major credit cards, but some surcharge for this. Occasionally a resort's affiliated dive school may need to be paid separately; the dive school may not take credit cards, so check with your tour operator before you set off. Mastercard and Visa are widely accepted at resorts; American Express is sometimes welcomed. Check the Regional Directories in this book for further details.

A number of banks in Malé will cash travellers' cheques into US dollars, and also exchange Rufiyaa for US dollars. If you wish to cash Sterling for Rufiyaa you must go to the Maldives Monetary Authority, which will convert the money to US dollars first – thus taking a double commission. Cash advances can be obtained on a credit card if you go to the relevant agent, who will issue a cheque that can be cashed at one of the Malé banks; this may take some time, so prepare to be patient. Banks are open Sunday–Thursday 09.30–16.00. There is a bank at the airport.

Below: *The locally inhabited island of Guraidhoo in South Malé Atoll is a popular tourist excursion.*

DHIVEHI LANGUAGE

The language of the Maldivians is called Dhivehi. It is believed to have developed from an Indo-Iranian language, displaying strong links with Sinhala (from Sri Lanka) and also with Sanskrit from northwest India. The script in which Dhivehi is written, Thaana, runs from left to right and is similar to Arabic. These days English is taught in all schools and many of the young children speak and write very good English.

GETTING AROUND

Maldives resorts are very popular and it is usually necessary to make a booking in advance, so it is generally a pre-booked resort that arranges for your transfer from the international airport. There are several ways of getting to the resorts. Transfer may be in a traditional local boat (*dhoani*), a speedboat, a helicopter or a seaplane, depending on how far away the resort island is. These services are not run on a scheduled basis, but connect with incoming flights whenever a resort knows it has pre-booked guests arriving. Resorts that are more than 40km (25 miles) from the airport tend to use either the helicopter service operated by Hummingbird Helicopters (tel 325708/fax 323161) or the seaplane operated by Maldivian Air Taxi (tel 315201/fax 315203); the latter's Twin Otters can land at most of the tourist resorts. Should you have the option, a transfer by air is worthwhile and highly enjoyable: if the day is clear, this is a great way to see the atolls – be sure you have your camera ready! Usually the seaplanes tie up to a floating platform anchored within the protected waters of the lagoon. Bear in mind that the platforms have no protection from the rain.

If you wish to hop between resorts, you often need to return to the airport to pick up a transfer, even when the next island you want to visit is nearer to you than the airport. A very few boats run between the resort islands; you may have better luck with the helicopter or the seaplane.

Independent travel in the tourist area of the Maldives is possible, but is difficult and can be expensive. The government currently allows tourist travel within all the atolls containing resort islands. This is subject to the proviso that tourists stay overnight on resort islands (or Malé Island) only – or on a registered live-aboard boat – somewhat limiting the options available. If you want to stay overnight on a locally inhabited fishing island, or if you wish to visit an atoll outside the tourist zone, you must apply specially to the Ministry of Atoll Administration (Faashanaa Building, Marine Drive, Malé; tel 323920). In your application you must state the purpose of your visit, and also you must have a letter from a 'sponsor' – i.e., an inhabitant of the fishing island concerned. Even then, it is unlikely you will ever be given permission to *dive* outside the tourist atolls.

If you do obtain a permit to travel to islands outside the tourist area, there are regular supply vessels to all the outer atolls. These boats can be picked up in the Old Harbour area of Malé, outside the covered market. Alternatively you could travel by air: four Maldivian

---

USEFUL PHRASES

Dhivehi is a difficult language. Luckily most Maldivians speak excellent English and will be delighted to have the opportunity to practise their language skills. However, here are some phrases that you may find useful:

Hello/goodbye	*Salaam alekum*	Today	*Miadhu*	Four	*Hathareh*
How are you?	*Kihineh tah?*	Tomorrow	*Maadhan*	Five	*Faheh*
Good	*Rangalu*	One	*Eke*	Banana	*Donkeyo*
Bad	*Sakarah*	Two	*Dhey*	Shark	*Miyaru*
Thank you	*Shukriyaa*	Three	*Tineh*	Dolphin	*Kormas*

Above: *Motorized* dhoanis *with their distinctive traditional prow are a regular sight.*
Below: *A seaplane discharges its passengers on a pontoon.*

TIME DIFFERENCES	
Australia	- 5hrs
Germany	+ 4hrs
Netherlands	+ 4hrs
South Africa	+ 3hrs
UK (GMT)	+ 5hrs
United States (EST)	+10hrs
United Sates (WST)	+16hrs

airports are well served by the domestic airline, Air Maldives. North of Malé, there is another airport on Hanimaadhoo Island (South Thiladhunmathee Atoll), while to the south there are airports on the islands of Kadhdhoo (Hadhdhunmathee Atoll), Kaadedhdhuvaa (South Huvadhoo Atoll) and Gan (Addu Atoll).

The best way to see more of the Maldives – and enjoy the very best of the diving – is by live-aboard boat. A number of registered 'safari' boats operate charters throughout the year. In many cases you do not need to book the whole boat: you can book as an individual or couple joining another group. Private yachts, by contrast, are likely to be restricted to travelling within North and South Malé atolls unless they have special permission from the Ministry of Transport.

ELECTRICITY

Most resort islands use 220/240V AC, 50Hz. There is no standard socket type and sockets can be either the three-square-pin British type or the two-pin European type, so take an international adaptor or check with your tour operator beforehand. If your equipment is designed for a 110V supply you will certainly need a small transformer. On most resort islands the electricity supply is quite reliable, but it is worth packing a flashlight just in case.

Below: *Windsurfers and sometimes catamarans are available for hire on many of the resort islands.*

Above: *Accommodation ranges from luxury suites to simple bungalows, all within feet of the sea.*

TELECOMMUNICATIONS AND MAIL

The international code for telephoning to the Maldives is 960. The telephone system within the Maldives is very efficient, with international telephone communications (access code 00) available from all the resort islands. However, beware the cost of telephoning from your resort, as the charges are sometimes very high. Most of the locally inhabited islands within the tourist zone have telephones at the island administration office, and some of them also have public telephones outside the office. International calls can be made from these callboxes, although you need a phonecard. In Malé, person-to-person and reverse-charge (collect) calls can be made from the Dhiraagu Office at 19 Medhuziyaaraiy Magu, Malé, which is open 08.00–20.00 Sunday–Thursday and 08.00–18.00 Friday–Saturday and during public holidays. Overseas mail can be sent from the resort islands; it usually reaches its destination within 7–10 days.

CRITERIA FOR CHOOSING YOUR ISLAND

With over 80 resort islands, all little tropical paradises, it can be difficult to choose any particular one. One of the first decisions to make is whether you want to stay on a larger, noisier island with more facilities or a smaller, quieter island.

As a general rule, the diving is likely to be better from the smaller resorts, containing about 70 beds. If you are a keen diver and snorkeller, choose an island with a good house reef that is easily accessible from the accommodation. Try to find out whether night diving is allowed, and ask your tour operator about the policy of the dive school regarding shore diving. Check page 26 regarding weather patterns to help you decide if your island is located in the best place, diving-wise, for the season you are staying there.

DESIGNATED RESORT ISLANDS	
North Malé (Kaafu)	27 resort islands
South Malé (Kaafu)	16 resort islands
Felidhoo (Vaavu)	2 resort islands
Mulaku (Meemu)	2 resort islands
Addu (Seenu)	1 resort island
South Nilandhoo (Dhaalu)	2 resort islands
North Nilandhoo (Faafu)	1 resort island
Ari (Alifu)	27 resort islands
South Maalhosmadulu (Baa)	5 resort islands
North Maalhosmadulu (Raa)	1 resort island
Faadhippolhu (Lhaviyani)	5 resort islands

DIVING AND SNORKELLING IN THE MALDIVES

In the comparatively short time since tourism began here, the Maldives has rapidly gained recognition as one of the top diving destinations in the world. Yet even now, only a tiny part of the nation has been explored by divers; thousands of kilometres of reefs have still to yield up their long-garnered secrets.

Some 65 million years ago the islands of the Maldives were part of a huge volcanic mountain range. When the volcanoes ceased to be active they submerged, sinking at a rate slow enough that coral formations could grow on their rims. This coral growth eventually became the fringing reefs of the atolls. Recent surveys have discovered that the depth of coral on the fringing reefs is as much as 2100m (6400ft), a remarkable statistic when you consider a coral massif may grow just 2mm (0.08in) annually.

As the oceanic currents eroded the atolls' rims they created channels, and today these channels provide some extraordinary diving. The tides of the Indian Ocean flow in and out through the channels, and in so doing concentrate millions and millions of microscopic plant cells, tiny marine animals and larvae, collectively called plankton. This rich soup provides food for many of the reef's inhabitants. In turn, creatures further up the food chain are attracted from the ocean by the prospect of a good meal, and a rich and diverse marine community builds.

Inside most of the atolls is a complex formation of reefs. A number of these reefs are circular, enclosing a shallow lagoon, others irregular and shallowly submerged. All offer interesting and usually easy diving and excellent snorkelling. Some of the best diving is on submerged reefs called *thilas*; usually located in the middle of a channel, these rise from the atoll floor to within 10m (33ft) of the surface.

Reef life is prolific, with over 700 common fish species and many more still to be discovered and classified; invertebrate species are reckoned to be in their tens of thousands. For the sharp-eyed diver there are encounters with species like frogfish, leaf fish, ghost pipefish and a multitude of nudibranchs. Whether it's the sight of the awesome manta ray, being face-to-face with a grey reef shark or spotting a tiny, brightly coloured flatworm, the Maldives has it all.

Opposite: *The dive sites of the Maldives offer plenty of photographic opportunities.*
Above: *Some islands' house reefs can only be reached by boat, due to their distance from the shore.*

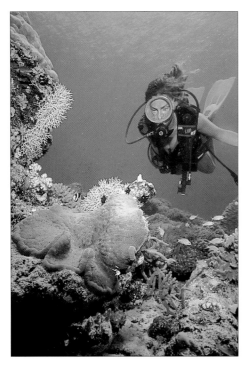

Above: *From May to November, sheltered sites inside the western rim of the atoll offer easy diving.*

THE DIVING SEASONS

Understanding the weather and currents in the Maldives is essential if you are to make the most of your diving.

As a general rule, in the months from May to November (southwest monsoon) you should try to choose a resort near or with access to dive sites on the west side of the atoll; from December to April (northeast monsoon) your resort should be situated near or have access to dive sites on the east side of the atoll. This ensures you enjoy the greatest variety of marine life and best visibility, as the currents bring clear water from the ocean according to the prevailing wind direction. The currents run from west to east during the southwest monsoon and east to west during the northeast monsoon.

THE SOUTHWEST SEASON

The diving on the west side of the atoll in the southwest season (*hulhagu*) is spectacular. You will regularly encounter large schools of pelagic fish like sharks, eagle rays and tuna.

Bear in mind that at this time of year there may be strong winds, ocean swells and rain, all of which can make conditions difficult for diving on exposed reefs. For this reason, most resorts on the west side also have a good selection of dive sites located within the atolls which are not affected by the strong winds. These sheltered areas, though they rarely feature large schools of pelagic species, are often more prolific in coral life than the ocean passes and can harbour a tremendous variety of reef fish, so offering excellent diving.

DHIVEHI REEF TERMS	
Falhu	a shallow reef rising up from the atoll floor and facing the inside of the atoll
Faro	a circular or elongated reef, rising up from the atoll sea bed, that forms inside the atoll lagoon or on the atoll perimeter
Faru	a circular reef that is exposed to the ocean and rises up from the ocean floor
Giri	a small area of coral, much smaller than a *thila*
Kandu	a break in the atoll rim connecting the waters of the atoll to the open sea
Thila	a coral reef just below the surface, much smaller than a *faro*, found inside the atoll; a *thila* makes a great dive site since you can often swim around in one dive

Another noticeable feature of the southwest season is that the water temperature is usually one or two degrees lower than the usual 28°C (82°F). This has an effect on both the behaviour of and sightings of marine life, particularly the grey reef sharks and hammerheads, which seem to congregate in larger numbers and in shallower water at this time of year.

On the eastern side of the atolls, the southwest season is the best time to see manta rays and whale sharks. Here your visibility is not so good, but this is compensated for by the wonderful experience of diving with mantas.

THE NORTHEAST SEASON

Known in Dhivehi as *iruvai*, or dry season, this is the Maldivian summer. The effect of the seasonal change on diving is dramatic. From November onward the currents begin to flow from the northeast, and by the beginning of January the Maldives has the most ferocious currents of the year. By-products are superb underwater visibility, plus lots of action in channels and on *thilas* on the eastern side of the atolls from the sharks and other pelagic species.

By the end of January the strength of the current begins to ease, the waters calm down and the surface of the sea is undisturbed by major wind or wave action. This is scenically the best time to visit the Maldives. The Doldrums continue through March, with easy diving and slack currents; the water surface resembles the face of a mirror. During April and into May the current begins to build and change direction. At this time large sperm whales, pilot whales and enormous schools of dolphins are often seen close to the atolls.

Throughout the northeast season, pelagic species such as sharks and jacks are to be found on the current points on the eastern side of the atoll. In addition there is usually a cornucopia of reef life. Manta rays and whale sharks, however, will only really be found on the west side during the northeast season.

It is this seasonal variation in sightings of mantas which makes the choice of diving complicated. While most sharks, barracuda and jackfish like to cruise the point of the current, mantas tend to be found at the back of the currents where the oceanic water is leaving the atoll. Ultimately, it might be said that the perfect divers' resort is one situated on the correct side of the atoll according to the prevailing wind and current direction, but which also offers access to a good manta point. Most resort islands offer full-day excursions, so you can travel further afield and experience the full range of Maldivian dive sites, but this can be time-consuming.

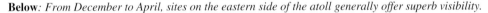

Below: *From December to April, sites on the eastern side of the atoll generally offer superb visibility.*

CURRENTS

On a more local scale, the strength and precise direction of the currents can be quite difficult to predict. Most times the dive guide jumps into the water first to check the strength and direction. In the Maldives there is a very small tidal range – usually no more than 1m (3ft) – but the currents can be very strong, the greatest generally being in January. Strong currents, when they happen, bring a dive site alive. If you are not experienced in these conditions, do not be frightened. Diving in strong currents is a technique that can be easily learned – although of course you should exercise caution and maintain respect for the power of the sea.

Here are a few tips for drift diving in a strong current:
- Listen carefully to the dive briefing and follow it closely.
- Once you have jumped into the water, spend as little time on the surface as possible; you will quickly be swept off the dive point, so get down safely to the reef as soon as you can. It may help to empty as much air as possible from your BC before you jump in the water.
- The slackest water is usually behind coral outcrops. If you need to rest or want to find a good viewing point, hide behind the coral outcrops – but do be careful not to damage the reef.
- Stay as low on the reef as you can without touching it, and without letting your contents gauge drag. The lower you are, the easier you'll find it to stay on the dive point.
- Your air consumption increases considerably when you are diving in a current: check your contents gauge more often than usual.
- Avoid decompression in open water: you could be swept for kilometres while waiting.
- All these matters should be thought about particularly carefully at night, when it is almost impossible for the boats to navigate through the water safely.
- Remember that the most exciting action will be at the point of the current, so it is worth the struggle to get there.
- Always carry a flag or an inflatable 'sausage' for safety.

Below: *Live-aboards such as the MV* Keema *offer greater access to dive sites than resort boats can.*

LIVE-ABOARD DIVING

Live-aboard diving has many advantages over shore-based diving, and anyone wanting to experience the very best of Maldivian diving should seriously consider this kind of holiday. A safari on a live-aboard can visit the best sites according to the prevailing wind and currents, whether divers are looking for sharks on the point of the current or for manta rays at the back. The better live-aboards steam a fair distance to ensure dives at a good selection of the best dive sites, visiting remote sites that are seen by relatively few divers.

Most of the live-aboards in the Maldives operate a system of 2–3 dives per day, plus some night diving. Usually there is a main vessel for accommodation and a dive-support *dhoani* to carry divers to and from the sites. This support vessel is important for your safety, as it can move easily in and out of the reefs and channels; your equipment is kept on it, which means carrying of heavy dive kit is kept to a minimum.

A great advantage of diving from a live-aboard is timing. Most resorts take their divers out at 09.30 and 14.30, but live-aboard divers can avoid these times to ensure they have the best dive sites to themselves. This makes an enormous difference at more popular sites, such as Fish Head (see page 124) and Ukulhus Thila (see page 118).

When booking your live-aboard holiday, bear in mind that the price you are quoted is usually all-inclusive; sometimes equipment hire may be extra. Nevertheless, by the end of the holiday you are likely to have enjoyed more dives for your money.

These are some of the vessels operating in the Maldives:

MV *Keema*

This 26m (86ft) boat, with six twin-berth cabins, caters specifically for divers and snorkellers; she has E6 film processing, a watermaker and 24-hour electricity, and offers 3–4 dives per day. The boat is available for individual and group bookings, and operates with an accompanying *dhoani*; she is run by a European Divemaster. *Keema* is operated by Maldives Scuba Tours, a specialist in the Maldives for many years.

Maldives Scuba Tours Ltd, Finningham Barns, Walsham Road, Finningham, Suffolk IP14 4JG, England (tel +44 (0)1449 780220/fax +44 (0)1449 780221; e-mail info@mst.keme.co.uk).

MV *Manthiri*

Over 27m (90ft) in length, with six twin-berth cabins, *Manthiri* runs nine-day safaris throughout the season. She has a watermaker and operates a separate diving *dhoani*. *Manthiri* is run by a local Maldivian crew and has a predominantly US and German clientèle. She offers 3–4 dives per day.

Sea & See pte Ltd, PO Box 210179, Malé, Republic of the Maldives (tel +960 320323/fax +960 325633).

SY *Jaariya*

Catering for up to 20 guests, the 30m (100ft) *Jaariya* has 10 twin-berth cabins, a watermaker, 24-hour electricity and a restaurant and coffee shop. All cabins have AC. Three dives a day are offered, and there is a separate diving *dhoani*. The boat is run by a German operator.

Contact Christian Neumann/Alfons Straub (Europe office), tel +43 6641000461, fax +43 6641031129.

MV *Moonima*

This is a 24m (80ft) boat with 12 berths in six twin cabins, and offers two dives per day. There is a separate diving *dhoani*. *Moonima* operates a schedule of sailings throughout the year. *Moonima* is run by an Italian with many years' experience in the Maldives.

Leuro Fresci, c/o Madoogali Resort Island, Republic of the Maldives (tel +960 450581/fax +960 450554).

MV *Al Pashah*

This 17m (56ft) boat is perfect for dive clubs, families or small groups. Accommodating six guests in three double cabins, she has a saloon with video playback facilities and a large deck area. *Al Pashah* operates on a schedule of one-week departures and is run by an English-speaking instructor.

Maldives Scuba Tours Ltd, Finningham Barns, Walsham Road, Finningham, Suffolk IP14 4JG, England (tel +44 (0)1449 780220/fax +44 (0)1449 780221; e-mail info@mst.keme.co.uk).

DIVING AND LEARNING TO DIVE FROM THE RESORT ISLANDS

Most resort islands in the Maldives have their own dive centre, usually managed as an independent enterprise from the resort itself. At all centres the diving follows a basic format: you get two boat dives per day, one at about 09.30 and the other at about 14.30. If you want more diving than this, choose an island with a good house reef, so you can enjoy some shore diving between boat dives. If you would like to be booked on a boat, most dive centres ask that you put your name down the night before. The chosen dive sites are generally no more than 30–40 minutes from the resort, and the boat returns after each dive. The dive boats are usually traditionally built Maldivian *dhoanis*: these are

> **SPARES TO PACK IN YOUR DIVE BAG**
>
> • Mask and spare straps
> • Fin straps
> • High-pressure hose
> • 'O' rings
> • Regulator mouthpiece
> • Spanner to change hoses

> **DIVERS' EAR DROPS**
>
> Many divers suffer from bad ear infections. To prevent this, always dry your ears thoroughly after diving. Some people find it helps to apply alcohol drops after diving. If an infection occurs, you should certainly stop diving and apply properly tested ear drops for several days. Possible ear drop solutions are listed in the Health and Safety section of this book (see page 169).

11–12m (35–40ft) in length and travel no faster than 5–6 knots. Because they travel so slowly, take your suntan lotion, towel, dry T-shirt/sweat shirt and sunglasses to keep yourself comfortable on the return journey. Watch out for dolphins and surfacing turtles on your ride home.

If booking a package holiday with a tour operator you may be able to book your diving in advance; but, if so, remember you will not be refunded for any days that you choose not to dive. Many islands offer an unlimited dive package, but this cost often does not include the charge made for a boat dive. On average, an additional US$10 per boat dive is charged. The unlimited package provides you with tank and weights, and as many air fills as you need. Of course, this is value for money only if there is a good house reef: check this with your tour operator first. If you wish to learn to dive or to take a further course, book in advance so you have a guaranteed start date.

The Maldives is a superb place to learn to scuba dive. All the schools are of international standard, and the beautiful lagoons and clear, warm blue water provide the perfect safe environment for the budding diver. Most of the dive centres in the Maldives offer PADI (Professional Association of Diving Instructors), SSI (Scuba Schools International), NAUI (National Association of Underwater Instructors) and CMAS (World Underwater Federation) training courses, with PADI leading the field.

The simplest course you can take is a Resort Course. This does not give you a qualification but does allow you to decide whether or not you like diving and would like to take it further. The Resort Course is usually over two days, and an average price is US$200, which includes four dives. The next stage is the Open Water Certificate, which takes about five days and involves classroom lectures plus practical instruction in the island lagoon, followed by a number of boat dives with your instructor. The Open Water Certificate allows you to dive in most countries of the world without further instruction; in the Maldives it costs about US$350, depending on your choice of resort island.

If you do not like the idea of spending five days of your holiday in training, you may want to complete the theory and pool work in your home country, leaving your first open-water dives until you arrive in the Maldives. This, called a Referral Course, is the best option for many people. Most Maldivian dive centres also offer more advanced courses as well as specialist courses like Night Diver and Wreck Diver.

Scuba courses do not generally require you to have a medical in advance, but nevertheless it is worth having a check with your doctor at home. The dive centre will certainly ask you to sign a disclaimer before you take a course or go diving; if you have ever suffered from asthma, epilepsy, heart disease, bronchitis or any other serious chest complaints you may be forbidden to dive.

EQUIPMENT

Standard scuba equipment can be hired from all the dive centres, although some do not have wetsuits; it is recommended you take your own mask, fins and snorkel. The hire equipment is usually of a good standard and well maintained, but check it carefully before your dive.

Above: *Snorkelling opportunities abound, including special excursions organized by resort islands, and the incredible experience of snorkelling with mantas when conditions are favourable.*
Below: *A 3mm wetsuit or a Lycra suit is ideal for scuba diving in the Maldives.*

If you take your own equipment, a 3mm full-length wetsuit or a lycra suit is perfect, whatever the time of year. Note that it is Maldivian law that divers must have octopus regulators; some live-aboards and resort islands make you comply with this. Carry some spares, as these can be difficult to get at the dive centres or even in Malé.

SNORKELLING FROM THE RESORT ISLANDS

All of the resort islands have access to some kind of snorkelling. Of course, some islands are better for this than others; if you want good snorkelling with unrestricted access, choose an island that has a good house reef. Islands which on the face of it may not be perfectly placed for good snorkelling often run a free and regular boat service to nearby reefs.

Snorkellers must be particularly careful of the strong currents – never underestimate them. Here are a few basic safety guidelines:

• Tell someone where you are going and when you expect to return.
• Always try to snorkel with a buddy.
• Do not lose sight of your boat or resort island.
• Always wear a T-shirt or some kind of protection against the sun.
• Carry a safety balloon or strobe light as a precaution.
• Be aware of other surface traffic, such as speedboats and windsurfers.

PROTECTED MARINE LIFE

All fishing or collection of these animals in the Maldives is prohibited:

• Black corals
• Conchs
• Giant clams
• Berried and small lobsters
• Turtles
• Napoleon wrasse
• Dolphins
• Whale sharks
• Whales

MARINE PRODUCTS PROHIBITED FOR EXPORT

These items may not be exported in any form, whether as souvenirs, souvenir products or for commercial use:

• Black coral
• All stony corals
• Triton shell
• Trochus shell
• Pearl oyster
• Lobster
• Turtle
• Eel
• Pufferfish
• Parrotfish
• Skate and ray
• Bigeye scad under 15cm (6in)
• Bait fish used in tuna fishery
• Dolphin
• Whale

PROTECTED DIVE SITES AND MARINE LIFE

Following pressure from the diving community, the government has protected a number of dive sites. These are officially designated 'Marine Protected Areas'. Here anchoring, coral- and sand-mining, dumping rubbish and fishing of any kind (with the exception of live-bait fishing) are prohibited. The removal of any natural object or live animal is forbidden, as is any activity which might cause damage to the area or its associated marine life.

Besides these protected areas, the government has also acted to protect species which are under threat. Turtle shells, for instance, were once widely sold in Malé, but the capture of turtles and export of souvenirs carved from turtle shell are now banned: you may find the odd item on sale, but importing turtle products to the USA, Australia, UK and all EC countries is illegal under CITES (Convention on International Trade in Endangered Species). The sale of all shell and coral products in their natural state is illegal, though craft products fashioned from certain shells and corals unfortunately are still sold.

Measures have also been put in place to protect species collected for other commercial uses. The napoleon wrasse was in danger of being wiped out when overseas demand pushed prices up, but fishing has since been banned. A similar situation now prevails with groupers, which are air-freighted live to the Far East for upwards of US$70 per kilo. Giant clams, which were under threat from over-collection, have been protected since 1991.

Opposite: *The magnificent giant clam is a protected species.*

NORTH MALÉ (KAAFU)

The sight of the Maldivian atolls from the air is spectacular. As your international flight descends, the view from the window clearly reveals the fringing reefs that make up the outer rim of North Malé Atoll. On one side of the reefs is the deep blue ocean; on the other is the turquoise water of the lagoon. Islands and sand bars are scattered across the atoll, and circular ring reefs look like blots of rich blue ink that have fallen into the sea.

North Malé Atoll, including the islands of Gaafaru and Kaashidhoo to the north, combines with South Malé Atoll to make up one administrative district, generally known by the old Dhivehi name, Kaafu. In this book we consider North Malé and South Malé separately, with Gaafaru and Kaashidhoo included in the discussion of North Malé. Furthermore, as North Malé was the first atoll to be developed for tourists and now has so many well known dives, we have divided the atoll into two areas: Southern and Northern.

As elsewhere in the Maldives, there is a strong and deeply rooted orthodox way of life here that survives Western influence. Yet the young people of North Malé Atoll are also well accustomed to embracing the new world that regularly arrives on their doorstep. You will find most of the Maldivians you meet are fascinated by new technology, and are superb linguists. It is possible to arrive at the airport and be greeted in English, German, Italian, Japanese, French or Russian – all by the same smiling representative who has just called his office on his mobile phone.

The capital city, Malé, and the airport are both in the southeastern corner of this atoll. Nevertheless, you need travel only a few kilometres to escape the hustle and bustle of the country's hub. Similarly, many excellent dive sites are to be found in North Malé; a safari around this large atoll can be very rewarding.

There are surprisingly few locally inhabited islands in North Malé, considering it is the principal atoll of the Maldives. Most are located on the southeast side. Although Malé Island is the country's capital, every atoll has its own administrative capital, and in the case of North Malé this is the island of Thulusdhoo. Thulusdhoo, a quarter of the

Opposite: *Children play off the locally inhabited island of Viligili, with Malé in the background.*
Above: *Yellow-saddled goatfish share a kiss.*

size of a small UK housing estate, is the industrial heart of the Maldives; it has a garment factory, a bottling plant and a glass-fibre boat-building centre.

The airport island was built in the late 1960s by joining two separate uninhabited islands, Hulhule and Gaadhoo. This huge reclamation project produced one of the most unusual airports in the world. Its single runway can accommodate the world's largest aircraft, and yet at its highest point it is only 1m (3ft) above sea level. You have an exciting landing when all you can see out of the window are coral reef and sea!

Separated by the Gaafaru Channel, and 3km (2 miles) to the north of Malé, is the ring reef of Gaafaru Falhu. On the eastern side of the reef is a large island, Gaafaru, with a local population of nearly 700. This is an important fishing island and a safe anchorage for boats making passage north or south. The ring reef of Gaafaru has two breaks and a big central lagoon.

The large, locally inhabited island of Kaashidhoo is famous for its good fishing. It lies 25km (15 miles) to the north of Malé Atoll but is included in the administrative district of Kaafu. This island is accessible to divers only by live-aboards, which often bring you to the outer reefs when making passage either to or from Faadhippolhu Atoll (see page 145). Unfortunately, the island does not have a good deep-water anchorage except in the most settled, calm conditions. The exposed location of Kaashidhoo means there is usually a strong swell, and breaking waves make anchoring extremely difficult.

There are few uninhabited islands in North Malé – most have been developed as resorts or are used for commercial purposes such as fuel storage. In total, there are 27 resorts, with the most intense concentration being in the southeast corner of the atoll, close to the international airport.

Compared with those of the other atolls, the resorts of North Malé range widely in style, from simple ones like Asdu, which has just 30 rooms, to the sophisticated Full Moon Resort, which features a conference centre, a gymnasium and floodlit tennis courts.

Diving in North Malé (Kaafu) Atoll

North Malé offers an exciting mixture of channel and *thila* diving. The high concentration of resorts in the southern area has acted as a magnet to large numbers of divers – possibly too many. However, most of the very best dive sites are exposed to strong currents, which continues to deter many divers and ensures the survival of the reef.

North Malé Atoll is separated from South Malé Atoll by the deep Vaadhoo Channel. This narrow ocean pass acts as a funnel for the prevailing currents. The dive sites that open onto the north or south side of Vaadhoo Channel are, by their geography, protected from the destructive elements of the southwest monsoon, and are thus pristine, with superb hard and soft corals, spectacular sheer reefs and prolific fish life.

In the northeast season, when clean oceanic waters flow into the atoll and visibility is often excellent, the diving in the narrow channels on the eastern fringing reef is very good. During the same season, many of the channels on the western side are favourite haunts of manta rays and whale sharks. In the southwestern season the opposite applies, and the western channels benefit from good visibility, although the mantas and whale sharks may be found on the east side.

Due to the high demand for building materials in this atoll, there has been an increase in coral-mining on the inner ring reefs. As a counter-measure, the government has recently introduced laws to control such mining.

Above: *The hovering cuttlefish is able to change colour at will, to blend in with a background.*
Below: *Red by nature, the scorpionfish also uses colour as a form of camouflage.*

North Malé (Kaafu): Northern Area

Even though this region is comparatively close to the international airport, it remains marvellously quiet. There is one fishing island on the northern ring reef of Gaafaru, separated from the main atoll by the Gaafaru Channel, which is 3km (2 miles) wide. The Gaafaru Reef has drawn a remarkable number of ships to their graves. At least seven wrecks are still to be seen on the reef, though many more have been smashed by years of relentless pounding by the ocean swells. The only other locally inhabited island in the region, Kaashidhoo, lies much further north.

Among the few uninhabited islands within the northern part of North Malé Atoll is Rasfari, on the atoll's exposed west side. There are also 10 resort islands in this section of the atoll. Most of them are small and were developed early on in the history of Maldivian tourism.

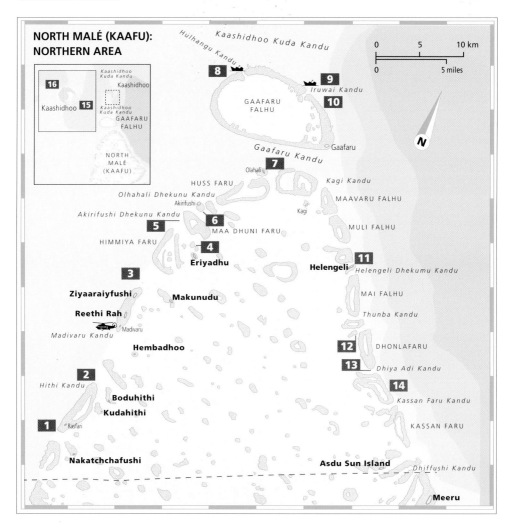

1 RASFARI
★★★★★

Location: Ocean reef of Rasfari uninhabited island.
Access: Nakatchafushi (15min), Kudahithi (25min), Boduhithi (35min), Hembadhoo (60min), Ihuru (60min).
Conditions: Very exposed in south and northwesterly winds: a big swell can build. Currents are moderate to strong. Sheltered during the northeast monsoon.
Average visibility: 25m (80ft).
Average depth: 25m (80ft).
Maximum depth: 40m+ (130ft+).

The reef gently slopes to a plateau with an average depth of 20–30m (65–100ft) before dropping off into the blue. The most interesting point of this dive is a small *thila* that sits on the plateau, with its reeftop at 25m (80ft). Divers descend onto the main reef and swim the 70m (230ft) over the plateau onto the top of the *thila*. Although the *thila* can be difficult to reach in strong currents it is worth the effort: it is a magnet for big fish and especially grey reef sharks (*Carcharhinus amblyrhynchos*), eagle rays, silvertip sharks, stingrays and some huge barracuda. On a good day you might see a wall of 25 grey reef shark. During the northeast monsoon the dive sites on the western side of the atoll lose some of their magic and the visibility deteriorates. After you leave the *thila* you can drift on the current back to the main reef. Take care over air consumption and decompression time: it is only too easy to be distracted by the excitement of the moment. This is a Protected Marine Area.

2 BODUHITHI THILA
★★★★★★★★★★★

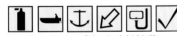

Location: Centre of the Boduhithi Channel.
Access: Nearly all resorts in North Malé Atoll send dive parties to this site during the northeast monsoon.
Conditions: Sheltered in the northeast monsoon, exposed otherwise. Currents can be very strong.
Average visibility: 20m (65ft).
Average depth: 12m (40ft).
Maximum depth: 30m (100ft).

In the northeast season this is a fantastic place to watch manta rays and sometimes whale sharks as, their mouths wide open, they scoop up the plankton like giant vacuum cleaners. The site is a large, round submerged reef some 300m (355yd) in diameter, with the reeftop at 12m (40ft). There are many *thilas* in this channel. The best one to dive, and the nearest to the ocean, is not particularly attractive on the top. However, during the northeast season the channel acts as a funnel for currents flowing out of the atoll, and when the outflow

---

CORAL-MINING

With the introduction of tourism, massive population growth and the increased wealth of the Maldives, demand for building material has grown substantially. Until recently, large *Porites* corals were being taken from the house reefs of locally inhabited islands. The government is deeply concerned about the environmental implications of this and in 1992 introduced regulations to control coral-mining activities. Mining can no longer be carried out on island house reefs, on atoll rim reefs or bait-fishing reefs. Permission is required by every applicant who wishes to mine coral and every island office must keep a log of the amount of coral mined.

hits the ocean it creates an upwelling of plankton-rich waters over the *thila*; consequently huge numbers of manta rays congregate to feed here, and whale sharks can also be seen. On the southeast corner are a number of huge coral heads which attract a tremendous variety of reef life. Whitetip sharks and batfish school at the current's point. Jump on this point and drift with the reef on your right, exploring the caves and overhangs as you go. When you meet the ocean at the southwest corner of the *thila* you may, if you're lucky, see the mantas hovering above and being cleaned by cleaner wrasse.

This is an excellent site for snorkelling with mantas, which often 'echelon' feed on the surface – feeding in formation.

3 FINGER POINT
★★★★

Location: The northern reef of the Makunudu Channel.
Access: Makunudu (15min), Eriyadhu (40min), Ziyaaraiyfushi (20min), Reethi Rah (35min), Hembadhoo (60min).
Conditions: Exposed in strong south or southwest winds; currents can be ferocious.
Average visibility: 25m (80ft).
Average depth: 20m (65ft).
Maximum depth: 40m+ (130ft+).

This is probably one of the best shark dives in the Maldives during the southwest season, when the current flows into the atoll through the narrow channel. The site is a small, oblong *thila* approximately 100m (330ft) long and 30m (100ft) wide; it protrudes out from the main reef like a finger. Jump in on the saddle of sand that links the *thila* to the main reef and, descending quickly, aim for the southern tip of the *thila*. This is most easily done by keeping the *thila* to your right; it offers you protection from the strong current. As usual, the current point is where you will find the action. This is a natural cleaning station for grey reef and whitetip sharks, and you can often see cleaner wrasse going right into the sharks' mouths. At times a squadron of up to 21 eagle rays patrol here. From this point, as you make your way back over the *thila* to the reef, there is a superb variety of fish and coral life to be seen. In the northeast season, when the currents are flowing out of the channel, this is a good site for coral and reef fish, but the pelagics are absent.

4 ERIYADHU THILA
★★ ★★★

Location: 1km (1/2 mile) west of Eriyadhu Resort Island.
Access: Eriyadhu Island Resort (10min).
Conditions: Protected in all wind states. Currents are usually small.
Average visibility: 18m (60ft).
Average depth: 10m (33ft).
Maximum depth: 35m (115ft).
This small round *thila* is shaped like an upside-down Christmas pudding; it is just 30m (100ft) in diameter. Though this is not a spectacular site, the variety of underwater life on view and the ease of the dive make it enjoyable. You can easily swim around the whole *thila* in a single dive; do this slowly and carefully, so as not to miss anything. There are usually pipefish (*Corythoichthys* spp) in great numbers and often nurse sharks, turtles and large morays. This is a superb night dive.

5 ERIYADHU CHANNEL
★★★

Location: 4km (2 1/2 miles) northwest of Eriyadhu Resort Island.
Access: Eriyadhu Resort (30min).
Conditions: Exposed in the south to northwesterly winds; there can be a big swell if these winds are strong. Currents can be very powerful, especially during the southwest monsoon.
Average visibility: 25m (80ft).
Average depth: 20m (65ft).
Maximum depth: 30m (100ft).
Eriyadhu Channel is scoured by the strong currents that flow in and out of the atoll. Over millions of years deposits from the currents have formed a cluster of small *thilas* in the centre of the channel. The best of these lies on the current point, its reeftop at 10m (33ft). A large section of this *thila* has broken away to form a gulley 40m (130ft) long and 10m (33ft) wide, with outcrops and overhangs. This whole gulley area is covered in fluorescent orange soft corals, black coral bushes and branching *Tubastrea*. Sweetlips, fusiliers, snappers, jackfish and a million others are to be seen here. If the current is flowing into the atoll you jump in on the current point, which is on top of the gulley, but your descent must be quick to ensure you are not carried off the best area.

6 AKIRIFUSHI CAVES
★★★ ★★★

Location: South side of Akirifushi uninhabited island.
Access: Eriyadhu (40min), Ziyaaraiyfushi (60min), Makunudu (60min).
Conditions: Exposed to southwest and northwest winds. Currents can be strong in the centre of the channel.
Average visibility: 25m (80ft).
Average depth: 25m (80ft).
Maximum depth: 40m+ (130ft+).
This site is a typical Maldivian ocean reef: gently sloping walls disappear into the blue. Between 25m (80ft) and 30m (100ft) you will find a series of large caves and overhangs which are washed by the ocean currents. The caves make an ideal shelter for reef fish, and you can often discover large groupers and sometimes nurse sharks resting in them. There are also many sea fans, black coral trees and whip corals. Descend on the outer corner of the reef and swim over the reeftop, which is at about 6m (20ft), to the dropoff. The current point is on the corner – it is here that you will see any large pelagics.

In calm conditions the reef can be rewarding for snorkellers. Turtles are regularly seen on the reeftop, and there is a massive school of red-toothed triggerfish (*Odonus niger*) on the shallow part of the reef.

7 OLAHALI BLUE CAVES
★★★ ★★★

Location: The north corner of Olahali Island Reef.
Access: Eriyadhu (60min).
Conditions: Sheltered in the southwest, but exposed to west and northwesterly winds. Choppy conditions can develop in easterly winds. Currents can be very strong.
Average visibility: 25m (80ft).
Average depth: 25m (80ft).
Maximum depth: 35m (115ft).
Beautiful blue soft corals hang like melted candlewax from the roof of this huge, long cave, which stretches for about 100m (330ft) along the Olahali Reef. When the currents are flowing into the channel, you descend onto the outer corner of the reef. If the currents are strong, don't hang around on the surface: make a rapid descent over the reeftop and, keeping the reef on the right, swim to the caves, which start at a depth of about 25m (80ft). They each extend into the reef for 10m (33ft) or so, therefore giving you great protection from the currents. The bottom of the area of caves, at 30m (100ft), is covered with a beautiful white undulating sandbank; here stingrays and sometimes even grey reef sharks can be found resting.

During the southwest season the point of the reef is a fabulous place to watch whitetip reef sharks dancing in the current. Note that, if the current is very strong, there can be overfalls and that, if you surface off the reef, you may find yourself being buffeted by currents heading in all directions.

If the current is small the reef is good for snorkelling.

8 THE LADY CHRISTINA WRECK
★★★

Location: Western channel of Gaafaru Reef.
Access: Some resort islands make day excursions to Gaafaru Atoll, but usually only live-aboards visit this site.
Conditions: Very exposed in the southwest season. Currents can be extremely strong along the reef.
Average visibility: 25m (80ft).
Average depth: 30m (100ft).
Maximum depth: 40m+ (130ft+).

The ocean channel between Gaafaru and the neighbouring atoll, Kaashidhoo, offers a clear passage, 50km (30 miles) wide, for ships travelling on this latitude through the Maldives. Occasionally mistakes are made, however, and the Gaafaru Reef has claimed a number of vessels through the years. The *Lady Christina*, an 863-tonne iron-survey vessel, was wrecked in 1974. At low water part of the wreckage can still be seen from the surface, and a mast and a small section of the ship lie scattered on the upper part of the reef. The reef wall slopes down steeply to a plateau at 55m (180ft). The main part of the wreck sprawls

down this wall, creating the perfect shelter for many species of reef fish and invertebrates. At 30m (100ft) are caves and small overhangs where you may see nurse sharks, rays and napoleon wrasse.

9 THE SEAGULL WRECK
★★★ ★★★

Location: Eastern channel of Gaafaru Atoll.
Access: Eriyadhu (2hr), Helengeli (2hr).
Conditions: Accessible in moderate conditions only. Currents can be very strong in the northeast season.
Average visibility: 30m (100ft).
Average depth: 25m (80ft).
Maximum depth: 45m (150ft).

The anchor winch and scattered deckplates of the steamship *Seagull* lie in 6m (20ft) on the reeftop. The reef shelves steeply, and the collapsed hull of the ship stands vertically against it, the ribs visible. As you descend to 30m (100ft) the reef plateaus out and you can see the giant boilers. The stern section of the steamship, sitting on its starboard side, remains intact. Look out for the binnacle; part of one of the ship's wheels remains. This interesting wreck dive is made spectacular by the coral and fish life around the debris.

Below: *Brilliant soft corals crowd together on the roof of a cave.*

🔟 HANS PASS
★★★

Location: Eastern channel of Gaafaru Atoll.
Access: Eriyadhu (2hr), Helengeli (2hr).
Conditions: Accessible in moderate conditions. There is usually a swell in the northeast season.
Average visibility: 25m (85ft).
Average depth: 20m (65ft).
Maximum depth: 45m (150ft).
This spectacular drift dive is across the mouth of the eastern channel which leads into Gaafaru Atoll. The site is best in the northeast season, when there is an uninterrupted flow of oceanic water running through the channel. The channel is 250m (275yd) wide and 20m (65ft) deep; the reef that forms the front of the channel starts at 20m (65ft) and drops down to a sand plateau at 45m (150ft). The plateau extends out 350m (380yd) before plunging into the depths of the ocean. Jump in on the eastern corner and descend to the front of the channel, at 25m (80ft); you can then drift across the channel to the other side. The channel funnels plankton-rich waters into the atoll, and this attracts pelagic fish. The sand plateau is a favourite spot for nurse sharks and stingrays. Eagle rays are often seen gliding in the current, and napoleon wrasse patrol the reeftops. The site was named after the great Hans Hass, who visited in search of tiger sharks; if you are lucky you might see one too.

🔟🔟 HELENGELI THILA
★★★★

Location: South channel of Helengeli Island Resort.
Access: Helengeli (10min).
Conditions: Calm seas are essential, as there is often a big swell driving in from the east.
Average visibility: 30m (100ft).
Average depth: 20m (65ft).
Maximum depth: 35m (115ft).
Shaped like a teardrop, this *thila* is 200m (220yd) long and just 70m (230ft) wide, its reeftop starting at 10m (33ft). The best time to dive is when the current is coming in from the ocean, bringing clear waters and a great profusion of fish life. You descend to 25m (80ft) at the front of the *thila*, on the eastern side, and drift from the current point, keeping the reef to your left. On the northern side the *thila* drops vertically down to meet the atoll plate, and here grey sharks, eagle rays and large schools of jackfish are often seen. On the reeftop the fish and corals are profuse – this site has some of the best hard-coral formations in North Malé Atoll. There are three very large massive coral heads in the central area of the reeftop, and in the southwest season manta rays can be seen at cleaning stations here.

🔟🔟 TRIXIE'S CAVES
★★★★ ★★★★★

Location: 6km (4 miles) south of Helengeli Resort Island in the Dhonlafaru Channel.
Access: Helengeli Island (45min).
Conditions: Sheltered in most conditions, although sometimes there can be strong currents.
Average visibility: 25m (80ft).
Average depth: 15m (50ft).
Maximum depth: 35m (115ft).
This reef lies in the centre of the Dhonlafaru Channel about 300m (330yd) from the edge of the atoll. The dive consists of a vertical wall, 300m (330yd) long, with caves set in at various depths. The most interesting part is where there are two large caverns, about 100m (110yd) long and linked by a swim-through. The roofs of all the caves are adorned with dense fluorescent yellow and blue soft corals. On the floors of the caves is brilliant white sand; here you can often find stingrays and nurse sharks. Whip corals, sea fans and black coral trees decorate the caverns.

Strong currents can run along the wall but, once you are inside the caves, you are well protected and can look out into the blue water to see schools of jackfish and tuna patrolling the reef. Take care not to stir up the sand.

🔟🔟 FAIRYTALE REEF BLUE CAVES
★★★★ ★★★★★

Location: South side of Dhiya Adi Kandu, 270m (300yd) inside the channel.
Access: Helengeli (60min), Asdu (40min).
Conditions: Mostly sheltered in the southwest season; exposed in the northeast season.
Average visibility: 20m (65ft).
Average depth: 15m (50ft).
Maximum depth: 35m (115ft).
Fabulous blue and yellow soft corals are the highlights of this beautiful drift dive. The westernmost part is a deep overhang that runs along the reef and teems with corals and fish life. You descend to the reef edge and, at 12m (40ft), can swim into the cavern formed by the overhang. On the ceiling are bright *Tubastrea* corals, plus schools of soldierfish swimming upside-down. The sandy floor of the overhang is at 20m (65ft), and here you can see stingrays and sometimes variegated sharks (*Stegostoma fasciatum*). To the east of this first section of overhang is a smaller but similar section of caves, marked by a large coral rock that has broken away from the main reef. Here the channel deepens, and this is a great area to see whitetip sharks feeding in the currents.

Opposite: *The grey reef shark is a common sight.*

14 FAIRYTALE REEF MANTA POINT
★★★★ ★★★★

Location: South side of Dhiya Adi Kandu, on the ocean corner.
Access: Helengeli Island (60min), Asdu Resort (40min).
Conditions: Mostly sheltered in the southwest season; exposed in the northeast season.
Average visibility: 20m (65ft).
Average depth: 15m (50ft).
Maximum depth: 35m (115ft).
During the southwest season this spectacular site is popular with divers who want to watch manta rays being cleaned by wrasse. The reef itself is not pretty: it is formed from massive corals that drop away into the ocean on a gentle gradient. At the ocean point is a large single coral head which is the mantas' main cleaning station. You should jump in well away from the corals, so as not to disturb the mantas, and then swim quietly to the cleaning station. When watching mantas being cleaned it is important to stay on the reef side rather than the ocean side of the cleaning station, and you should never swim onto the coral heads.

Below: *When threatened, the Christmas-tree worm can dart back into its tube.*

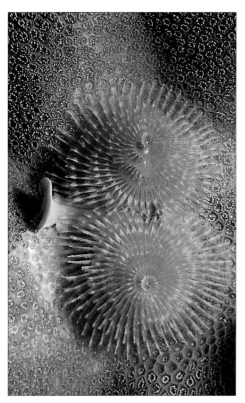

CHRISTMAS-TREE WORMS

On almost every *Porites* coral massif, you are likely to find Christmas-tree worms (*Spirobranchus giganteus*) of the phylum Annelida. This worm can be any colour imaginable. It embeds its tube in a live coral, leaving two brightly coloured whorls protruding from its hole. Whenever threatened it darts back into its protective calcareous tube.

15 KAASHIDHOO EAST FARU
★★★ ★★★

Location: Northeast corner of Kaashidhoo fishing island.
Access: Live-aboard only.
Conditions: Very exposed – there can be a huge swell.
Average visibility: 30m (100ft).
Average depth: 15m (50ft).
Maximum depth: 30m+ (100ft+).
The most noticeable part of this exposed site is that all the fish and corals appear to be unusually large. The drift dive on the northeast section of the reef is fantastic, with kilometre after kilometre of stunning coral formations, thousands of fish and the possibility of big pelagic species coming in from the ocean. The top of the reef is 10–15m (33–50ft) deep, and extends out from the island for at least 500m (550yd). At this point it drops steeply down to 40m (130ft) and then, more gradually, off into the ocean. The wall of the dropoff is not particularly interesting, having been scoured by the currents, but the reeftop and shoulder are superb. This is a site where you could see anything: there have been many reports of mantas, hammerheads and a variety of sharks here.

The site is also good for snorkelling if the conditions are right and there is not too much swell.

16 KAASHIDHOO WEST WALL
★★★

Location: Northwest point of Kaashidhoo Atoll.
Access: Live-aboard only.
Conditions: A huge swell can run over this reef.
Average visibility: 30m (100ft).
Average depth: 25m (80ft).
Maximum depth: 30m+ (100ft+).
This site can be dived only when the conditions are calm and the weather settled. At first sight, the reef appears quite broken and barren in areas, but on the top there are many coral massifs; under these you can often find resting nurse sharks and big stingrays. The reef slopes steeply down from 10m (33ft) to 30m (100ft), then plateaus onto a small step, and thereafter plummets to the ocean depths. It is an incredible feeling to know you have so much water between you and the sea bed.

HOW TO GET THERE

By air: All international flights land at the airport on Hulhule Island, in the southern part of North Malé Atoll. Most transfers to the northern part of the atoll are usually made by speedboat or *dhoani* rather than by air. The helipad in this region of the atoll is on the uninhabited island of Madivaru. The helicopters are operated by Hummingbird Helicopters (tel 325708/fax 323161). As an indication, flying time by helicopter from the international airport to Madivaru Island is 20 minutes.

By boat: Most of the resorts in this part of North Malé Atoll use speedboats for their transfers rather than the much slower *dhoanis*. It is possible to book a private speedboat to transfer you to your island (a number of companies offer this service from Malé), but the price may be quite high. As an indication, a speedboat transfer to Makunudu takes 50 minutes and to Helengeli one hour.

WHERE TO STAY AND EAT

Visitors normally stay on registered tourist islands, in other words at a resort. Every resort provides its own dining facilities.

Asdu Sun Island
tel 445051/fax 445051; 30 rooms; 30km (20 miles) from airport
Small island with a good, easily accessed house reef and 30 bungalows on beach front, plus water bungalows. All rooms have AC, hot and cold water, bath, minibar, telephone. Facilities include catamaran sailing, windsurfing, waterskiing, parasailing. The dive school offers a small range of PADI and CMAS courses. Visa, American Express, Mastercard, JCB, Diners' Club.

Boduhithi Coral Island
tel 442637/fax 442634; 87 rooms; 25km (17 miles) from airport
Medium-sized island with lush vegetation and beautiful beaches. Most accommodation is in brick-built bungalows; there are also four water bungalows. Some rooms have AC, hot and cold water, telephones. Catamaran sailing, windsurfing and canoeing. The dive school teaches a range of PADI and CMAS courses. There is limited access to the house reef on the southern side. The guests are predominantly Italian. American Express, MasterCard.

Eriyadhu Island Resort
tel 444487/fax 445926; 48 rooms; 42km (26 miles) from airport
Small, quiet island with beautiful lagoon and beaches. Simple accommodation in 48 thatched, semi-detached standard rooms situated on the water's edge, all with ceiling fan and small fridge. The bar is set partly over the water on stilts; there is a small coffee shop. The dive school offers a small range of PADI and CMAS courses. The excellent house reef is easily accessible. Visa, American Express, MasterCard.

Helengeli Tourist Village
tel 444615/fax 444615; 32 rooms; 42km (27 miles) from airport
The northernmost resort island in North Malé Atoll, this small resort offers simple accommodation in semi-detached thatched coral bungalows. Beautiful beaches and lagoon. Very limited watersports facilities aside from the superb diving: excellent house reef plus some exceptional dive sites nearby. Visa, American Express, MasterCard.

Taj Coral Reef Resort (Hembadhoo Island Resort)
tel 443884/fax 441948; 70 rooms; 30km (20 miles) from airport
Recently taken over by the Taj group, this large island offers a high standard of accommodation in thatched cottages; all rooms have AC, minibar, telephone. The Garden Villas have a small terrace; there are a number of water bungalows. Restaurant and coffee bar. Facilities include catamaran sailing, windsurfing, waterskiing, parasailing, canoeing, fishing, swimming pool. The PADI dive school offers a range of courses. Good house reef, plus small wreck at end of the jetty. Visa, American Express, MasterCard.

Kudahithi Tourist Resort
tel 444613/fax 441992; 7 rooms; 25km (17 miles) from airport
Ultimate hideaway island: beautiful beach, and fabulous house reef for snorkelling. The atmosphere is exclusive, accommodation of high standard. All rooms have AC, hot and cold water, telephone; some have a bath. Diving is organized in conjunction with the sister island resort Boduhithi to the north. Facilities include canoeing, windsurfing. Visa, American Express.

Nakatchchafushi Tourist Resort
tel 443847/fax 442665; 51 rooms; 25km (15 miles) from airport
Good accommodation in 51 thatched, round bungalows on the beach front. Some rooms have AC, hot and cold water, minibar. Two restaurants, coffee shop, beach grill, freshwater swimming pool. Facilities include catamaran sailing, windsurfing and waterskiing. The PADI dive school offers a range of courses. The house reef suffered an attack from crown-of-thorns starfish in the early 1990s but is now slowly recovering and is good on the southern side. Visa, American Express, Mastercard, Diners' Club.

Makunudu Island
tel 446464/fax 446565; 37 rooms; 37km (23 miles) from airport
Beautiful beaches and lagoon. Mostly Italian guests. Accommodation is in individual thatched bungalows on the beach. All rooms have ceiling fan, telephone. There is one suite. Catamaran sailing, windsurfing and waterskiing available. The dive centre offers a range of PADI and CMAS courses. Limited access to the house reef. Visa, MasterCard.

Reethi Rah Resort
tel 441905/fax 441906; 60 rooms; 35km (22 miles) from airport
50 individual thatched bungalows and 10 semi-detached water bungalows. All rooms have ceiling fans, hot and cold water; the water bungalows have AC and a shared sitting area. Windsurfing, catamaran sailing and waterskiing are offered. The dive centre is run by Eurodivers. The house reef can only be reached by boat.

Ziyaaraiyfushi (Summer Island Resort)
tel 443088/fax 441910; 93 rooms; 37km (23 miles) from airport
Low-budget accommodation in thatched bungalows and two-storey blocks of rooms. No hot and cold water in the rooms; very few have AC. Facilities available are windsurfing and catamaran sailing. The house reef can only be reached by boat. The dive centre offers PADI courses.

DIVING EMERGENCIES

There are no hospitals in this part of North Malé Atoll. Some of the resort islands run general medical surgeries, but they are mainly for the treatment of ear infections and simple cuts. If you require any kind of medical assistance you can transfer reasonably quickly by speedboat, helicopter (from Madivaru Island) or seaplane to the main hospital or private clinic in Malé (AMDC Clinic tel 325979; ADK Medical Centre tel 324332). There are no recompression facilities in northern North Malé; divers in difficulties are taken by speedboat to the Hyperbaric Centre on Bandos Island Resort (tel 440088/fax 440060).

EXCURSIONS

There are five **uninhabited islands** in this part of North Malé Atoll: Olhahali, Kagi, Akirifushi, Madivaru and Rasfari; some resort islands offer half- and full-day excursions. Take insect repellant, sun cream, sun hat, plenty of drinking water, shoes suitable for walking over shallow broken reef, mask, fins, snorkel and camera. Many resorts also offer **fishing** excursions aboard a *dhoani*. Most resorts offer excursions to **Malé** for souvenir shopping. When making a trip to Malé, remember this is a Muslim country and respect the local laws and customs, one of the most important being to dress modestly.

North Malé (Kaafu):
Southern Area

The southern part of North Malé Atoll is home to both the capital of the Maldives and the international airport, and is consequently the busiest part of the country. There are few uninhabited islands, but no less than 17 resorts, making it a popular tourist area.

The resorts close to Malé are among the most developed in the Maldives. As the distance from the airport and capital is relatively small, transfers can be made by speedboat, and visitors to these resorts are not necessarily looking for the informal island atmosphere the Maldives has come to represent. Many resorts offer sophisticated facilities, including conference rooms, freshwater swimming pools, tennis and squash courts and a choice of international restaurants. Kurumba Village, Paradise Island Resort, Full Moon Resort and Bandos each offers this style of accommodation. Club Med, just to the north of the airport, stands on its own in terms of management and style, with evening cabarets and karaoke nights. Another range comprises those large islands that offer a two- to three-star standard of accommodation, such as the resorts of Kanifinolhu, Meeru and Lohifushi. Here you find a good variety of sports – such as catamaran sailing and tennis – plus simple accommodation and an informal atmosphere. The remaining resorts are much smaller and quieter, with fewer guests, and offer a more relaxed style of holiday. Ihuru and Vabbinfaru occupy particularly beautiful small islands.

This southern part of North Malé Atoll has five of the Marine Protected Areas designated by the Maldivian Government: Hans Hass Place, Lion's Head, Kuda Haa, Banana Reef and HP Reef.

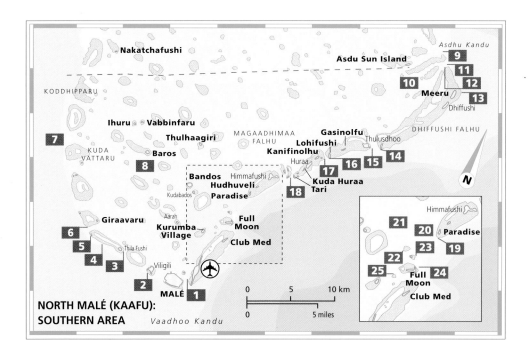

1 MALDIVES VICTORY

★★★★

Location: Western reef of Hulhule Airport Island.
Access: Club Med (30min), Kurumba (30min), Bandos (55min), Baros (60min), Full Moon (50min), Embudhu Finolhu (60min), Embudhu Village (60min), Giraavaru (60min).
Conditions: Surface conditions are usually calm, but may be choppy with incoming current from the Vaadhoo Channel against a northwesterly wind. Currents can be very strong on the wreck.
Average visibility: 15m (50ft).
Average depth: 25m (80ft).
Maximum depth: 35m (115ft).
The wreck of this 3500-tonne, 110m (360ft) cargo ship lies parallel to the reef of the airport island. The vessel is bolt upright, its bow pointing due north just 70m (230ft) off the reef. The midships mast stands intact, reaching to 12m (40ft), where a shotline is attached. You descend to the crosstrees of the mast at 15m (50ft), then down to the deck, at 25m (80ft), where you are sheltered from the current. Here you can either look at the open holds or stay on the ship's rail and survey the outside. At the bow, where one of the main anchors lies on the sand, you can see turtles, large groupers, jackfish, giant trevallies and masses of fusiliers. You can explore the accommodation block and bridge, but take great care when entering the wreck. Make the ascent back up the shotline: this is a busy area with a great deal of surface traffic. Make sure you allow plenty of time and air for your ascent, as the currents can be deceptively strong on the shotline; it is important to make a safety stop.

There is much speculation about the cause of the sinking of the *Maldives Victory*. All we know is that on Friday 13 February 1981 the vessel made a navigational error as it approached the deep channel between Hulhule and Malé. The 35 crew members escaped unhurt.

2 VILIGILI FARU

★★★ ★★★★

Location: South side of Viligili fishing island.
Access: Kurumba (20min), Giraavaru (30min), Club Med (30min), Full Moon (35min), Bandos (35min).
Conditions: Sheltered from northwesterlies but exposed to westerly and southerly winds. Currents can be strong, and there may be chop when the tide outflows from the atoll.
Average visibility: 20m (65ft).
Average depth: 10m (33ft).
Maximum depth: 40m (130ft).
This site, an outer ocean reef, is shaped like a basin, with an east and west point. The west point is formed by a break in the reef that has created a section of caves at 10–30m (33–100ft). The east point has a coral pinnacle which stands 10m (33ft) proud of the reeftop and is shaped like a banana. The reef is exposed to the ocean and is almost vertical, its shallowest point being at 10m (33ft). As the current swirls around the point you can find shelter in the caves and overhangs. All types of reef life are abundant, including different-coloured leaf fish; off the reef in the blue are schools of bluefin jackfish *(Caranx melampygus)*. Tuna, whitetip sharks *(Triaenodon obesus)* and eagle rays are common on the current points. If you look carefully you may find the white-spotted nudibranch *Chromodoris tritos.*

3 OLD SHARK POINT

★★★ ★★★

Location: Southeast corner of Thila Fushi Channel.
Access: Giraavaru (20min), Kurumba (30min), Laguna Beach (30min), Vaadhoo (30min).
Conditions: Exposed in southwesterly conditions, but sheltered from northwesterlies. There can be a strong current; surface can be rough if wind is against tide.
Average visibility: 20m (65ft).
Average depth: 25m (85ft).
Maximum depth: 40m (130ft).
There are large broken rocks 12–30m (40–100ft) down on the corner of this reef, which form an obstruction to the currents and attract all types of marine life. You are best to dive on a westerly travelling tide, the ocean water flowing in through the narrow channel to the atoll. The top of the reef starts at 5m (16ft); descend the steep reef and make your way to the corner that has the broken rocks. Here you will see the most action, including grey sharks *(Carcharhinus amblyrhynchos)*, eagle rays *(Aetobatus narinari)* and schooling jackfish.

While the reef can offer exciting snorkelling, take great care when there is a strong current because the surface conditions could become rough.

TYPES OF CORAL	
Coral is described by its shape, of which there are seven principal forms:	
Massive	big, round boulder-shaped corals of a form that enables them to withstand strong wave action
Columnar	corals that form columns
Encrusting	corals that form flattish growths closely applied to the sea bed
Branching	corals consisting of clumps of thin or thick branches
Foliaceous	corals that are thin and brittle with a sharp edge
Laminar	corals that are plate-like in appearance
Mushroom	solitary corals that do not attach themselves to a substrate

4 HANS HASS PLACE

★★★ ☆☆☆

Location: Southern, ocean side of Gulhi Faru.
Access: Giraavaru (20min), Kurumba (30min), Laguna Beach (30min), Vaadhoo (30min), Club Med (40min), Full Moon (45min), Bandos (45min), Embudhu Finolhu (50min).
Conditions: Protected from northerly winds but exposed during southwesterlies. Sheltered from currents.
Average visibility: 25m (80ft).
Average depth: 12m (40ft).
Maximum depth: 25m (80ft).
Named after the famous explorer, this very beautiful site offers a tremendous variety of corals and reef fish. Although the reef faces the deep Vaadhoo Channel, Hans Hass Place is a shallow dive. For about 100m (110yd) a section of the main reef has fallen away, leaving a basin with overhangs and caves beginning at a depth of 5m (16ft). The site is suitable for all levels of diver and a great place for snorkellers as the top of the reef, at a mere 4m (13ft), is in excellent condition, particularly at the point of the dropoff. There is often the opportunity to see larger fish swimming by in the blue.

5 LION'S HEAD

★★★★ ☆☆☆☆

Location: Southern, ocean side of Thila Fushi Reef.
Access: Giraavaru (15min), Kurumba (40min), Club Med (45min), Full Moon (45min), Bandos (50min).
Conditions: Sheltered from northerly winds but difficult in strong southwesterlies. Often a strong current runs along the reef.
Average visibility: 20m (65ft).
Average depth: 15m (50ft).
Maximum depth: 40m (130ft).
This is a thrilling dive. You can see schooling grey reef sharks as well as some superb hard and soft corals and a mass of colourful reef life. The overhang, shaped like a lion's head, is the pinnacle of a natural break in the reef which interrupts the tidal flow and causes upwellings.

The reeftop is at 3m (10ft) and shelves off steeply to 40m (130ft), before plunging into the depths. There are caves and overhangs in the first 25m (80ft). From the point of entry, where most of the sharks are seen, you can follow the reef either west or east, depending on the direction of the current. On the reef wall you can find a huge variety of invertebrates and fishes. Look out for the unusual leaf fish *(Taenianotus triacanthus)* and the false stonefish *(Scorpaenopsis diabolus)*. Hawksbill turtles are common. Resorts used to shark-feed here (do not take along any food yourself). The site is now a Protected Marine Area.

6 KUDA HAA

★★★

Location: Central part of Giraavaru Channel.
Access: Giraavaru (10min), Baros (40min), Kurumba (45min), Bandos (50min).
Conditions: Very exposed to southwesterlies but sheltered during northwesterlies. Can be strong currents during the southwest season, and uncomfortable surface conditions if wind is against tide.
Average visibility: 25m (80ft).
Average depth: 20m (65ft).
Maximum depth: 40m (130ft).
This small *thila* rises up from the atoll bed, looking like a camel's back. The larger of the two humps is about 30m (33yd) in diameter, with steep sides; its top is at 8m (25ft). To the north, the second has its shallowest point at 15m (50ft). Between the two is a saddle of coral reef. The *thila* provides protection to many species of reef fish. Large schools of blue-lined snappers *(Lutjanus kasmira)* congregate in the saddle area, and on the current point you can see schools of jackfish and batfish. There are sea fans and soft corals on the *thila* sides; look out for the long-nosed hawkfish *(Oxycirrhites typus)* in the black coral trees. The top of the reef is home to anemones and their symbiotic clownfish, including the Maldives anemonefish *(Amphiprion nigripes)*. This site is a Protected Marine Area.

7 WATTARU KANDU

★★★★ ☆☆☆

Location: Northern side of Kuda Vattaru Reef.
Access: Baros (20min), Giraavaru (30min), Bandos (30min), Kurumba (40min), Nakatchafushi (35min).
Conditions: Exposed when winds are south to northwesterly. Currents can be very strong during the southwest season, sometimes with a moderate swell.
Average visibility: 25m (80ft).
Average depth: 20m (65ft).
Maximum depth: 35m (115ft).
This site is best dived when the tide is flowing into the atoll. The reef is marked by a small sandbank, and the shallow reeftop is clearly visible. You descend on the ocean side of the channel towards the atoll bed at 30m (100ft), keeping the reef on your right. The best part of the dive is a section of large, broken rocks that form a crevice running up the reef at an angle of 45°. Here you can see stingrays in the sand on the channel floor, whitetip reef sharks and a meadow of garden eels *(Heteroconger hassi)*. If the current is strong the crevice provides good shelter, and you can swim up it to the top of the reef, which is at 6m (20ft).

The reeftop is excellent for snorkelling if the current is not too strong.

Above: *The leaf fish is naturally well disguised and is usually very difficult to spot.*

8 BAROS THILA
★★

Location: 1km (½ mile) south of Baros Resort Island.
Access: Baros (10min), Bandos (20min), Ihuru (20min), Vabbinfaru (20min), Giraavaru (30min), Nakatchafushi (40min), Kurumba (40min).
Conditions: Can be dived in almost all weathers.
Average visibility: 20m (65ft).
Average depth: 15m (50ft).
Maximum depth: 30m (100ft).
Located inside the atoll, Baros Thila forms a circular reef that rises gently up to a shallow plateau at 8m (25ft). The top of the *thila*, which is about 50m (165ft) in diameter, is at first sight quite uninteresting, as it is made up of large and bare coral rock. However, this area is home to a huge variety of fish life. You can easily swim all the way around the *thila* in one dive. On the current point are shoals of batfish and masses of blue-striped and red snappers. Stonefish hide between the boulders on the reeftop, and very large anemones shelter their clownfish. Look carefully at the anemones and you may also see another symbiotic partner, the tiny spotted anemone crab.

On the whole the site is too deep to be enjoyed by snorkellers, although there have been many dolphin sightings in this area.

9 ASDU KANDU
★★★ ★★★

Location: South corner of Asdu Channel.
Access: Asdu (10min), Meeru (25min), Helengeli (60min).
Conditions: Sheltered from south to northwesterly winds but exposed in strong northeasterlies, when an ocean swell may also be present.
Average visibility: 20m (65ft).
Average depth: 18m (60ft).
Maximum depth: 35m (115ft).
On the corner of the Asdu ocean reef there are many massive *Porites* corals, in the shape of mushrooms. During the southwest season, when the currents flow to the east, these become cleaning stations for a great variety of reef fish and manta rays (*Manta birostris*). In the northeast season the ocean currents flow into the atoll through this channel and bring good visibility as well as pelagic fish like tuna, sharks and bluefin jacks. When the current is running into the atoll you descend on the corner of the channel; when it is running out you descend at a place 200–300m (220–330yd) inside the channel. The reef, which shallows to 5m (16ft), is in very good condition, and just drifting along with the current makes a super dive.

In moderate to calm conditions this is an excellent reef for snorkellers.

RECOMPRESSION CHAMBER

A private medical practice called AMDC has established a two-person recompression chamber on the resort island of Bandos in North Malé Atoll. This is the only chamber in the Maldives that is operated 24 hours a day by technicians and doctors fully trained in hyperbaric medicine. Evacuation of divers from the outer atolls is usually by seaplane or helicopter flying at low levels, although flights are generally restricted to daylight hours. All the dive centres have pure oxygen available for use in diving emergencies. The telephone number for the recompression chamber on Bandos is 440088.

10 ASDU ROCK
★★ ☆☆☆

Location: 1km (1/2 mile) south of Asdu Resort Island on the southwest side of Maabadhi Faru.
Access: Asdu (10min), Meerufenfushi (20min).
Conditions: Sheltered in all conditions other than extreme winds.
Average visibility: 20m (65ft).
Average depth: 15m (50ft).
Maximum depth: 30m (100ft).
Situated well inside the atoll, this submerged oblong reef is approximately 100m (110yd) long and 60m (65yd) wide. The reeftop is covered by *Acropora* corals, and the walls, which drop away gently to the atoll floor, are full of interesting nooks and crannies, with small caves and overhangs alive with invertebrates and fish. This is a great site for divers of all standards, and is also suitable for snorkellers – the reeftop starts at just 3m (10ft).

11 MAABADHI FARU (LONG REEF AND PRISCA HEAD)
★★★ ☆☆☆

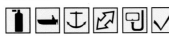

Location: North reef of Dhiffushi Kandu.
Access: Meeru (20min), Asdu (20min).
Conditions: Sheltered in the southwest season. Can be exposed during strong winds in the northeast season, when there may be a swell on the ocean corner.
Average visibility: 30m (100ft).
Average depth: 15m (50ft).
Maximum depth: 30m (100ft).
In the southwest season, when the current is flowing out of the channel, you might see manta rays being cleaned on the large coral heads that form the corner of this reef. From here the ocean reef slopes gently down to the atoll plate at 35m (115ft). An abundance of fish life, including schooling blue-lined snappers and yellowfin fusiliers (*Caesio xanthonotus*), swarms around

the large coral heads. Groupers, stingrays and coral trout are also to be seen in this area. As you move into the channel the gradient of the reef wall increases, as does the current. When the current is flowing into the channel, in the northeast season, this long reef is a very enjoyable drift dive. Between 15m (50ft) and 20m (65ft) there are several large caves and overhangs. Look out for hawksbill turtles and napoleon wrasse (*Cheilinus undulatus*).

This is a great site for snorkelling and just going with the flow.

12 MEERU KANDU
★★★ ☆☆

Location: South reef of Dhiffushi Kandu.
Access: Meeru (20min), Asdu (25min), Lohifushi (50min).
Conditions: Sheltered from south to northwesterly winds, but exposed in strong northeasterly winds. Strong currents can cause eddies and overflows on the point, so snorkellers should take care.
Average visibility: 30m (100ft).
Average depth: 15m (50ft).
Maximum depth: 30m (100ft).
This is a pretty wall dive with plenty of reef fish and invertebrates. Depending on the current flow, you descend either on the ocean side, keeping the reef on your left, or in the channel, keeping the reef on your right. The reeftop is at 8m (25ft), and the reef then slopes steeply down to a sandy floor, at 30m (100ft), where stingrays and whitetip reef sharks can be seen resting. In a number of small caves and overhangs along the reef you can see moorish idols (*Zanclus cornutus*), blue-faced angelfish (*Pomacanthus xanthometopon*) and large schools of squirrelfish (*Holocentridae* family). The wall is covered in *Dendronephthya* soft corals, brightly coloured sponges and orange and green *Tubastrea* corals. Nudibranchs, flatworms and pipefish are commonly found among the corals.

The top of the reef is not in particularly good condition, so the site is not great for snorkelling.

HOUSE REEF ETIQUETTE

The tops of the house reefs that fringe many of the tourist islands are very shallow and at some states of the tide may have less than 50cm (20in) of water above them. All islands with accessible house reefs have designated channels to show divers and snorkellers the way across the reeftop. Make sure you always use these channels when diving or snorkelling on the house reef. Sometimes the resort has even marked the channels with submerged buoys so that they can be easily navigated underwater.

13 THE STEPS
★★★

Location: Outer reef of Meerufenfushi, the easternmost point of North Malé Atoll.
Access: Meeru (35min), Asdu (40min).
Conditions: Sheltered in the southwest season; accessible only in moderate to good conditions in the northeast season. At all times of year there can be a large rolling swell.
Average visibility: 30m (100ft).
Average depth: 15m (50ft).
Maximum depth: 35m (115ft).
This wild, exposed ocean reef drops down from 10m (33ft) in steps, as its name suggests, to a sandy plateau at 35m (115ft). Large coral outcrops on the sand floor are homes to the usual array of reef fish. This is a site where you can expect to see just about anything as you look out into the blue; if you're lucky you'll spot whale sharks and schools of eagle rays. If there is a swell, diving in the shallow parts of the reef may be uncomfortable; swim well off the reef when surfacing.

14 VILINGILLI CORNER (CHICKEN ISLAND)
★★★

Location: North side of Thulusdhoo Kandu.
Access: Meeru (40min), Asdu (40min), Lohifushi (30min), Kanifinolhu (40min).
Conditions: Sheltered in the southwest season but exposed in strong northeasterly winds, when a large swell may be present.
Average visibility: 20m (65ft).
Average depth: 20m (65ft).
Maximum depth: 35m (115ft).
The corner of Vilingilli Reef protrudes 200m (220yd) from the island, gradually falling away to 15m (50ft); at this point it becomes a vertical wall, dropping steeply into the ocean. As the reef turns the corner into Thulusdhoo Channel a ridge of coral extends out from the main reef some 100m (110yd) across the channel entrance. It is on this corner that all the action takes place, with schools of grey sharks, whitetip sharks, eagle rays and napoleon wrasse competing for food. If you drift inside the channel 200m (220yd) or so you'll see a giant coral head, about 15m (50ft) in diameter; this is home to a huge variety of life.

The top of the reef is in the surf line, and the consequent strong swell makes the site unsuitable for snorkellers. However, there is good snorkelling further into the channel, where the reef is not affected by the swell.

15 THULUSDHOO KANDU (THE COLOSSEUM)
★★★

Location: Northeast corner of Thulusdhoo Island Reef.
Access: Lohifushi (40min), Kanifinolhu (40min), Asdu (55min), Meeru (55min).
Conditions: Always sheltered in the southwest season, but exposed in strong northeasterly winds.
Average visibility: 30m (100ft).
Average depth: 20m (65ft).
Maximum depth: 35m (115ft).
This fabulous ocean reef drops gently down to a sand floor at 35m (115ft). The corner of the channel is shaped like a semicircular basin. At the top of this, at 10m (33ft), are large coral heads. You descend on the point of the reef and watch the show; here sharks, squadrons of eagle rays and napoleon wrasse are commonly seen. Watch out for the large shoal of huge bumphead parrotfish which patrols the reef. In the southwest season you may see manta rays being cleaned as they hover above the coral heads. Although currents can be strong, they are reasonably predictable.

16 LOHIFUSHI CORNER (THE AQUARIUM)
★★★ ★★★

Location: North corner of Lohifushi Kandu.
Access: Lohifushi (10min), Kanifinolhu (15min), Gasfinolhu (20min), Kuda Huraa (35min).
Conditions: Usually sheltered in the southwest monsoon, although wind against tide can cause a short, choppy sea. Exposed in strong northeasterlies.
Average visibility: 30m (100ft).
Average depth: 25m (80ft).
Maximum depth: 35m (115ft).
The channel between Lohifushi and Kanifinolhu, 500m (550yd) wide and 40m (130ft) deep, acts as a funnel for the currents running in and out of the atoll. The site is best dived when the current is flowing into the atoll: you descend on the ocean side and continue into the channel. The reef slopes gently down to a sand floor at 35m (115ft), where you can see stingrays, whitetip sharks and garden eels. Outcrops of coral rocks scattered along the reef provide shelter to a host of small fishes and invertebrates. Swarms of glassfish hide in the overhangs, along with moray eels. Keep your eyes open for the handsome honeycomb moray (*Gymnothorax favagineus*). In the southwest monsoon this is a good site for mantas, which come in to feed on the surface and to be attended by the cleaner wrasse on the reeftop.

This is an excellent site for snorkelling.

A meeting with a majestic manta ray will leave you awe-inspired. A gentle and inquisitive creature, the manta moves through the water with the grace of a large bird, little deserving the alternative name, 'devil ray'.

The Maldives is fortunate enough to enjoy a long season for manta sightings. From June to November, when the ocean currents and the trade winds come from the southwest, mantas can be found on points to the eastern side of each atoll. As the winds then veer to the northeast in early December, mantas migrate to the western side of the atoll.

Very little research has been carried out on the manta ray but there are certainly more than ten species worldwide. In the Maldives the most commonly sighted species is *Manta birostris*, a giant animal that may weigh up to two tonnes and reach a width of at least 6.5m (22ft) – although there have been some reported at 9m (30ft). Also present is the much smaller *Mobula mobulae*, which grows to a width of at least 3m (10ft). The species are easily distinguished by size and the placing of the mouth on the body, the smaller species having its mouth set back much further than *Manta birostris*.

Manta Physiology

Manta rays are filter feeders, eating plankton that they strain out of the water with their fine gill rakers. They need to take in huge quantities of food to survive, for which they have a well adapted method of feeding. On either side of the mouth are two cephalic fins which sweep the plankton-rich waters in the right direction. These fins curl and uncurl according to the activity taking place, so if the manta is feeding they will be stretched out to increase the surface area and thereby the catching potential. They are then curled up like croissants when feeding finishes, lending a more streamlined effect. As a relative of the shark the manta ray is an elasmobranch with a

Below: *Cleaner fish nibble away small organisms and debris that have become attached to a manta.*

cartilaginous skeleton and plate-like gills. Its skin is composed of hundreds of microscopic teeth which help to improve its passage through water – stroke a manta and it feels smooth in one direction and like a cat's tongue in the other. The eyes are located far apart, either side of the cephalic fins. They peer out at you with curiosity and a gentle acceptance of your presence in their world.

Although all *Manta birostris* have the same dark saddle pattern on their backs, each manta has a distinctive pattern on its white belly. These markings usually take the form of grey or black spots and are very useful for identifying individuals. If you see a manta ray, try to memorize those markings, so that when you dive the site again you can check to see if the manta has stayed in the same place.

The Marine Research section of the Ministry of Fisheries in Malé and Bathala Resort Dive Base have jointly begun a manta ray migration study through which they hope to learn about the seasonal migration of mantas as well as other aspects of their behaviour. A number of mantas have been successfully tagged close to their tails with colour-coded tags. If you see a tagged manta while you are diving you should note down the colour of the tag, the time, depth, date, name of the dive site and as many details of the manta that you can. This information should then be relayed either to the dive centre or to the Marine Research section in Malé (tel 322509/fax 326558).

CLEANING RITUALS

Generally we see mantas when they are either feeding or cleaning. Cleaning stations are boulders of massive corals set on the channel perimeters, usually no more than 10m (33ft) deep. They attract a great variety of reef life, but most importantly they harbour the cleaner wrasse *Labroides dimidiatus* and *Labroides bicolor* which provide such a vital function to our devils of the deep. As well as the cleaner wrasse, moon wrasse (*Thalassoma lunare*) often join in the cleaning process. The mantas line up, waiting their turn at the cleaning

Above: *The manta is an extraordinarily graceful animal, swooping through the sea.*

station. Then, when it is all clear, they glide in and hover over the coral massif. The cleaner fish set to work, dashing into the mouth and gill cavities, nibbling at the small organisms and debris which have become attached to the manta. This cleaning ritual provides an unbelievable opportunity to spend hours in the presence of the gentle manta ray. Patience is paramount for divers who wish to enjoy the spectacle. Initially the mantas are naturally wary of the divers and their bubbles, but as time passes they become braver and the need for cleaning overrides their fear.

If mantas are not cleaning, they are eating – a manta ray weighing over a tonne needs to capture an awful lot of those little plankton to satiate its huge appetite. The rays can often be found on the current points feeding in shallow water, voraciously gulping plankton and small fish. They are seen feeding during the day, but it is believed they feed mostly at night.

17 KANI CORNER
★★★ ☆☆☆

Location: South corner of Lohifushi Kandu.
Access: Lohifushi (10min), Kanifinolhu (15min), Gasfinolhu (20min), Kuda Huraa (35min).
Conditions: Usually sheltered in the southwest season, although wind against tide can cause a short, choppy sea. Exposed in strong northeasterly winds; there is often an ocean swell.
Average visibility: 30m (100ft).
Average depth: 20m (65ft).
Maximum depth: 30m (100ft).
The reef wall on this side of the channel drops steeply away from 8m (25ft) to the ocean depths. When the current is flowing into the atoll you should drift with the reef on your left towards the corner of the outer reef and the channel. It is at this point that most of the action occurs: you can see fantastic schools of eagle rays, grey sharks and barracuda and, if you're lucky, you may also spot hammerhead sharks cruising off the point. During the southwest season, when the current is flowing out of the atoll, mantas come in to feed and be cleaned.

Snorkellers may be put off by the large swell that is usually present here.

18 GIRIFUSHI THILA (HP REEF)
★★★★★

Location: Between Girifushi and Himmafushi islands.
Access: Tari Village (15min), Hudhuveli (30min), Kanifinolhu (45min), Lohifushi (45min), Paradise Island (45min). Many other resorts in the atoll offer trips here.
Conditions: Wind against tide can raise a short, choppy sea, but otherwise this site is usually good for diving. There are very strong currents in this channel, and these can cause surface eddies.
Average visibility: 30m (100ft).
Average depth: 20m (65ft).
Maximum depth: 35m (115ft).
Located just off the main reef of Himmafushi Island, this site offers one of the best dives in the Maldives. The *thila* is made up of house-sized boulders with many overhangs, caves and crevices. One section of the reef forms a chimney from 25m (80ft) to the reeftop at 12m (40ft). The whole area is covered in blue, yellow and orange *Dendronephthya* soft corals as well as stunning sea fans and black coral trees (*Antipathes* spp). The currents flowing in and out of the atoll wash the *thila* and provide the perfect environment for reef and pelagic fish. On the point of the current you can see a spectacular variety of fish life in considerable numbers, including schooling grey reef shark, eagle rays, tuna and barracuda (*Sphyraena*

spp). To enjoy this dive you must be confident in strong currents; it is not suitable for beginners or snorkellers.

Girifushi is an army training camp where rifle practice sometimes takes place; when an exercise is planned a red flag is flown from the island and it is forbidden to dive in the channel. This site is a Protected Marine Area.

19 LANKANFINOLHU FARU (MANTA POINT)
★★★★★ ★★★

Location: Southeast corner of Lankanfinolhu Reef.
Access: Visited in the southwest season from most resorts in the southern part of North Malé Atoll and from South Malé Atoll. Paradise Island (10min), Full Moon (25min), Bandos (25min), Club Med (30min), Kurumba (30min), Baros (50min).
Conditions: There is often a strong swell and surge, which can make it an uncomfortable dive for novices and snorkellers. There is often a strong current along the reef.
Average visibility: 20m (65ft).
Average depth: 15m (50ft).
Maximum depth: 40m (130ft).
In the southwest season an astonishing number of manta rays can be seen here when they come to be cleaned. The top of the reef is at 12m (40ft); the reef then slopes gently down to 40m (130ft). It is interspersed with massive *Porites* corals which are homes to the colonies of cleaner fish. The manta rays come in from the deep water and hover over the coral heads while the wrasse set to work. To ensure the best sighting you need to be patient and position yourself close to, but not on top of, the coral heads. If you do not crowd the mantas they will perform their cleaning ritual in front of your eyes. It is common for encounters to last half an hour or more, but if you try to touch the mantas you will scare them away. Should you be unlucky enough not to see mantas, this is still a tremendous dive site: huge schools of bullseyefish (*Priacanthus hamrur*), oriental sweetlips and napoleon wrasse, plus heaps of turtles and various species of moray eels. The western point of the reef has beautiful table corals and a large section of caves. On surfacing you may need to swim away from the reef as the swell can make life very difficult for the boat captain.

20 NASSIMO THILA (PARADISE ROCK)
★★★★

Location: In the centre of the channel to the southwest of Lankanfinolhu Resort Island.
Access: Visited from most resorts in the southern part of North Malé Atoll. Paradise Island (15min), Huduveli (20min), Bandos (20min), Full Moon (35min), Baros (35min), Ihuru (50min), Vabbinfaru (50min).

Above: *Hundreds of sweepers flash by in a blinding moment of irridescence.*
Below: *The clown triggerfish is one of the most distinctive inhabitants of the reef.*

Conditions: Sheltered from all but extreme weather conditions, although there is sometimes a short, choppy sea created by wind over tide. Currents can sometimes be very strong.
Average visibility: 25m (80ft).
Average depth: 20m (65ft).
Maximum depth: 40m (130ft).
This *thila*, situated inside the Bodu Kalhi Channel between Lankanfinolhu and Furana Island, offers one of the most spectacular dives in the Maldives. It is a comparatively large reef, 200m (220yd) by 100m (110yd), with its top at 9m (30ft). The main point of interest is on the eastern side of the reef, facing the ocean currents. Here a large section, about 100m (110yd) long, has broken away, depositing a series of house-sized coral heads that rise up from the sea bed at 45m (150ft). Where the coral rocks have fallen away, a long series of caves, crevices and overhangs remain. The whole area is constantly washed by ocean currents and the overhangs are packed with wonderful blue hanging soft corals and colourful sponges. The rocks themselves are festooned with sea fans, black corals and a mass of other coral species. The fish life is prolific, with almost every cave a home to schools of snappers, violet soldierfish (*Myripristis violacea*) and oriental sweetlips – to name but a few. With so much activity, the site attracts its fair share of pelagic fish: grey and whitetip reef sharks are a common sight here, as are bigeye trevallies (*Caranx sexfasciatus*) and tuna, feeding on the massive schools of fusiliers. In the southwest season manta rays can sometimes be seen at the cleaning stations on top of the *thila*.

21 OCCABOLI THILA (BARRACUDA GIRI)
★★★★

Location: Inside the Bodu Kalhi Channel, east of Bandos Resort Island.
Access: Paradise Island (25min), Huduveli (30min), Bandos (25min), Thulhaagiri (25min), Full Moon (30min), Baros (40min), Ihuru (50min), Vabbinfaru (50min).
Conditions: Usually sheltered, though there can be chop created by wind over tide. Currents can be very strong.
Average visibility: 15m (50ft).
Average depth: 20m (65ft).
Maximum depth: 40m (130ft).
There are two parts to this site: the main reef, which is 200m (220yd) in circumference and has an average depth of 10m (33ft), and a small narrow *thila* lying 50m (55yd) off the southeastern corner. During the southwest season manta rays may be seen around the coral heads of the main reef as they are cleaned by the resident wrasse. On the reeftop are anemones with symbiotic clownfish.

The second part of the dive, the *thila*, is about 75m (82yd) long and only a few metres wide at the top; one end comes up to 12m (40ft), the other to 18m (60ft). A coral rock has broken off to create a canyon between the *thila* and the main reef, and this is covered in soft corals. When the current flows into the canyon, schools of fusiliers swarm into the gap. Bigeye trevallies, tuna and reef sharks hunt here, and there is a family of napoleon wrasse. Jump into the water onto the small *thila* and, having explored its caves and overhangs, cross to the shallow reef. The *thila* sits well inside the atoll and so visibility is not always great.

Below: *The conspicuous colouration of this nudibranch warns of its poisonous nature.*

22 HANNAS REEF

★★★ ★★★★

Location: West of Maagiri uninhabited island.
Access: Full Moon (20min), Bandos (30min), Paradise Island (30min), Huduveli (30min), Club Med (30min), Kurumba (30min), Baros (45min).
Conditions: Sheltered in both seasons. Moderate currents.
Average visibility: 25m (80ft).
Average depth: 15m (50ft).
Maximum depth: 25m (80ft).
This comprises three small *thilas* connected by sandbars; you can swim to all of them during one dive. The middle *thila* is the most interesting; it has a diameter of 50m (55yd) and a reeftop at about 6m (20ft), and the gently sloping sides drop down to the sandy atoll bed at 25m (80ft). The reef is home to many rare species, including ribbon eels (*Rhinomuraena* spp), stonefish, juvenile rockmover wrasse (*Novaculichthys taeniourus*) and leaf fish. The smaller outside *thilas* are less worth exploring: they act only as a funnel to the currents. This is a beautiful dive with masses to see. Suitable for all levels of divers, and great for snorkelling.

23 MAAGIRI CAVES

★★★

Location: North side of Maagiri Reef.
Access: Full Moon (15min), Club Med (30min), Paradise Island (30min), Bandos (30min), Kurumba (20min).
Conditions: Mostly good.
Average visibility: 20m (65ft).
Average depth: 20m (65ft).
Maximum depth: 30m (100ft).
Maagiri Reef is a large submerged reef sitting inside the channel between Chicken Island and Lankanfinolhu. The best part of the dive is the northern side of the reef, which has a series of caves and overhangs from 10m (33ft) to 30m (100ft). There is a great bow in this northern section of the reef that concentrates the fish life, and you can expect to see tawny nurse sharks (*Nebrius ferrugineus*) and stingrays in the sand – plus a tremendous population of reef fish and hard and soft corals.

24 FURANA THILA

★★★

Location: 300m (330yd) north of the Furana (Full Moon Resort) house reef.
Access: Full Moon (15min), Club Med (30min), Paradise Island (30min), Kurumba (30min), Bandos (35min), Baros (50min).

Conditions: Sheltered in southwest to northwest winds, although a short, choppy sea may develop if wind is against tide. Currents can be very strong.
Average visibility: 25m (80ft).
Average depth: 15m (50ft).
Maximum depth: 30m (100ft).
This is a thin *thila*, 350m (385yd) long, with a reeftop at 10m (33ft). Its eastern point faces the ocean and slopes down to the atoll plate. When the current is funnelling into the atoll through the narrow channel, the point of the *thila* attracts all types of pelagic fish. The top of the *thila* is in poor condition but there is plenty to see on the reef slopes and in the caves. Following the current with the *thila* on your right, you drift along the southern wall, which is interspersed with caves and overhangs. Here you can see tawny nurse sharks and turtles. In the southwest season, when the currents are flowing out of the atoll, manta rays use the *thila* as a cleaning station and whale sharks are frequently sighted.
    The site is a little too deep for snorkelling, but is worth a visit during the manta season.

25 BODU BANANA REEF

★★★★ ★★★★★

Location: 1.6km (1 mile) northwest of Club Med Island.
Access: Club Med (10min), Kurumba (15min), Full Moon (15min), Bandos (30min), Paradise (35min), Thulhaagiri (40min), Vabinfaru (50min), Ihuru (50min).
Conditions: Sheltered in all seasons. Very strong currents can bring eddies.
Average visibility: 20m (65ft).
Average depth: 15m (50ft).
Maximum depth: 40m (115ft).
As its name suggests, the site is shaped like a big banana, with the reef facing the ocean channel between the islands of Full Moon and Club Med. This is a spectacular dive, but take great care if there is a strong current coming in from the ocean: part of the reef has been nicknamed The Washing Machine! At the eastern point of the site, between 10m (33ft) and 23m (75ft), large rocks have broken away from the main reef, so creating a series of gullies. Here you can see big schools of oriental sweetlips, red snappers (*Lutjanus bohar*) and fusiliers. Every centimetre of the rock is covered in life of some sort, and all sizes of moray eels are to be found in the many cracks and crevices. The middle of the reef, the area known just as The Banana, is a huge overhanging cave created by the eddying current. From here to the western point of the reef there is a vertical wall that drops to 45m (150ft) and is home to literally thousands of red-toothed triggerfish. The whole site makes for a fabulous dive, the fish are friendly and the shallow reeftop provides great entertainment for snorkellers. The site is a Protected Marine Area.

HOW TO GET THERE

By air: All international flights land at the airport on Hulhule Island, in the southeastern part of North Malé Atoll. Transfers from the airport to the islands are usually by boat rather than by air.

By boat: Transfers to this part of the atoll are made by speedboat or by *dhoani*. As an indication, the transfer to Bandos Island Resort takes 20min by speedboat and 55min by *dhoani*; to Gasfinolhu it takes 35min by speedboat and 90min by *dhoani*. You can book a private speedboat to transfer you to your island from Malé (Prestige Launch Services [tel 322774] and Sea Tracs [tel 324566]).

WHERE TO STAY AND EAT

Visitors normally stay on registered tourist islands, in other words at a resort, or on the capital island, Malé. Resorts provide their own dining facilities, and there is also a limited number of eating options on Malé.

Bandos Island Resort

tel 440088/fax 443877; 221 rooms; 8km (5 miles) from airport
A large island with good facilities and a bustling atmosphere. Accommodation is in 177 deluxe rooms, all with AC, hot and cold water, minibar and telephone. There are also 44 suites, which have an additional seating area and a bath. There are five restaurants, a convention centre, business centre, crèche, beauty salon and a small selection of stores, including a photographic shop that provides film developing. Facilities include tennis, squash, badminton, aerobics, gym, freshwater swimming pool. Nearby is the tiny uninhabited island of Kuda Bandos. Windsurfing, snorkelling and catamaran sailing are also available. The Hyperbaric Centre, with the only 24-hour recompression chamber in the Maldives, is located on this resort island. Dive Bandos offers a comprehensive range of PADI and CMAS courses. The house reef is good, with a small wreck opposite the dive centre.

Baros Holiday Resort

tel 442672/fax 443497; 75 rooms; 15km (9 miles) from airport
A small, round island with a relaxed atmosphere and good accommodation in 53 deluxe rooms and 12 water bungalows built on stilts over the large lagoon. All rooms have AC, minibar and shower; the water bungalows have telephone and sunbathing platform. Facilities include catamaran sailing, windsurfing. The dive school offers a range of PADI courses. The house reef is good for diving and snorkelling.

Club Med (Farukolhu Fushi)

tel 444552/fax 441997; 152 rooms; 2km (1 mile) from airport
Recently renovated following a fire, this resort is managed in the classic Club Med style. Accommodation is in simple two-storey blocks in the centre of the island. Some rooms have AC. There are two restaurants and two bars; the food is good. Sports and leisure activities are organized throughout the day and evening. A very large lagoon to the east of the island is excellent for windsurfing and catamaran sailing. The dive centre, managed by Eurodivers, offers a good range of PADI courses. The house reef is not directly accessible from the beach. Visa, American Express, MasterCard, JCB.

Full Moon Beach Resort

tel 441976/fax 441979; 156 rooms; 8km (5 miles) from airport
A recently refurbished resort with 104 standard rooms in two-storey blocks, each of four rooms, set back from the beach; also 52 water bungalows built on stilts in the lagoon on the northern side of the island. All rooms have AC, ceiling fan, hot and cold water, minibar, tea- and coffee-making facilities, bath, shower and telephone. Facilities are comprehensive, including floodlit tennis court, gym, freshwater swimming pool, catamaran sailing, windsurfing. The dive school, run by Eurodivers, offers a good range of PADI courses. The house reef is accessible only from the north side of the island. Most main credit cards.

Gasfinolhu Island Resort

tel 442078/fax 445941; 40 rooms; 25km (14 miles) from airport
Small, exclusive island; the rooms are built on the beach; all have AC and hot and cold water. The resort has mostly Italian guests, so the food is of Italian style. Facilities include catamaran sailing, windsurfing, canoeing. A PADI dive centre offers the usual range of courses, but the house reef can only be reached by boat. Visa, American Express, MasterCard.

Giraavaru Tourist Resort

tel 440440/fax 444818; 48 rooms; 12km (7 miles) from airport
This island's bungalows, all on the water's edge, have simple facilities. The island is tiny but the beaches are very pretty. Facilities include tennis, table tennis, windsurfing, catamaran sailing, fishing, freshwater swimming pool. The house reef is good for snorkelling and diving. Visa, American Express, MasterCard.

Hudhuveli Beach Resort

tel 442982/fax 443849; 44 rooms; 13km (8 miles) from airport
A long, thin island offering accommodation in 34 thatched waterfront bungalows and 10 terraced rooms, which have AC. All rooms have hot and cold water. Facilities include tennis court, catamaran sailing, windsurfing, waterskiing, fishing. The island has a large lagoon, perfect for sailing and windsurfing; this means that the house reef can only be reached by boat. A range of PADI courses is offered. Visa, American Express, MasterCard.

Ihuru Tourist Resort

tel 443502/fax 445933; 40 rooms; 16km (10 miles) from airport
Very pretty, tiny resort island offering good accommodation in individual, modern-style cottages with thatched roofs; only three rooms, built in a block, have AC. All rooms have hot and cold water, ceiling fan, minibar and safe. The island's beach is excellent. Facilities include catamaran sailing, windsurfing, waterskiing, canoeing, fishing. The dive school is run by a German with many years' experience of the Maldives. The house reef of Ihuru is very good, with easy access through five channels. Visa, American Express, MasterCard, JCB.

Kanifinolhu Resort

tel 443152/fax 444859; 150 rooms; 19km (12 miles) from airport
A large island offering three types of rooms: deluxe, superior, standard. All have ceiling fan and minibar; deluxe and superior rooms also have AC, telephone, hot and cold water. Exceptional facilities: they include windsurfing, catamaran sailing, parasailing, waterskiing, canoeing, tennis, table tennis. The 5-star PADI dive base is run by Eurodivers with German-, English- and Italian-speaking instructors; also on offer are PADI IDCs. The house reef can only be reached by boat.

Kuda Huraa Reef Resort

tel 444888/fax 441188; 106 rooms; 16km (10 miles) from airport
Exclusive and expensive resort offering a range of high-standard accommodation and facilities. There are five different types of room, from the standard Beach Villas to the Water Villa Suites. All rooms have AC, minibar, telephone and hot and cold water. Facilities include large swimming pool, herbal spa, small gym, windsurfing, catamaran sailing, waterskiing. The Kuda Huraa Dive Centre offers PADI courses from Open Water to Divemaster in a wide range of languages including English, Japanese, French, Spanish. Nitrox diving available. The house reef can only be reached by boat.

Kurumba Village
tel 442324/fax 443885; 187 rooms; 5km (3 miles) from airport
The first resort opened in the Maldives; now a sophisticated, bustling resort offering a high standard of accommodation in standard rooms, presidential suites and minisuites. All rooms have AC, hot and cold water, bath, minibar, telephone. Being close to Malé, the resort caters for a large proportion of short-stay and day guests. There are six restaurants, barbecue terrace, coffee shop, two bars, fully equipped convention centre. Facilities include freshwater swimming pool, catamaran sailing, windsurfing, tennis, gym. The dive school, run by Eurodivers, offers a good range of PADI courses. The house reef, accessible from the resort, is good for both snorkelling and diving.

Lhohifushi Island Resort
tel 441909/fax 441908; 127 rooms; 35km (22 miles) from airport
Situated on the edge of the atoll in a very large shallow lagoon, this island is excellent for windsurfing and catamaran sailing. Accommodation is in thatched standard rooms, which have ceiling fan, hot and cold water, minibar and telephone; modern-style superior rooms are larger and have AC; deluxe rooms have TV and larger terrace area. There are two restaurants, bar, coffee shop. Facilities include swimming pool, floodlit tennis court, squash court, gym, waterskiing, windsurfing, catamaran sailing. The dive school offers a range of PADI courses. Access to the house reef is limited, and involves entering the water at the end of a jetty 200m (220yd) long.

Meeru Island Resort
tel 443157/fax 445946; 214 rooms; 40km (24 miles) from airport
Lovely beaches and a beautiful lagoon. Accommodation is in simple rooms of two types: standard rooms with ceiling fan and superior rooms which have also AC. Three bars. This is a quiet and unsophisticated island; windsurfing and catamaran sailing are available. The dive school is run by Eurodivers. The house reef can only be reached by boat.

Paradise Island (Lankanfinolhu)
tel 440011/fax 440022; 260 rooms; 10km (6 miles) from airport
A busy resort with a massive area reclaimed from the lagoon to increase the size of the island. Accommodation is in modern-style bungalows and water bungalows all with AC, hot and cold water, bath, minibar and telephone. There are three restaurants, including a Japanese restaurant. Facilities include large freshwater swimming pool, tennis court, catamaran sailing, windsurfing, waterskiing, parasailing, canoeing, aerobics. The dive centre offers PADI courses. Limited access to the western side of the house reef. Visa, American Express, MasterCard, Diners' Club.

Tari Village (Kanu Huraa Island)
tel 440012/fax 440013; 24 rooms; 16km (10 miles) from airport
An island with a beautiful beach and simple accommodation in individual bungalows. Some rooms have AC, hot and cold water and minibar. Facilities include catamaran sailing, windsurfing, waterskiing, canoeing, fishing, tennis court. The dive school offers PADI and CMAS courses. Guests are mostly Italian. The house reef, on the southwest of the island, is excellent. Visa, American Express, MasterCard.

Thulhaagiri Island Resort
tel 445960/fax 445939; 58 rooms; 12km (7 miles) from airport
Small and beautiful island with a very relaxed atmosphere. Accommodation in individual thatched cottages on the water's edge. Rooms have AC, hot and cold water, minibar and telephone. Facilities include small freshwater swimming pool, pool bar, catamaran sailing, windsurfing, waterskiing, parasailing. The dive centre offers PADI courses. The house reef is good for snorkelling and diving. Visa, MasterCard, American Express, Diners' Club.

Vabbinfaru (Banyan Tree)
tel 443147/fax 443843; 48 rooms; 16km (10 miles) from airport
This exclusive resort is part of the Banyan Tree group. The island has 48 beachfront villas each with open terrace and private garden. All rooms have hot and cold water, minibar, hair dryer and telephone. Two restaurants. Facilities include catamaran sailing, windsurfing, canoeing. The house reef is good for snorkelling and diving. Visa, American Express, MasterCard.

DIVING EMERGENCIES
All medical facilities for resorts in this part of the atoll are in Malé. Some resort islands run general medical surgeries, but these are mainly for the treatment of ear infections and simple cuts. Guests requiring any kind of medical assistance can transfer reasonably quickly by speedboat or helicopter from their resort island to either the main hospital or a private clinic in Malé (AMDC Clinic tel 325979/ADK Medical Centre tel 324332). Divers in real difficulties are carried by speedboat to the Hyperbaric Centre on Bandos Island Resort (tel 440088/fax 440060)

EXCURSIONS
There are only a few uninhabited islands in this part of the atoll, so resorts are limited in the kind of excursion they can offer. Nonetheless, most resorts offer **fishing** excursions aboard a *dhoani*, while all offer excursions to the fascinating capital island of the Maldives, **Malé**. A visit to the capital is well worthwhile for sightseeing as well as shopping. If it is souvenirs you are looking for, the best area to browse is on Orchid Magu and Fareedhee Magu, but please do not purchase turtle-shell or coral goods. For all other goods the main shopping area is Majeedhee Magu in the centre of the island. Make sure you dress modestly for your excursion and take plenty of suntan lotion and a hat. The best way to get around is on foot but you can call a taxi from most shop premises: they have a standard charge of 10 Rufiyaa (US$1) per trip.

MALÉ CAPITAL

As well as being the centre of government, Malé is the hub of both domestic and international commerce. Most tourists will have just 4 or 5 hours here and should take time to visit the local produce market on Marine Drive.

Next door is the fish market, where selling begins at about 15.00 as fishermen come in from the oceans. This whole section of town, known as the 'bazaar', is the main trading area for the islanders, and all along the harbour boats are moored two or three thick, with islanders of all ages unloading their bananas and papaya or loading newly purchased building materials.

Just east of here is the Islamic Centre with its large golden dome. It contains not only the Grand Mosque, but also a library and education centre. The National Museum can be found in Sultan's Park, close to the Islamic Centre. This small museum is open from 09.00 to 15.00 except on Friday and public holidays and, although rather disorganized, provides a fascinating insight into Maldivian history.

A number of other, very beautiful mosques are dotted around the city, the most interesting of which is the Friday Mosque or Hukuru Miskiiy, dating from 1656. Here many sultans and characters of Maldivian history lie buried; the wood carvings inside tell the story of the conversion of the Maldives to Islam.

Finally, on a visit to Malé you may like to try visiting one of the teashops for a cup of tea and some 'short eats', savoury or sweet snacks.

SOUTH MALÉ (KAAFU)

Though under the administrative cloak of North Malé Atoll, South Malé Atoll has its own strong style and personality. Its three locally inhabited islands each play an important role in the economic and social structure of the country as a whole. The capital island, Maafushi, is a traditional Maldivian fishing island and is relatively unaffected by the comings and goings of the tourists. Its large fleet of boats (*mas dhoanis*) harvests the tuna shoals and sells the fish at the marketplace in Malé, just two hours away.

To the north, the island of Gulhi, with a population of over 500, has developed a strong link with Malé and the national economy by providing a dry-dock facility to small coastal boats. The privately owned Gulhi Shipyard is renowned for its ability to slip surprisingly large vessels with just a rope, a winch and a lot of manpower.

Guraidhoo is a big island that offers a safe anchorage; it is still a natural staging post for sailors going to and from the trading post of Malé. Here voyagers who may have travelled for hundreds of kilometres from the southern atolls of Huvadhoo and Addu have traditionally replenished their stocks or sought shelter from the rough seas. The island also houses a Maldivian hospital for the handicapped and infirm who have no families to care for them. As nearby islands have been developed into resorts, Guraidhoo is now popular for tourists on excursions. A helicopter pad here serves all the tourist islands in the southern part of the atoll. Souvenir shops line Guraidhoo's main street and most of the men have left fishing behind in order to be employed on the tourist islands. Nevertheless, some boat-building and boat-maintenance still goes on.

There are 11 uninhabited islands in the atoll. All except Maniyafushi are located on the fringing reef. Access to these islands by boat is difficult if not impossible: many can be reached only by wading through shallow lagoons. Some of the resort islands, such as Rihiveli and Fun Island, have their own uninhabited island just a few hundred metres away; at low tide you may be able to wade out to them.

Opposite: *The circular* faros *of South Malé Atoll are clearly visible when viewed from the air.*
Above: *Nudibranchs come in all shapes and colours, though few are as exuberant as this.*

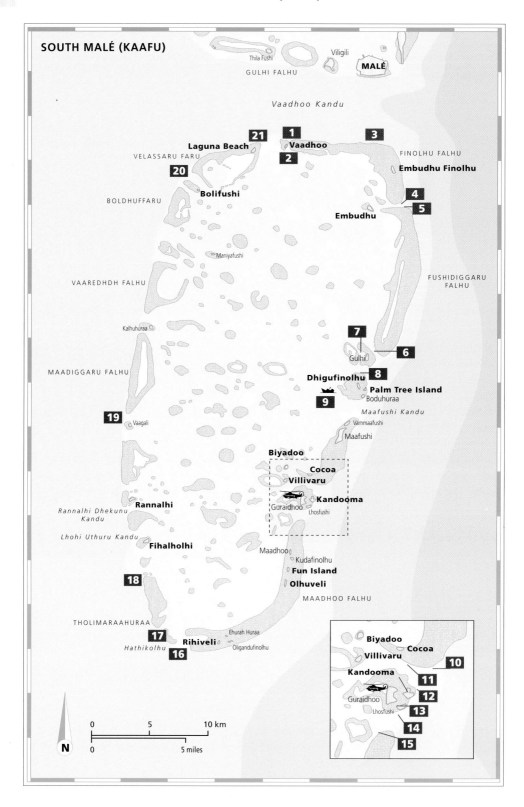

SOUTH MALÉ (KAAFU)

Viligili

Thila Fushi

MALÉ

GULHI FALHU

Vaadhoo Kandu

21 **1** **3**

Laguna Beach **Vaadhoo**

VELASSARU FARU **2**

FINOLHU FALHU

20 **Embudhu Finolhu**

BOLDHUFFARU **Bolifushi**

4

Embudhu **5**

Maniyafushi

FUSHIDIGGARU FALHU

VAAREDHDH FALHU

Kalhuhuraa

7

MAADIGGARU FALHU Gulhi **6**

Dhigufinolhu **8**

Palm Tree Island

Boduhuraa

9

Maafushi Kandu

19 Vaagali Vammaafushi

Maafushi

Biyadoo

Cocoa

Villivaru

Kandooma

Guraidhoo Lhosfushi

Rannalhi Dhekunu **Rannalhi**
Kandu

Lhohi Uthuru Kandu

Fihalholhi

Maadhoo

Kudafinolhu

Fun Island

Olhuveli

MAADHOO FALHU

18

THOLIMARAAHURAA

17 Ehurah Huraa

Hathikolhu **Rihiveli** Oligandufinolhu

16

0 5 10 km

0 5 miles

N

Biyadoo

Cocoa

Villivaru **10**

Kandooma **11**

12

Guraidhoo **13**

Lhosfushi **14**

15

Most of the 16 resort islands that have been developed in South Malé are concentrated in the southern part. On the eastern side all the resort islands are long and narrow, with wide fringing reefs and large, shallow lagoons. On the western side Fihalhohi and Rannalhi are both small pear-shaped islands separated by wide channels in the atoll rim.

South Malé Atoll was one of the first atolls to accept tourism, and all the resort islands were opened in the late 1970s or the early 1980s. It is only in the last five years, however, that navigational buoys have been erected to allow night transfers to take place.

> **NATURE'S MINT**
>
> The Maldives were once the mint of the Indian Ocean. In the eleventh century, records of the Arab traveller Al-Biruni show that the Maldives were known as the 'Cowrie Islands', thanks to an abundance of the small cowrie. Used as money on the subcontinent and beyond, the cowrie shell was exchanged with traders for food and building materials. *Cypraea moneta* is found mainly in shallow water and is often exposed during the day.

DIVING IN SOUTH MALÉ (KAAFU) ATOLL

Regardless of weather or season, South Malé Atoll offers tremendously exciting diving and snorkelling. Most of the best dive sites are on the east side of the atoll in the narrow channels that break the fringing reef. During the northeast season, when the currents flow predominantly into the atoll through the eastern channels, visibility is usually superb and the reef and pelagic life is thrilling. During the southwest season, when the currents mainly flow out of the eastern channels, visibility may be reduced but there is compensation: snorkellers and divers on the outer reefs frequently encounter lots of manta rays.

North Malé Atoll acts as a buffer against the strong and destructive wave action from the northeast and, as a result, much of the coral life on the fringing reefs is in very good condition. The deep Vaadhoo Channel separating North and South Malé atolls has some excellent dive sites with steep reef walls and interesting topography.

Strong currents are a characteristic of many Maldivian dive sites, and particularly so in South Malé Atoll. From Vaadhoo in the north to Rihiveli in the south there are only six breaks in the outer reef on the eastern side, which means that huge volumes of water have just these few narrow channels through which to ebb and flow. This causes powerful currents – and fabulous diving.

Below: *Large schools of dark-banded fusiliers are a frequent sight all over the Maldives.*

1 VAADHOO CAVES
★★★ ★★★

Location: North side of Vaadhoo Resort house reef.
Access: Vaadhoo (10min), Laguna Beach (20min), Bolifushi (35min), Embudhu Finolhu (40min), Embudhu Village (45min). Some resorts in North Malé Atoll run day trips to this site.
Conditions: A very strong current and large swell can sometimes be present.
Average visibility: 25m (80ft).
Average depth: 20m (65ft).
Maximum depth: 40m+ (130ft+).
The extreme north point of the Vaadhoo Reef drops off steeply to the great depths of the Vaadhoo Channel. Here the reef is honeycombed with caves and overhangs from 8m (25ft) down to 40m (130ft). At one point a very large overhang starts at a depth of 15m (50ft) and curves down to 30m (100ft), cutting into the reef for about 7m (23ft). The overhang's ceiling is completely covered in beautiful iridescent blue soft corals, and inside the cave is a mass of squirrelfish and soldierfish. When the current is flowing strongly into the atoll you can shelter within this large cave and watch trevallies and tuna schooling on the eddies. Keeping the reef on your right, you can then go on to the shallows at 8m (25ft), where you can drift along and explore the nooks and crannies on the reef. There is another large overhang at the shallow corner of the eastern reef.

The site is excellent for snorkelling, although beware of the strong currents and confused waters that sometimes develop in the channel.

2 CORAL GARDENS
★★ ★★★★

Location: Southern side of Vaadhoo Resort house reef.
Access: Vaadhoo (10min), Laguna Beach (20min).
Conditions: Can be rough in strong southwest winds, at which times visibility will be reduced.
Average visibility: 15m (50ft).
Average depth: 15m (50ft).
Maximum depth: 30m (100ft).
This section of the Vaadhoo house reef slopes gently down to the atoll plate and is protected from destructive wave action. Consequently the corals on top of the reef are superb. Divers usually begin the dive opposite the resort's water bungalows and drift with the reef on their right. The start of the dive is a gently sloping section where turtles and sometimes eagle rays can be seen feeding. The gradient of the reef then increases until it is a wall full of shallow caves and small overhangs. As you approach the outer corner of the atoll you may find the direction of the current changes so that it is flowing against you; at this point it is best to ascend to shallower areas to finish the dive.

3 THE CANYON
★★★ ★★★

Location: 4km (2½ miles) northwest of Embudhu Finolhu Resort, on the fringing reef of Vaadhoo Channel.
Access: Embudhu Finolhu (25min), Embudhu Village (35min), Vaadhoo (30min).

Below: *The handsome honeycomb moray eel is a formidable predator for little fishes.*

CONE SHELL

It is hard to believe that such a small, innocuous looking creature could be so dangerous to divers, yet cone shells have a venomous sting powerful enough to kill a person. This small sea snail, around 10cm (4in) in length, lives on the reef down to a depth of 50m (165ft) and feeds on worms and small fish. It kills its prey by darting out its proboscal tube and injecting the victim with a strong poison, causing paralysis. Always follow the basic rule that if you do not know what something is, don't touch.

Conditions: Very exposed. A big swell can develop if winds are strong.
Average visibility: 30m (100ft).
Average depth: 15m (50ft).
Maximum depth: 40m+ (130ft+).
This is a super dive with interesting topography and masses of fish life, the views usually enhanced by dramatic visibility. A section of the reef has fallen away, leaving an indentation about 250m (275yd) long. At the eastern end is a huge rock the size of a house; between the rock and the main reef is a canyon about 5m (16ft) wide and 20m (65ft) deep. Jump in on the ocean side of the large rock and explore the caves and crevices at 35m (115ft) before swimming up through the canyon and along the wall at 10m (33ft), with the reef on the left. Most of the fish life is concentrated around the rock. As well as a mass of reef fish you should see a lot of schooling fish including fusiliers, midnight snappers and jackfish.

The shallowest part of the reef, above the canyon, is excellent for snorkelling.

4 EMBUDHU THILA
★★★

Location: The north side of Embudhu Kandu.
Access: Embudhu Village (15min), Embudhu Finolhu (15min), Vaadhoo (45min), Laguna Beach (50min).
Conditions: Overfalls may occur if wind is against tide.
Average visibility: 25m (80ft).
Average depth: 15m (50ft).
Maximum depth: 35m (115ft).
The best diving is on the east and southeast side of this large *thila*. At times the current can rip across the reeftop, which is at 12m (40ft), and in such conditions this is certainly not a dive for the faint-hearted. With the current flowing into the atoll, you jump in on the northeast corner and follow the face of the *thila* at 25m (80ft), with the reef on your right. Along this face is a wonderful set of caves and overhangs. At the southeast corner the *thila* is divided at a depth of 18m (60ft) by a canyon, 60m (200ft) long, about 10m (33ft) wide at its widest point and no more than 2m (6ft) at its narrowest. You can swim through this section to emerge on the southern point of the *thila*, where there are three coral rocks covered in hard and soft corals of all descriptions. The fish life in this area can be incredible, with

large schools of big-eye trevallies and snappers. For safety, make your return to the reeftop by swimming either back through the gulley or along the face of the *thila*.

5 EMBUDHU KANDU
★★★★ ★★★

Location: The south corner of Embudhu Kandu.
Access: Embudhu Village (15min), Embudhu Finolhu (15min), Vaadhoo (45min), Laguna Beach (50min).
Conditions: Overfalls may occur if wind is against tide.
Average visibility: 30m (100ft).
Average depth: 25m (80ft).
Maximum depth: 35m (115ft).
The whole Embudhu Channel is a Protected Marine Area because of its excellent shark life. As the powerful northeast currents stream through the channel this is one of the best places to see grey sharks, whitetip sharks and schools of eagle rays. You jump in on the northeast corner of the south side of the channel and descend to 30m (100ft), keeping the reef on your left. At 30m (100ft) the ocean reef meets the atoll plate and drops away vertically into the deep blue. It is here you can see the best pelagic life. Leaving the dropoff and ascending back up the reef wall to 15m (50ft), you can enjoy a fabulous drift dive through the narrow channel before surfacing in the shallows of the reef in 6m (20ft).

6 GULHI KANDU
★★★ ★★★

Location: North channel of Gulhi fishing island.
Access: Palm Tree Island (20min), Dhigufinolhu (20min).
Conditions: There can be a big swell on the outer reef, but conditions in the channel are usually good.
Average visibility: 30m (100ft).
Average depth: 20m (65ft).
Maximum depth: 40m (130ft).
This classic Maldivian channel offers a thrilling and spectacular dive, with grey reef sharks and large pelagic species on the current point, and a diversity of fish life along the wall of the reef. Jump in on the southeast corner of the north side of the channel and descend to 35m (115ft), where the atoll plate drops away to the ocean; here are to be found most of the pelagic fish. Leaving the greater depths, you can drift into the channel, keeping the reef to your right. This reef wall has many soft corals and healthy hard-coral formations in the shallows at 6m (20ft). On the corner of the channel the current can sometimes push you off the reef; take care to stay close to the reef to avoid making an open-water ascent.

The inside of the channel, where the reef offers some protection to swimmers, is good for snorkelling.

7 GULHI FARU
★★★ ★★★

Location: The eastern side of Gulhi house reef.
Access: Palm Tree Island (20min), Dhigufinolhu (20min).
Conditions: There can be a big swell on the·reef in either season.
Average visibility: 30m (100ft).
Average depth: 20m (65ft).
Maximum depth: 40m (130ft).

This reef, 1km (¹/₂ mile) long, between the north and south channels of Gulhi starts at 8m (25ft) and drops steeply away into the ocean blue. The reeftop is made up of excellent hard-coral formations and large blocks of massive corals, and harbours a profusion of fish life. Between 20m (65ft) and 30m (100ft) are a number of interesting caves and overhangs, decorated with many varieties of soft corals, black coral trees and whip corals laden with featherstars. One cave of particular interest is at 25m (80ft); it looks like a large porthole in the reef. You can swim inside this overhang at 30m (100ft) and look out through the porthole, which is 3m (10ft) wide and covered in soft corals and gorgonians. (Note the hole is too narrow to swim through without damaging the coral.) Hawksbill turtles are often seen feeding on the reeftop.

As long as the swell is not too strong, the shallow part of the reef is super for snorkelling.

8 DHIGUFINOLHU
★★★ ★★

Location: Northeast corner of Dhigufinolhu Reef.
Access: Palm Tree Island (10min), Dhigufinolhu (15min), Biyadoo (45min), Cocoa (45min).
Conditions: Sheltered in the southwest season, although a long rolling swell can be present at any time.
Average visibility: 20m (65ft).
Average depth: 15m (50ft).
Maximum depth: 30m (100ft).

The southeast corner of this reef slopes at a gentle gradient for at least 1km (¹/₂ mile) before reaching the ocean dropoff. The channel between Dhigufinolhu and Gulhi is very shallow, with a sandy bottom at a depth of just 20m (65ft), rising in one place to a long narrow *thila* with its reeftop at 15m (50ft). In the southwest season, when the current is flowing predominantly out of the atoll, manta rays are often seen feeding on the surface or being cleaned on the reef's numerous coral heads. The reef does not boast tremendous coral or fish life but, if the mantas are around, this is an excellent dive.

If the mantas are feeding on the surface in the channel it is often best just to snorkel with them. If they are being cleaned they are likely to be found on Dhigufinolhu Reef.

9 YACHT THILA
★★★ ★★★★

Location: 1km (¹/₂ mile) east of Dhigufinolhu Resort Island.
Access: Dhigufinolhu (10min), Palm Tree Island (15min), Biyadoo (25min), Villivaru (30min), Kandooma (30min).
Conditions: Good in all seasons.
Average visibility: 15m (50ft).
Average depth: 20m (65ft).
Maximum depth: 35m (115ft).

This is a small *thila*, just 50m (55yd) in diameter, with a reeftop at a depth of 3m (10ft). You can easily swim around the whole *thila* in a single dive, also surveying the wreck of a small freighter that was deliberately sunk by the local resort islands as an attraction to divers. The wreck lies upright on the southwest side of the *thila* with its bow at 15m (50ft) and its stern at 27m (86ft). Although there is very little hard-coral growth on the ship, the fish life is interestingly varied – with some large groupers, morays and a school of batfish.

There is good coral growth on the *thila*, and the usual hordes of reef fish make this a great site for snorkelling. It is also a very good night dive.

10 COCOA FARU
★★★ ★★★★

Location: Southern side of Cocoa Resort house reef.
Access: Kandooma (10min), Cocoa (10min), Villivaru (15min), Biyadoo (15min).
Conditions: Ferocious currents at times. A short, choppy sea may develop if there is wind over tide.
Average visibility: 30m (100ft).
Average depth: 20m (65ft).
Maximum depth: 40m (130ft).

You jump in on the ocean corner of Cocoa Faru and drift with the reef to your right. Most of the pelagic fish are to be found at the corner where the atoll plate meets the ocean dropoff; grey reef sharks, eagle rays and whitetip sharks are often seen here. From the corner you can swim out across the mouth of the channel to a small coral ridge, sitting at a depth of 30m (100ft), that seems to be a haven for whitetip sharks. Leaving the deep water you follow the reef into the atoll and can enjoy a spectacular drift dive along the reef wall, which is covered in colourful soft corals. Between 15m (50ft) and 25m (80ft) there are a number of large caves and overhangs to explore.

If the current is moderate this is a good site for snorkelling as the hard corals on the reeftop, at 6m (20ft), are superb. Watch out for green and hawksbill turtles feeding on the reeftop.

Above: *A long-nosed hawkfish rests above a gorgonian with delicate polyps extended.*
Below: *Most soft corals rely on numerous tiny pale spicules for support.*

11 COCOA THILA
★★★★★

Location: In the middle of Biyadhoo Kandu.
Access: Kandooma (10min), Cocoa (10min), Villivaru (15min), Biyadoo (15min).
Conditions: Ferocious currents at times. A short, choppy sea may develop if there is wind over tide.
Average visibility: 25m (80ft).
Average depth: 20m (65ft).
Maximum depth: 35m (115ft).

This can be a very rewarding dive, though challenging. As with many *thila* dives, it is best done when there is a moderate current: if the current is too strong it becomes difficult to stay on the dive site; conversely, if there is no current, there are few fish. The western end of this *thila*, which is 400m (440yd) long, has steeply sloping sides undercut down to 30m (100ft) by large caves and overhangs. This is where you see the main action, principally trevallies, tuna and eagle rays. Lying off this point are three huge coral rocks and smaller coral outcrops. The current flowing around these rocks creates a cauldron of activity, with a mass of rock cod (*Cephalopholis miniata*), oriental sweetlips and just about every other reef fish you can think of. There are caves and overhangs along both north and south sides of the *thila*. At another big coral outcrop on the northern side, 200m (220yd) from the point, grey reef shark are often seen. The eastern side of the *thila* slopes off to the ocean at 45° and is less interesting than the west side.

Below: *The distinctive silhouettes of batfish can be an eerie sight.*

12 KANDOOMA POINT
★★★

Location: Northeast corner of Kandooma Faru.
Access: Kandooma (10min), Villivaru (15min), Biyadoo (15min), Cocoa (15min).
Conditions: There can be ferocious currents. A short, choppy sea may develop if there is wind over tide.
Average visibility: 30m (100ft).
Average depth: 20m (65ft).
Maximum depth: 40m+ (130ft+).

This is a fantastic dive when the current is running into the atoll. The site is a reef corner with huge caves and overhangs at 15–25m (50–80ft), and is full of life. Jump in on the northeast corner of the reef and descend to 30m (100ft), keeping the reef on your left. As you round the corner inside the atoll, the currents try to push you off the reef into deep water, so take care here. Hammerhead sharks are often seen at this point, but don't be tempted to leave the reef to follow them! About 70m (77yd) from the corner is a long set of caves. Two of the caves are huge, with big domed ceilings and lots of reef fish inside. The caves are dark: take a torch if you want to make the best of this part of the dive.

13 LHOSFUSHI KANDU
★★★ ★★★★

Location: The small channel between Guraidhoo fishing island and Medhu Faru.
Access: Kandooma (15min), Villivaru (20min), Biyadoo (20min), Cocoa (25min).
Conditions: Often a large rolling swell. The waves can break on the reef in the shallows.
Average visibility: 30m (100ft).
Average depth: 15m (50ft).
Maximum depth: 25m (80ft).

A ridge of sand and coral spans the narrow entrance to this channel. The ridge is 12m (40ft) deep at its shallowest point, and slopes down on the eastern side to the ocean dropoff at 30m (100ft). Stingrays and whitetip sharks rest on this sandy slope. On the north corner of the channel are a number of huge coral heads; here a school of humpback snappers (*Lutjanus gibbus*) and blue-striped snappers is often seen. As the channel is extremely narrow and shallow, the current accelerates as it passes over the ridge; the channel thereafter drops gently down to the sandy atoll bed. The reefs on both north and south sides of the channel are very healthy, with excellent hard and soft corals and an abundance of reef life. In the southwest season, when the currents predominantly flow out of the channel, manta rays are quite often seen waiting to be cleaned.

Both sides of the channel offer excellent snorkelling.

14 MEDHU FARU

★★★ ☆☆☆☆

Location: North corner of Guraidhoo Kandu.
Access: Kandooma (15min), Villivaru (20min), Biyadoo (20min), Cocoa (25min).
Conditions: Often a large rolling swell. The waves can break on the reef in the shallows.
Average visibility: 30m (100ft).
Average depth: 15m (50ft).
Maximum depth: 30m (100ft).
The ocean front of this reef is 200m (220yd) across and slopes gently down to 30m (100ft), where a long shallow cave with a sandy bottom runs just about the entire length of the front section of the reef. You can find stingrays in the sand and, if you look carefully, may be rewarded with the sight of ribbon eels in burrows at the back of the cave. Around the southern corner the reef is much steeper, and has lots of caves and overhangs full of soft corals and colourful fishes.

The channel wall makes an exciting drift dive, with plenty of action. Take your time exploring a coral rock which has fallen away from the reef about 100m (110yd) inside the channel. As you approach the corner of the channel, you might be pushed off the reef if the current is strong, so stay close to the reef.

The inside of the channel is good for snorkellers.

15 GURAIDHOO KANDU SOUTH

★★★★★ ☆☆☆

Location: Southern corner of Guraidhoo Kandu.
Access: Kandooma (15min), Villivaru (20min), Biyadoo (20min), Cocoa (25min).
Conditions: Frequently a rolling swell: The waves often break on the reef in the shallows.
Average visibility: 30m (100ft).
Average depth: 20m (65ft).
Maximum depth: 40m (130ft).
This site is well known for sightings of grey sharks and eagle rays. The break in the atoll rim south of Guraidhoo is a complex structure of two channels with a large reef in the middle. The southern channel, Guraidhoo Kandu, is 300m (330yd) across, and has sheer sides; its sea bed meets the ocean dropoff at 35m (115ft). Jump in on the outer reef of the south corner and drift with the current into the atoll. Most of the pelagic action can be observed on the ocean dropoff, where the oceanic water enters the channel. Inside the channel, all along the reef wall, are overhangs with plenty of sea fans and black coral bushes. Keep an eye open for the family of friendly and curious napoleon wrasse that patrols the reef. About 100m (110yd) inside the channel there is a basin in the reef, with a large coral outcrop in its

---

CROWN-OF-THORNS

When you first come across the crown-of-thorns starfish (*Acanthaster planci*) you can't help but admire its bright purple colour and sharp black spines. However, this animal can cause untold damage to a coral reef. The starfish feeds on and kills coral. It can push its whole stomach out through its mouth and secrete digestive juices onto the coral polyps to break them down. It then pulls the stomach back into its body, leaving the white limestone skeleton of the coral behind. The starfish prefer branching species such as *Acropora*. Since an outbreak of crown-of-thorns in parts of the Maldives in the 1980s, dive centres have been on their guard against the species. Today, measures to protect some of their natural predators, the giant triton (*Charonia tritonis*), triggerfish and humphead wrasse, have helped redress the ecological balance of the reef.

centre; take great care to stay close to the reef as the currents here can be unpredictable and it is easy to be swept off the reef and be forced to make an open-water ascent.

16 HATHIKOLHU KANDU EAST

★★★ ☆☆☆

Location: Eastern side of Hathikolhu Kandu.
Access: Rihiveli (20min), Fihalhohi (35min).
Conditions: Chop can develop if wind is against tide.
Average visibility: 25m (80ft).
Average depth: 15m (50ft).
Maximum depth: 30m (100ft).
The eastern side of this channel is the southernmost point of South Malé Atoll. It is exposed to the ocean currents that flow through Fulidhoo Kandu. On the point of the reef are a number of caves and ledges that drop down steeply across the channel. On a plateau set out from the main reef is a large rock with its top at 25m (80ft); here schooling grey reef sharks and hammerheads can sometimes be seen. This is a good dive if the currents are running into the atoll, which they are likely to be doing during the southwest season.

17 HATHIKOLHU KANDU WEST

★★★ ☆☆☆

Location: Western side of Hathikolhu Kandu.
Access: Rihiveli (20min), Fihalhohi (35min).
Conditions: Sheltered in most conditions. A short, choppy sea can develop when wind is against tide.
Average visibility: 25m (80ft).
Average depth: 15m (50ft).
Maximum depth: 30m (100ft).
At first sight this reef appears quite uninteresting, but in fact it is great for seeing some of the more unusual

underwater species in the Maldives. The corner of the reef slopes gently down from the reeftop, at 8m (25ft), in a series of ledges to reach the atoll bed at 30m (100ft). Look carefully and you may see pairs of ribbon eels. Many lionfish shelter and feed on the reef ledges, and you may also find leaf fish. The corner of the channel is marked by a large coral head on the reeftop, and here midnight and red snappers can be found schooling.

The inside of the channel is good for snorkelling.

18 FIHALHOHI FARU
★★★ ★★★

Location: 1km (1/2 mile) southwest of Fihalhohi Resort.
Access: Fihalhohi (10min), Rannalhi (20min).
Conditions: Exposed in southwest winds.
Average visibility: 25m (80ft).
Average depth: 20m (65ft).
Maximum depth: 35m (115ft).
This long narrow reef in the middle of the wide Lohi Channel offers a lovely dive in calm conditions during the southwest season. The western side of the reef, shaped like a basin, drops quickly down from 6m (20ft) to the sandy atoll floor at 30m (100ft). Coral outcrops are scattered around the edge of the basin and along the reef wall; there are several caves and overhangs. The eastern side of the reef is not as interesting, but the coral formations on the top of the whole area are good.

19 VAAGALI THILA
★★★

Location: 300m (330yd) southeast of Vaagali uninhabited island.
Access: Rannalhi (30min), Fihalhohi (40min).
Conditions: Exposed during southwest season.
Average visibility: 25m (80ft).
Average depth: 20m (65ft).
Maximum depth: 35m (115ft).
You never know what you might see at Vaagali Thila, which faces the ocean: you might spot sharks, eagle rays and schooling fish in the southwest season or manta rays in the northeast season. When the currents are flowing into the atoll, visibility can be extremely good, and large schools of snappers, fusiliers and jackfish may be seen on the point of the *thila*. The reeftop is at 10m (33ft); from here the walls slope gradually to the atoll floor at 30m (100ft). The best part of the dive is on the northern side of the *thila*, where there is a basin in the reef. This is full of soft corals and masses of reef fish. On the western side the coral is quite broken, and there is fire coral on the reeftop.

In the northeast season, when mantas can be found feeding in the channel, you may be better off snorkelling with them.

20 BOLIFUSHI THILA
★★★

Location: North of Bolifushi Resort Island.
Access: Bolifushi (10min), Laguna Beach (20min).
Conditions: Can be very choppy if wind is against tide.
Average visibility: 25m (80ft).
Average depth: 15m (50ft).
Maximum depth: 35m (115ft).
The hard corals on the top of this *thila*, 200m (220yd) in diameter and with its top at a depth of 10m (33ft), are particularly healthy. You can see fine foliaceous corals as well as good reef-fish life. The best diving is to the north and west, where the sides slope down moderately. There are some large coral outcrops at 28m (100ft) on the western side; there are often napoleon wrasse and some large saddleback groupers. The best plan is to visit the *thila* when the current is gently flowing into the atoll, to jump in on the northwest corner and then descend to the coral heads to explore the western slopes. From here, ascend to the reeftop, where there is a ridge of coral.

This *thila* is not good for snorkelling.

21 VELASSARU FARU
★★★ ★★★

Location: Velassaru Faru.
Access: Laguna Beach (15min), Vaadhoo (20min), Bolifushi (25min).
Conditions: There can be a swell and uncomfortable conditions in northwesterly winds.
Average visibility: 25m (80ft).
Average depth: 15m (50ft).
Maximum depth: 40m (130ft).
This site is part of the long fringing southern reef of the Vaadhoo Channel. It has steeply sloping walls that fall away to the ocean depths. The best section of the reef is found directly opposite the westernmost point of Laguna Beach Island. Here there are caves and swim-throughs between 20m (65ft) and 35m (115ft) and a fantastic variety of hard and soft corals and fishes. Watch out for the many species of moray eels, including the unusual honeycomb moray (*Gymnothorax favagineus*), masked moray (*Gymnothorax breedeni*) and yellow margin moray (*Gymnothorax flavimarginatus*). Sightings of hammerhead and thresher sharks are common at the point where the Velassaru Channel opens out to the ocean. Whitetip sharks are frequently seen patrolling the reeftop.

The site is very good for snorkelling.

Diving in the Maldives is always a wonderful experience but nothing quite matches your first time on the coral reefs when you find yourself surrounded by a myriad of reef fish and corals of every imaginable colour, shape and size. Colour has a very important and sometimes vital part to play in the life of the fishes and plants that live in the ocean. In order to survive, fish have developed colours which camouflage and protect them from their natural predators; some reef fish are even able to change colour to blend in with their surroundings.

Bars and stripes on fish appear to play a role in helping them to become invisible to their predators – bars across the body help slower-moving fish to remain unseen amongst the corals, plants and encrustations found on a coral reef. The deep-bodied angelfish, butterflyfish and triggerfish have bars going across their back which present a confusing target as they move amongst the rocks and crevasses of the reef. Such fish cannot swim particularly fast but are adept at manoeuvring amongst the corals in a way that creates confusing visual patterns. Their strategy appears to be successful; experiments have shown that no large numbers of these types of fish are to be found in the stomachs of predators.

Certain species of fish send messages of aggression or territorial warnings by a change in their body hues or by altering their patterns, while others use colour to establish their gender to fish of the same species, or to attract a mate. While bars and spots can act as camouflage, it seems they can also help as a positive means of recognition both within species and to other types of fish. The dainty and brightly painted butterflyfish, for example, tends to have only one partner and, when they greet each other, they often tip slightly to one side to show their patterning. It has also been observed that these little fish often tend to swim one behind the other: viewed from behind like this, the bars may help the trailing fish to identify the one in front, despite the fact that it has only a very slim profile.

There is still a great deal that we do not know about why fish sport such dashing livery. Not yet established is just how much colour is actually seen by the fish, and more quantitative behavioural studies need to be done to evaluate the abilities of reef fishes to discriminate colours. One thing, however, is certain – observing the colours and changing patterns of fish in the Indian Ocean can afford hours of pleasure and interest.

Below: *This sailfin tang displays a mesmerizing array of bars and spots.*

How to Get There

By air: All international flights land at the airport on Hulhule Island in the southern part of North Malé Atoll. Most transfers from the airport are made by speedboat or *dhoani*. There is a helipad on Guraidhoo Island, in the southeast of South Malé Atoll. The helicopters are operated by Hummingbird Helicopters (tel 325708/fax 323161). As an indication, flying time by helicopter from the airport to Guraidhoo is 15min. A local boat meets you at the helipad and transfers you to your resort.

By boat: Most of the resorts in South Malé Atoll use speedboats for their transfers rather than the much slower *dhoanis*. All resorts have their own arrangements regarding transfers; when you book your island resort, check the transfer at the same time. You can book a private speedboat – a number of speedboat companies offer this service from Malé – but the price may be quite high. As indications, a speedboat transfer to Biyadoo takes 50min and to Rihiveli 80min.

Where to Stay and Eat

Visitors normally stay on registered tourist islands, in other words at a resort. Every resort provides its own dining facilities.

Biyadoo Island Resort

tel 447171/fax 447272; 96 rooms; 30km (21 miles) from airport
The larger sister of Villivaru (see page 73). Biyadoo's accommodation is based in six two-storey buildings, all close to the water's edge. Ground-floor rooms have a private patio leading to the beach; first-floor rooms have a private balcony. All rooms have AC, hot and cold water, minibar. Facilities include windsurfing, catamaran sailing, waterskiing. The dive centre, run by Nautico, is a PADI 5-star IDC. The house reef is excellent for both snorkelling and diving. Visa, American Express, Mastercard, JCB.

Bolifushi Island

tel 443517/fax 445924; 40 rooms; 16km (10 miles) from airport
A tiny round island offering quite sophisticated accommodation in 32 AC rooms and eight bungalows. All rooms have hot and cold water, minibar, telephone. The thatched bar and coffee shop are built over the lagoon. Karaoke, live music and cultural shows on a regular basis. Facilities include windsurfing, canoeing, catamaran sailing, parasailing. The dive school offers PADI and CMAS courses. The house reef is good. Visa, American Express, MasterCard.

Cocoa Island

tel 443713/fax 441919; 8 rooms; 30km (20 miles) from airport

An exclusive resort on a small island with stunning beaches, a beautiful lagoon and a price tag to fit. The thatched rooms have few facilities and are made as simply as possible, from local woods. No AC. Facilities include catamaran sailing, windsurfing, waterskiing. There is a small dive school. The house reef can only be reached by boat. Visa, American Express, MasterCard, EuroCard.

Dhigufinolhu Tourist Resort

tel 443599/fax 443886; 64 rooms; 25km (15 miles) from airport
This resort is linked to Palm Tree Island by a wooden walkway that runs across the lagoon for almost 1km (½ mile). Some of the beachfront bungalows have AC; all have hot and cold water, bath, minibar and telephone. Facilities include windsurfing, catamaran sailing, waterskiing. The dive school offers a range of PADI and CMAS courses. Access to the house reef is limited.

Taj Lagoon Resort (Embudhu Finolhu)

tel 444451/fax 445925; 64 rooms; 12km (7 miles) from airport
Recently taken over by the Taj group of hotels, this remarkably long, thin island has beautiful beaches and a huge shallow lagoon. There are two types of accommodation. The 48 beach bungalows are simple thatched cottages on stilts at the water's edge; each has its own sundeck area and ladder into the lagoon; all have AC, ceiling fan, hot and cold water, coffee-making facilities, minibar and telephone. The 16 lagoon rooms, set on the beach, have a bath in addition to the above amenities. Facilities include waterskiing, windsurfing, catamaran sailing. There is a PADI dive school. The house reef can only be reached by boat. Visa, American Express, MasterCard.

Embudhu Village

tel 444776/fax 442673; 120 rooms; 11km (7 miles) from airport
A round island with beautiful beaches. There are 62 non-AC rooms and 42 AC rooms on the water's edge, facing the beach, plus 16 water bungalows built over the lagoon. Some rooms have hot and cold water, and some have a bath and minibar. Facilities include catamaran sailing, windsurfing, parasailing. The dive school offers a range of PADI courses. The house reef is reasonable and easily accessible. Visa, American Express, MasterCard.

Fihalhohi Tourist Resort

tel 442903/fax 443803; 92 rooms; 30km (22 miles) from airport
On the western side of the atoll, a small island offering accommodation in 92 thatched beachfront rooms. Only 18 of the rooms have AC, hot and cold water and a

fridge. Facilities include catamaran sailing, windsurfing, canoeing, waterskiing. The house reef is good. The PADI dive school offers a range of courses. Visa, American Express, MasterCard, Diners' Club.

Fun Island Resort (Bodufinolhu)

tel 444558/fax 443958; 100 rooms; 35km (22 miles) from airport
Well established resort with modern buildings; accommodation is in 100 rooms built along the beach. The rooms are built in terraces and are of good standard, all with AC, hot and cold water shower, telephone, minibar. There are three bars, including a karaoke bar, and a coffee shop. The long, thin island has very pretty beaches. The large lagoon is good for windsurfing, catamaran sailing. When the tide is low you can walk to the uninhabited islands of Kudafinolhu and Maadhoo. The dive school offers BSAC courses as well as PADI and CMAS diving courses. The house reef can only be reached by boat. Visa, American Express, MasterCard, Diners' Club.

Kandooma Tourist Resort

tel 444452/fax 445948; 58 rooms; 30km (18 miles) from airport
Across the reef from Guraidhoo, this small, low-budget resort, with thick vegetation at its centre, provides simple accommodation. Some rooms have AC and hot and cold water. Facilities include catamaran sailing, windsurfing, waterskiing. The dive school offers a range of PADI courses. There is limited access to the house reef, which is on the northern side; it has caves and often strong currents. Visa, American Express, MasterCard.

Laguna Beach Resort (Velassaru)

tel 443042/fax 443041; 115 rooms; 11km (7 miles) from airport
A sophisticated, busy resort with five restaurants, swimming pool and choice of bars. Accommodation is in semidetached tiled bungalows. All rooms have AC, ceiling fan, hot and cold water, telephone, minibar. Facilities include tennis court, gymnasium, windsurfing, catamaran sailing, small freshwater swimming pool. The dive school, run by Inter Aqua, offers PADI courses. The house reef is excellent.

Olhuveli View Hotel

tel 441957/fax 445942; 125 rooms; 40km (22 miles) from airport
Built on a small, narrow island, this Japanese-run resort provides accommodation in 112 superior and standard rooms, plus 12 water bungalows. The main rooms are built in two-storey blocks; the water bungalows are set well out over the lagoon. Facilities include large freshwater swimming pool, tennis court, mini-golf, billiards, karaoke, disco, live music,

Above: *Biyadoo Resort Island's beautiful palm-fringed beach is easily accessible by boat.*

windsurfing, catamaran sailing, canoeing. The dive school offers PADI courses. The house reef can only be reached by boat. Visa, American Express, MasterCard, EuroCard.

Palm Tree Island (Veliganduhuraa)
tel 443882/fax 440009; 16 rooms; 25km (17 miles) from airport
This tiny island is part of a group of three islands connected by walkways across the water. The 16 large thatched rooms have AC, hot and cold water and telephone. The dive centre is located on one of the satellite islands, Bushy Island. The resort island Dhigufinolhu is the third in the group. Access to the house reef is limited.

Club Rannalhi
tel 442034/fax 442035; 72 rooms; 35km (21 miles) from airport
On the western side of the atoll, Rannalhi has many tall palm trees and thick vegetation at its centre. Accommodation is in 100 rooms, some of which have AC, hot and cold water, bath, hair-dryer, minibar. There are two restaurants and a coffee shop. Facilities include catamaran sailing, windsurfing, waterskiing. The dive centre offers PADI and CMAS courses. The easily accessible house reef is excellent for both snorkelling and diving. Visa, American Express, MasterCard.

Rihiveli Beach Resort
tel 443731/fax 440052; 47 rooms; 40km (25 miles) from airport
The southernmost resort in the atoll, Rihiveli has a good atmosphere and

beautiful beaches and lagoon. Run by a Frenchman, the resort has become well known for its good food. Accommodation is in bungalows at the water's edge; all have a small private terrace. Facilities include catamaran sailing, windsurfing, waterskiing, parasailing, tennis court, games room. The dive centre offers a range of PADI and CMAS courses. The house reef can only be reached by boat. Visa, American Express.

Vaadhoo Diving Paradise
tel 443976/fax 443397; 31 rooms; 10km (6 miles) from airport
A very small island situated on the edge of the Vaadhoo Channel. Accommodation is in three types of rooms: the Sunrise Wing has 24 rooms built on two floors; the Sunset Wing comprises five water bungalows and two suites built on stilts above the water. All rooms have AC, hot and cold water; the Sunset Wing rooms have a bath. Facilities are limited: only windsurfing and scuba diving. The dive school offers PADI courses. The house reef is excellent. Visa, American Express, MasterCard.

Villivaru Island Resort
tel 447070/fax 447272; 60 rooms; 30km (21 miles) from airport
Smaller sister of Biyadoo (see page 72), this is an unsophisticated, quiet island with accommodation in terraced rooms which have verandahs that open onto the beach. Each room has AC, ceiling fan, minibar, hot and cold water. Good range of

watersports, including catamaran sailing, windsurfing. There are regular transfers to Biyadoo Resort. The dive centre, run by Nautico, is a PADI 5-star IDC. The easily accessed house reef offers good diving and snorkelling.

DIVING EMERGENCIES
There is a very small hospital on Guraidhoo; its facilities are limited. Some of the resort islands run general medical surgeries, but these are mainly for the treatment of ear infections and simple cuts. Guests requiring any kind of medical assistance can transfer reasonably quickly by speedboat, helicopter (from Guraidhoo) or seaplane to the main hospital or a private clinic in Malé (AMDC Clinic tel 325979/ADK Medical Centre tel 324332). There are no recompression facilities in South Malé Atoll: any divers in trouble are carried by speedboat to the Hyperbaric Centre on Bandos Island Resort (tel 440088/fax 440060)

EXCURSIONS
There are 11 **uninhabited islands** in South Malé Atoll; some can be reached from nearby resorts by wading through the lagoon. The **fishing islands** of Gulhi, Maafushi and Guraidhoo can be visited from resort islands in the southern part of South Malé Atoll. There are souvenir shops on all these islands, plus small supply shops stocking a limited quantity of fresh and tinned foods. Most resorts also offer **fishing excursions** aboard a *dhoani*.

FELIDHOO (VAAVU) AND MULAKU (MEEMU)

Felidhoo and Mulaku atolls are extraordinarily quiet and, in terms of both tourist resorts and fishing islands, only barely developed. Indeed, as far as Mulaku is concerned, only recently did the government agree to the opening of the first resorts here, and Mulaku Atoll remains to be properly explored. Felidhoo Atoll, including the single reef to the south, Vattaru, has always been a great favourite with safari boat operators. Not only are there several superb dive sites but the area is beautiful and close to Malé.

Felidhoo Atoll's locally inhabited islands are Fulidhoo in the north, Thinadhoo, Felidhoo and Keyodhoo on the east, and Rakeedhoo in the south. The islanders all rely heavily on tuna fishing; besides supplying the needs of the two resorts in the atoll, the fishermen smoke or dry part of their catch to be sold in the dried fish market in Malé. These islands have small populations – Thinadhoo has a population of just 150. Although the influence of tourism has had some impact on Fulidhoo and Felidhoo, the other islands remain relatively unaffected.

The capital of the atoll is Felidhoo, well known for the hospitality it offers to international visitors, its *bodu beru* performances and its excellent football team. In the southern part of the atoll, Rakeedhoo is a traditional fishing village with a big fleet. The island was once renowned for its tiger shark fishery, in the days when oil from the sharks' liver was used on fishing boats as a waterproofing agent.

The main part of boot-shaped Felidhoo Atoll has a number of uninhabited islands. Fotteyo, the largest, is the easternmost point of the Maldives. Bodumohoraa and Hulhidhoo are both stunning islands, with beautiful beaches and excellent snorkelling. Kudiboli, a small uninhabited island on the western side, has a safe anchorage and offers good snorkelling for guests aboard safari boats. Many of the other uninhabited islands are smaller – often no more than a patch of sand and a few bushes. The large reef to the south of the main atoll, Vattaru, has a single uninhabited island, Vattaruhuraa, which lies adjacent to the only entrance to the big lagoon. The island is densely vegetated and has no beaches; the shallow fringing reef around it makes access extremely difficult.

Opposite: *Peaceful Felidhoo Atoll has several stunning uninhabited islands.*
Above: *The blue ribbon eel is a secretive animal, usually only seen with its head protruding.*

DIVING IN FELIDHOO (VAAVU) AND MULAKU (MEEMU) ATOLLS

There are exceptions, but generally speaking the most exciting diving here is in the many channels that break the outer rim of the reef. Consequently the diving is on average a little deeper than the *thila* diving predominant in the northern atolls, and the success of a dive is more often dependent on the direction and strength of the current. Given good conditions in either the southwest or the northeast season, the diving in Felidhoo Atoll is both exciting and rewarding. Mulaku Atoll has only recently become a diving possibility, though channels along the northern fringing reef are already known to be good sites.

The fringing reef of Felidhoo Atoll on both east and west sides drops steeply to great depths. In many of the northern atolls the reef drops to a shelf at about 40m (130ft) before sloping off to the ocean. However, in Felidhoo Atoll this is not the case: the reef is truly a vertical dropoff. With the combination of deep water, narrow channels and the natural funnelling effect caused by the shape of the atoll, the diving can be superb.

During the northeast season the east side of the atoll benefits from the clear, blue oceanic water flowing in through the narrow channels. Here at the front of the current, pelagic species, especially grey reef sharks, are seen in great numbers. The reefs on the east side are mostly in pristine condition with very little wave damage. For encounters with manta rays and whale sharks, look to the western side of the atoll, where these

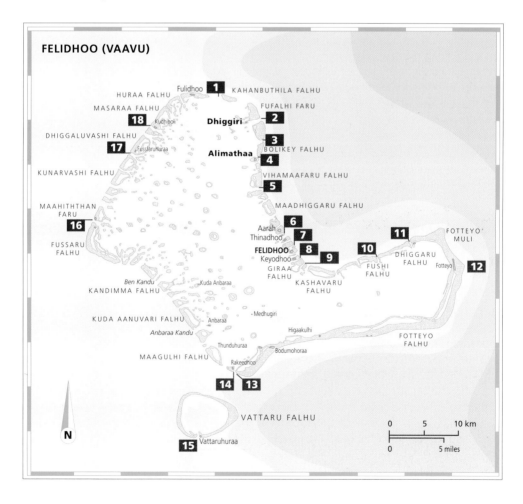

FELIDHOO (VAAVU)

animals are to be found feeding on the plankton-rich currents as they flow out of the atoll.

In the southwest season the channels on the west side of the atoll offer superb diving, with excellent visibility and great pelagic life. At this time of year the seas can be rough, so diving the channels may be difficult; if so, there are some cleaning and feeding stations on the east side of the atoll where mantas are regularly seen.

Felidhoo (Vaavu)

Felidhoo Atoll has five locally inhabited islands, 12 uninhabited islands and two resorts. The resorts are both owned by the same Italian tour operator. Alimathaa is a beautiful island with lovely beaches and lagoon. Dhiggiri is as beautiful but very small, and caters for a more exclusive market.

Both islands offer excellent diving, especially in the northeast season when visibility is very good. Many of the reefs on the eastern side of Felidhoo Atoll are in perfect condition and wonderful for snorkellers and divers alike. There are several thrilling shark dives in the atoll, where divers may be lucky enough to see hammerhead sharks as well as more common grey sharks. Fotteyo Kandu (Site 11) is probably the best-known dive site in the Maldives, and is considered by some to be among the best dive sites in the world.

1 FARUKOLHU KANDU
★★★★ ★★★★

Location: 2km (1½ miles) east of Fulidhoo fishing island.
Access: Dhiggiri (30min), Alimathaa (50min).
Conditions: Exposed. Can be very choppy if there is wind against tide.
Average visibility: 25m (80ft).
Average depth: 20m (65ft).
Maximum depth: 40m+ (130ft+).
At the northernmost point of Felidhoo Atoll, a wide channel separates Felidhoo Island from Farukolhu Reef. Unlike many of the Maldivian channels, this is very shallow, at just 12m (40ft). The face of the channel fronts the ocean, and a powerful current brings plankton-rich water into the atoll; with this comes a host of reef and pelagic fish life. The channel, leading from the atoll into the ocean, slopes gently down from 12m (40ft) to 15m (50ft), where it meets the ocean dropoff, which is vertical down to at least 60m (200ft). This wall is interspersed with small caves and soft corals, sea fans, whip corals and colourful sponges. The best part of the dive is the edge of the step that runs across the mouth of the channel, where there are many different species of hard and soft corals in very good condition. Whitetip sharks, eagle rays and many napoleon wrasse live in the channel. Expect to see four or five turtles.

2 DHIGGIRI KANDU
★★★

Location: 1km (½ mile) due east of Dhiggiri Island Resort.
Access: Dhiggiri (10min), Alimathaa (40min).
Conditions: Generally good. A short, choppy sea may develop with wind against tide. Very strong currents can run through the channel at times.
Average visibility: 30m (100ft).
Average depth: 30m (100ft).
Maximum depth: 40m+ (130ft+).
This channel is too deep and too wide to cross safely in one dive. You can jump in on either the north or the south corner, then descend to the atoll plate and to the edge of the dropoff at 35m (115ft). Depending on the strength of the current, you can thereafter follow the line of the dropoff for about 50m (55yd) into the centre of the channel. This is a big fish dive. Grey reef sharks are often found cruising in the channel along with jackfish, rainbow runners and sometimes hammerhead sharks. Then you should retrace your steps back to the reef, ready for your ascent. The drift along the reef into the channel is interesting, and the reef is full of life – although the corals are not that spectacular. If the current is running out of the atoll, you will not see the sharks and pelagic species.

TURTLES

The two species of turtle seen most often by divers in the Maldives are the hawksbill turtle (*Eretmochelys imbricata*) and the green turtle (*Chelonia mydas*). It is easy to tell the difference between the two if you remember that hawksbill turtles have a hooked beak and a narrow head, whereas the green turtle has a blunt head that is also longer. The hawksbill turtle has two claws on each flipper whilst the green turtle has only one. The plates on the shell of the hawksbill turtle overlap; those on the green turtle do not. Hawksbill turtles are found on the reeftop feeding on sponges and soft corals, whereas green turtles usually feed on seagrasses found in the lagoons.

---

3 MEDHU KANDU (DHIGGIRI KUDA KANDU)

★★★★ ☆☆☆

Location: First channel, 4km (2 miles) south of Dhiggiri Kandu.
Access: Alimathaa (20min), Dhiggiri (20min).
Conditions: Usually calm, although conditions can be choppy if there is wind against tide. Strong currents can run into the channel.
Average visibility: 30m (100ft).
Average depth: 20m (65ft).
Maximum depth: 30m (100ft).
The underwater equivalent of a cinema, Medhu Kandu is about 250m (275yd) wide. In the centre is a *thila* which almost spans the width of the channel. The front of the *thila*, which faces the ocean, is semicircular and shaped like an auditorium. The top of the reef is at 10m (33ft) and steps down to 20m (65ft); from here it drops down gently to the ocean depths. On the slopes several coral outcrops attract a marvellous variety of schooling fish. Whitetip sharks, eagle rays and turtles are common here, as are large schools of bannerfish and oriental sweetlips. All this action is set against a backdrop of colourful hard and soft corals.

The snorkelling on both the *thila* and the reef is usually excellent.

4 MIYARU KANDU

★★★★ ☆☆☆

Location: North channel of Alimathaa Resort.
Access: Alimathaa (5min), Dhiggiri (30min).
Conditions: Usually calm, although conditions can be choppy if there is wind against tide. Strong currents can run into the channel.
Average visibility: 30m (100ft).
Average depth: 30m (100ft).
Maximum depth: 40m+ (130ft+).

Miyaru means 'shark' in Dhivehi. In this channel you may see large numbers of schooling grey reef sharks, plus hammerheads. The channel is about 100m (110yd) wide, narrow enough for experienced divers to swim across from one side to the other. Always make the dive with the current flowing into the atoll from the ocean; your best dive plan is to jump in on the north corner of the channel and descend quickly down to 30m (100ft), where the atoll plate meets the ocean dropoff. This is the lip of the channel, and you can swim along this ridge to the other side. Keep below the level of the lip to stay sheltered from any strong incoming currents.

This is a big fish dive; expect to see large pelagic species, particularly grey reef sharks, rainbow runners, jackfish and tuna. On reaching the other side, drift into the atoll and make a safe ascent onto the top of the reef, which is at 6m (20ft).

The southern side of the channel offers an enjoyable drift dive, with good coral and fish life. Be careful of air consumption and decompression requirements when making the channel crossing, as it is all too easy to be distracted by the thrilling and spectacular fish life.

The snorkelling is enjoyable on either side of the fringing reefs.

5 DEVANA KANDU

★★★★ ☆☆☆☆

Location: Second channel south of Alimathaa Island Resort.
Access: Alimathaa (15min), Dhiggiri (30min).
Conditions: Usually calm, although can be choppy if there is wind against tide. Strong currents can run into the channel.
Average visibility: 30m (100ft).
Average depth: 25m (80ft).
Maximum depth: 40m+ (130ft+). ·
Devana Channel has two ocean passes, with a long, narrow *thila* between them. The best part of the dive is the southern channel, some 150m (165yd) wide and with its floor at 20m (65ft). You can swim across both northern and southern channels in one dive. In the centre of the southern channel, set back from the ocean dropoff, is a huge stack of coral that must be centuries old. This coral head rises from 20m (65ft) to within 6m (20ft) of the surface and supports a massive amount of reef fish, particularly a colony of large moray eels. From the base of the stack the channel slopes gently down towards the dropoff, at 30m (100ft). You can cross the channel along the lip of the dropoff and, with an incoming current, can expect to see grey reef sharks, whitetip sharks, rainbow runners and eagle rays. This is a Protected Marine Area.

6 THINADHOO FARU

★★★ ☆☆☆☆

Location: Northeastern point of Thinadhoo Reef.
Access: Alimathaa (60min).
Conditions: Usually calm, although can be choppy if there is wind against tide. Strong currents can run into the channel.
Average visibility: 30m (100ft).
Average depth: 20m (65ft).
Maximum depth: 35m (115ft).

The northeast corner of this reef faces the ocean. The reeftop starts at about 6m (20ft) and slopes gently down in a series of ledges to a sandy plateau at 35m (115ft). This area of the reef and the ledges are packed with life, and there are many shallow caves from 25m (80ft) down to 35m (115ft). On the edge of the reef are great clouds of schooling fish, including red snappers, surgeonfish and dark-banded fusiliers. Stingrays and whitetip sharks are often seen on the plateau. The branching and massive corals on the reeftop are healthy and colourful. Leaving the current point with the reef to either right or left, you can drift around the house reef; this is great for both diving and snorkelling, offering above-average corals and fish life.

7 FELIDHOO KANDU

★★★ ☆☆☆☆

Location: South channel of Felidhoo fishing island.
Access: Live-aboard only.
Conditions: Usually calm, although can be choppy if there is wind against tide. Strong currents can run into the channel in the northeast season.
Average visibility: 30m (100ft).
Average depth: 30m (100ft).
Maximum depth: 40m+ (130ft+).

During the northeast season, ocean currents flow into the channel between Felidhoo and Keyodhoo. A long submerged reef rising from 30m (100ft) to within 3m (10ft) divides this channel into two smaller ones. The narrower, northern channel offers the best diving. The ideal dive plan is to descend to the atoll plate at the southeast corner of Felidhoo Island and make the 100m (110yd) crossing to the other side of the channel, staying on the edge of the dropoff. You can then make a safe ascent to the reeftop. On either side, the reefs are in excellent condition and have fabulous branching and laminar corals. There is an abundance of reef fish on the reef slope. You can usually see turtles feeding on the reeftop.

The best snorkelling is on either side of the channel.

Below: *The hawksbill turtle is easily identifiable by its hooked beak and narrow head.*

8 KEYODHOO BODU THILA
★★★

Location: In the first channel south of Keyodhoo fishing island.
Access: Live-aboard only.
Conditions: Usually calm, but can be choppy if there is wind against tide. Strong currents can run into the channel in the northeast season.
Average visibility: 30m (100ft).
Average depth: 20m (50ft).
Maximum depth: 40m+ (130ft+).
This long narrow *thila*, close to the atoll rim, is washed by ocean currents in the northeast season. The top of the *thila* is at 5m (16ft); the western side slopes steeply down to the channel floor, at 25m (80ft). The eastern end of the *thila* faces the ocean, sloping down at 45° to the channel dropoff, which is at 40m (130ft). With an incoming current, you should jump in well up-current to have the best opportunity to reach the front of the *thila*, where numerous pelagic species are commonly seen. From here you can drift along either side of the *thila* and thus back onto the reeftop, where the coral life is good.

9 KEYODHOO KUDA KANDU
★★★ ★★★★★

Location: The second channel south of Keyodhoo fishing island.
Access: Live-aboard only.
Conditions: Usually calm, but can be choppy if there is wind against tide. Strong currents can run into the channel in the northeast season.
Average visibility: 30m (100ft).
Average depth: 15m (50ft).
Maximum depth: 30m (100ft).
Best done when there is a strong in-current, this is an excellent drift dive, with unusual topography. Jump in on the southern corner of the channel and follow the reef, keeping it to your left. The channel bed shallows from 30m (100ft) at its entrance to just 15m (50ft) after about 300m (330yd). Here the reef follows a bend to the left, and there is a separate reef, like an island, to the right. On entering this passage the sandy floor shallows up to 10m (33ft); it feels as if you are in a natural swimming pool. The corals on the side of the fringing reef are in excellent condition; the reflection of the sunlight on the white sand brings the site alive with colour.

Opposite: *A large group of fusiliers school above the reef and its resident anthias.*

10 FOTTEYO WEST CHANNEL (FUSHI KANDU)
★★★★ ★★★

Location: Second channel west of Fotteyo uninhabited island.
Access: Alimathaa (120min), Dhiggiri (150min).
Conditions: Usually calm, but can be choppy if there is wind against tide. Very strong currents can run into the channel in the northeast season.
Average visibility: 30m (100ft).
Average depth: 20m (65ft).
Maximum depth: 35m (115ft).
This channel is about 80m (88yd) wide, and it can be crossed easily in one dive if you follow the edge of the dropoff, which is at 30m (100ft). After the dropoff, the mouth of the channel is like a huge coral bank, sloping upwards to form the channel bed at about 20m (65ft). Below this is the vertical wall of the outer ocean reef.

Set 50m (55yd) back in the middle of the channel is a long, narrow *thila*, which rises from 20m (65ft) to within 10m (33ft) of the surface. The whole channel floor is covered in excellent branching, massive and laminar corals of all types. Out on the dropoff eagle rays, schooling jacks, snappers and tuna, to name but a few, cruise on the currents.

The *thila* and fringing reef, at a depth of just 2m (6ft), are both superb snorkelling sites that harbour a mass of reef fish.

11 FOTTEYO KANDU
★★★★★ ★★★★★

Location: First channel to the west of Fotteyo uninhabited island in the north fringing reef of the atoll.
Access: Many resorts offer day excursions to this site.
Conditions: Generally calm, although big overfalls can build up if there is wind against tide. Currents into and out of the channel can be very strong.
Average visibility: 30m (100ft).
Average depth: 20m (65ft).
Maximum depth: 40m+ (130ft+).
This is a stunning, remote place, and it is well worth diving here at least twice and ideally four or five times to fully appreciate its beauty. The site is part of the vertical wall of the fringing reef, and it is the funnelling effect of the currents flowing into the channel that concentrates the superb marine life. Fotteyo Kandu, about 200m (220yd) wide, is divided into two narrow passages by a large *thila* that shallows to within 3m (10ft) of the surface. The west pass is some 100m (110yd) wide; the *thila* extends across the mouth of the channel for 70m (77yd), leaving just 30m (33yd) for the eastern pass. The

average depth of the channel is 20m (65ft), and it meets the ocean with a vertical dropoff descending to many hundreds of metres. In the western channel, the wall of the ocean dropoff hosts a stack of caves at depths from 20m (65ft) to over 50m (165ft). The roofs of the caves and the overhangs are festooned with beautiful iridescent yellow soft corals. A number of swim-throughs are packed with fishes, and hammerhead sharks are often seen off this wall. The top of the *thila* is covered in hard corals of all types, colours and sizes.

Eagle rays frequently hang in the currents that flow through the narrow eastern passage. The *thila* extends southwards for 150m (165yd), its sides gently sloping down to the channel bed, which is at 20m (65ft).

A drift over the sandy floor of the channel, known by many as Triggerfish Alley, is another thrilling dive. Dolphins can often be seen and heard swimming through the channel.

12 FOTTEYO EAST POINT
★★★

Location: The easternmost point of Felidhoo Atoll.
Access: Live-aboard only.
Conditions: A moderate swell is usually present on the shallows close to the reef. Currents can be very strong along the reef.
Average visibility: 30m (100ft).
Average depth: 25m (80ft).
Maximum depth: 40m+ (130ft+).

This, the easternmost point of the Maldives, is like the toe of a boot that divides the currents as they hit the atoll rim. A drift along this reef is a thrilling dive; this is one of the most exposed reefs in the Indian Ocean, and simply anything could come by. The massive corals on the reef slope, going down to 40m (130ft), are home to an abundance of marine life. As you might expect at such an exposed site, the reeftop is rugged in appearance. At 40m (130ft) the reef begins to slope more steeply, descending quickly towards the blue depths. Silvertip and silky sharks, naturally shy, flirt with divers on the edge of visibility.

SURVIVAL BAG

For a small fish on the reef, dozing at night time is a perilous activity, as this is the time when predatory hunters such as jackfish and whitetip sharks are hoping for an easy meal. However, some species of parrotfish have developed a sophisticated protection in the form of a mucous cocoon. As night falls, glands in the skin of the parrotfish secrete a mucous membrane that encloses the entire body like a cellophane wrapper. As well as being poisonous to other fish, the membrane may prevent the parrotfish attracting predatory species with its odour.

---

13 RAKEEDHOO KANDU EAST
★★★★ ★★★★

Location: Eastern side of Rakeedhoo Kandu.
Access: A number of resort islands make day excursions to this site.
Conditions: There are often confused currents that create turbulence and overfalls across the entrance to the channel.
Average visibility: 30m (100ft).
Average depth: 25m (80ft).
Maximum depth: 40m+ (130ft+).

Rakeedhoo is the southernmost point of Felidhoo Atoll; there is a huge flow of water in and out of this channel, which is narrow but 50m (165ft) deep. The channel is a little too wide and a little too deep to cross, but the dives on each of its corners are superb. The eastern corner and the outer fringing reef are vertical walls with many large caves at depths of 20–40m (65–130ft). These caves are resting places for stingrays, nurse sharks and an abundance of reef life. Large groupers, turtles and big families of napoleon wrasse live on the reeftop. The site is best dived with the current running into the channel; jump in on the outer fringing reef and drift into the channel with the reef on the right.

If the conditions are calm, the snorkelling on the reeftop is excellent.

14 RAKEEDHOO KANDU WEST
★★★★ ★★★★

Location: Western side of Rakeedhoo Kandu.
Access: A number of resort islands make day excursions to this site.
Conditions: There are often confused currents that create turbulence and overfalls across the entrance to the channel.
Average visibility: 30m (100ft).
Average depth: 25m (80ft).
Maximum depth: 40m+ (130ft+).

This corner of the channel slopes quickly down to the atoll plate, where it meets the ocean dropoff at 30m (100ft). From 20m (65ft) to 50m (165ft) there is a series of large caves lined with stunning blue hanging soft corals; many of the caves have huge sea fans and whip corals swaying in the current. In the right conditions, you can hang in the ocean at a depth of 35m (115ft) and look up at the stack of caves, the deep blue water beneath you and the brightly coloured caves above you – a fabulous scenario. A large school of big-eye trevallies usually circles on the current point, and all manner of pelagic species may be seen in this channel.

Above: *The gorgonian positions itself so that it can trap nutrients flowing with the current.*

15 VATTARU KANDU

★★★★ ☆☆☆☆

Location: Southern channel of Vattaru Falhu.
Access: Live-aboard only.
Conditions: Exposed in the southwest season, sheltered in the northeast. Surface conditions may be choppy if the current is running to the south.
Average visibility: 30m (100ft).
Average depth: 25m (80ft).
Maximum depth: 40m+ (130ft+).

This narrow channel, just 100m (110yd) wide, is the only break in the circular Vattaru Falhu. On the ocean side of the eastern corner the reef drops vertically down to great depths, and here the wall is punctuated with many shallow caves and fractures. The whole area is decorated with beautiful blue iridescent soft corals. Keeping the reef on your right, enter the channel, which is 30m (100ft) deep, and follow the sandy slope up to a section of overhangs which spans the channel like a step. From here you can cross to the other side of the channel or continue to drift on to the top of the overhangs, at 20m (65ft), and into the atoll.

In the northeast season manta rays may be seen feeding in the shallow waters close to the house reef of Vattaru Island, which makes for good snorkelling.

16 MAAFUSSARU KANDU

★★★ ☆☆

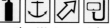

Location: Westernmost channel of Felidhoo Atoll.
Access: Live-aboard only.
Conditions: Very exposed in southwest winds. Very strong currents at times.
Average visibility: 30m (100ft).
Average depth: 25m (80ft).
Maximum depth: 35m (115ft).

About 200m (220yd) wide, this channel is narrow enough and shallow enough – its sea floor is at 30m (100ft) – for divers to cross from one side to the other. Ideally, you should make the crossing from the south to the north. Two-thirds of the way across you find a large *thila*, which rises from 30m (100ft) to within 10m (33ft) of the surface. Numerous coral outcrops are scattered around the channel bed and the shoulder of the reef; these are encrusted with brightly coloured soft corals. Snappers and fusiliers school on the current point; tuna, grey sharks and whitetip sharks are often seen hunting along the ocean dropoff.

Although the top of the *thila* is too deep for snorkelling, the fringing reefs offer reasonable snorkelling territory.

Above: *Powderblue surgeonfish mill around the shallow reef, home to healthy branching corals.*

17 KUNARVASHI KANDU
★★★ ★★★

Location: Third channel south of Kudiboli uninhabited island.

Access: Live-aboard only.

Conditions: Exposed in the southwest season. Strong currents can sometimes run into and out of the channel. Out-currents sometimes cause severe overfalls at the channel mouth.

Average visibility: 30m (100ft).

Average depth: 20m (65ft).

Maximum depth: 40m+ (130ft+).

Kunarvashi Channel is divided in two by a long submerged reef. The passage to the south of the reef offers the best dive; here you can swim across the mouth of a narrow – 80m (260ft) wide – channel in one dive. Jump in on the southern corner and cross to the *thila* (whose top is not particularly good) along the edge of the ocean dropoff, which is at 35m (115ft). The face of the dropoff has many beautiful caves, full of black coral trees, whip corals and sea fans. Between the reef and the *thila* the channel bed rises in a gentle sand slope, covered with coral outcrops and large table corals. Barracuda, sharks and eagle rays are often seen in the shallows of the channel, as are massive schools of blue-lined snapper – sometimes so dense in the water that you can lose sight of your buddy!

18 KUDIBOLI THILA
★★★★ ★★★★

Location: 1km (1/2 mile) west of Kudiboli uninhabited island.

Access: Alimathaa (90min), Dhiggiri (90min).

Conditions: Very exposed in southwest winds; very strong currents at times cause big eddies and overfalls.

Average visibility: 20m (65ft).

Average depth: 15m (50ft).

Maximum depth: 30m (100ft).

This *thila* is shaped like a teardrop. The bulb faces the ocean. On the north side a huge slab of rock has broken away to stand vertically just off the reef. The base of the slab is at 30m (100ft), its top at 12m (40ft). A number of coral heads are scattered on the channel floor. The rocks and pinnacle are covered in orange soft corals and excellent branching coral formations. Around them large schools of jackfish and red snappers circle in the eddies created by the pinnacle. Between the pinnacle and the *thila* is a gulley about 5m (16ft) wide. There are caves and overhangs between 25m (80ft) and 15m (50ft) on the north side of the main *thila*. The top of the *thila* is at 8m (25ft) and, although it is broken in areas, there is a huge amount of fish life, including stonefish and scorpionfish. This is a favourite haunt of octopus.

The snorkelling over the top of the *thila* is excellent. Manta rays are commonly seen in the northeast season.

Felidhoo (Vaavu)

HOW TO GET THERE

By air: All international flights land at the airport on Hulhule Island in the southern part of North Malé Atoll. There is no helipad in Felidhoo Atoll, so transfers from the airport are made by seaplane or by speedboat. The seaplanes are operated by Maldivian Air Taxi (tel 315201/fax 315203); their Twin Otters can land at most of the tourist resorts. As an indication, flying time by seaplane from the airport to Alimathaa is 35min.

By boat: There are no scheduled boat departures to Felidhoo Atoll. The resorts arrange their transfers according to guests' arrival time. You can book a private speedboat to transfer you to your island: a number of speedboat companies offer this service from Malé, though prices can be expensive. As an indication, a speedboat transfer to Alimathaa takes 50min.

WHERE TO STAY AND EAT

Visitors normally stay on registered tourist islands, in other words at a resort. Every resort provides its own dining facilities.

Alimathaa Island Resort
tel 450544/fax 450575; 70 rooms; 55km (36 miles) from airport
This resort has recently been taken over by an Italian tour operator, and the accommodation and facilities have been renovated. A beautiful island with superb beaches and a lovely lagoon. The simple accommodation is in thatched beachfront bungalows. All rooms have AC, hot and cold water, minibar. Facilities include catamaran sailing, windsurfing, canoeing. The dive school offers PADI courses. There is limited access to the house reef. Visa, American Express, MasterCard.

Dhiggiri Island Resort
tel 45059/fax 450592; 55 rooms; 68km (42 miles) from airport
A small, exclusive resort that has been redeveloped by the Italian tour operator who also manages Alimathaa. Dhiggiri is a very beautiful island, with a lovely lagoon and a tranquil atmosphere.
Accommodation is in 45 circular coral cottages. Facilities are limited to windsurfing. The dive school offers PADI courses. The house reef is excellent for both snorkelling and diving.

DIVING EMERGENCIES

There is no hospital in Felidhoo Atoll: if you require any kind of medical assistance you will need to travel to Malé. Transfer can be made reasonably quickly by speedboat or seaplane to the main hospital or private clinic in Malé (AMDC Clinic tel 325979/ADK Medical Centre tel 324332).

There are no recompression facilities in Felidhoo Atoll. Any divers in trouble are evacuated to the Hyperbaric Centre on Bandos Island Resort (tel 440088/fax 440060).

EXCURSIONS

The five **inhabited fishing islands** of Felidhoo Atoll can be visited by tourists from the resort islands. There are souvenir shops on some of the fishing islands, plus small supply shops stocking a limited quantity of fresh and tinned foods. Please remember to dress modestly. Both Alimathaa and Dhiggiri resorts offer excursions to some of the 12 **uninhabited islands** in Felidhoo Atoll. Both resorts offer **fishing excursions** aboard a *dhoani*.

Below: *Several gorgeous uninhabited islands in Felidhoo Atoll are accessible on a boat excursion.*

Divers and snorkellers seem to fall into two camps when it comes to sharks – those who say 'Wow!' and those who say 'Oh no!' Sharks have always inspired a degree of fear, a shame as more often than not they are certainly more frightened of humans than the other way around.

Maldivian waters are home to a large range of shark species, and few visitors return from a snorkelling or diving holiday without having seen at least one. Novice shark watchers should not be nervous: there are very few records of shark attacks in the Maldives and all those that have occurred have been the result of careless shark feeding by dive instructors or overzealous fishermen.

Veteran shark researcher Chas Anderson, author of *Diver's Guide to Sharks of the Maldives*, believes that while there are 25 recorded shark species in the Maldives, many more still await to be positively identified. The three most common sharks are the whitetip reef shark (*Triaenodon obesus*), the blacktip reef shark (*Carcharhinus melanopterus*) and the grey reef shark

(*Carcharhinus amblyrhynchos*). Also seen on a fairly regular basis are the scalloped hammerhead shark (*Sphyrna lewini*), the variegated shark (*Stegostoma fasciatum*) and the tawny nurse shark (*Nebrius ferrugineus*).

If you do see a shark and want to identify which species it might be, you should make careful note of its fin markings, overall shape and colour. The following guide should help you to identify your shark species:

REEF SHARKS
Whitetip shark (*Triaenodon obesus*)
This is easily distinguished from other sharks by its long thin body and blunt nose. It also has distinct white tips on the first dorsal fin and upper part of the tail fin. The body is grey in colour but may have small, irregular darker blotches on its side. These sharks are found exclusively on the reef. They feed on reef fish and octopus and commonly grow up to 1.3m (4ft).

Blacktip shark (*Carcharhinus melanopterus*)
These sharks commonly grow up to 1.3m (4ft). The species is pale brown in colour

Below: *The grey reef shark is pale on its under side and noticeably stocky in shape.*

with large black tips on all its fins – but most noticeably on its first dorsal fin and the lower part of the tail fin. The blacktip is often seen in very shallow water in island lagoons, where they patrol the sandy areas in search of shrimps and small fish life. They also eat octopus and other reef life.

Grey reef shark (*Carcharhinus amblyrhynchos*)
Thrilling to see, this stocky shark is grey in colour on the upper part of its body and paler on the lower part. It has a white tip to the trailing edge of its dorsal fin and a black edge to its tail fin. It commonly grows to 1.5m (5ft) and has a maximum size of 2m (6ft). This shark feeds on reef fish, octopus, lobsters and crabs.

BOTTOM-DWELLING SHARKS
Variegated shark (*Stegostoma fasciatum*)
Usually seen resting on the sandy sea floor, this shark also goes by the names of zebra shark and leopard shark. It is a beautifully marked species, very light brown in colour with large dark brown spots of varying size on a distinctly ridged back. The juveniles of the species are dark with pale stripes. It is a relatively large shark, commonly growing to 2.3m (7ft) and with a maximum recorded size in the region of 3.5m (12ft). Living on the bottom, it feeds on molluscs and crustaceans.

Tawny Nurse shark (*Nebrius ferrugineus*)
Sometimes growing up to more than 3m (10ft), nurse sharks are usually found resting in caves during the day. They are easily approached and unlikely to react unless severely provoked. As a bottom-dwelling species, they feed on octopus, crabs, sea urchins and small fish. Their first dorsal fin is located well back on the brown body and they have a long tail, measuring almost one-third of the total length of the shark.

OCEANIC SHARKS
Scalloped hammerhead shark (*Sphyrna lewini*)
Hammerheads are bizarre-looking animals with an eye at each end of their great hammer-shaped heads. Reaching up to 4m (13ft) in length, they are heavily built and grey in colour. The species may be found alone or in schools of great number on known hammerhead points such as Madivaru in the northern part of Ari Atoll (see page 119) or Fotteyo in Felidhoo Atoll (see page 82). It is thought that electroreceptors found in the hammer part of their heads helps them to locate fish and crustaceans buried in the sand.

Silky shark (*Carcharhinus falciformis*)
This is probably the most commonly occurring shark in the Maldives but is not often seen by divers as it inhabits oceanic waters rather than reefs. The silky commonly grows to 2.5m (8ft). A slender shark, it is dark grey with no fin markings. Silky sharks have a reputation for being very fast swimmers. We have seen a school of more than 100 silky sharks at Fotteyo Channel in Felidhoo Atoll.

Tiger shark (*Galeocerdo cuvier*)
This is a very large shark, growing up to more than 7m (23ft) in size and with a reputation for being dangerous. The tiger shark is grey in colour, with distinctive dark bars on its side and a broad head that tapers to a slender sharp-pointed tail. They will eat almost anything including turtles, marine mammals and sea birds, but visitors to the Maldives should not be worried since the species is rarely seen by divers.

PLANKTON-FEEDING SHARKS
Whale shark (*Rhincodon typus*)
It is the dream of every diver and snorkeller to see the largest fish in the sea. The great whale shark commonly grows to 9m (30ft) and often reaches a length of more than 12m (40ft). It has a broad head with a wide mouth, perfectly adapted for filter feeding on plankton and small fish. The shark is dark grey in colour with distinct ridges on its side and large white spots and stripes along the length of its body.

Mulaku (Meemu)

Sixteen kilometres (10 miles) to the south of Rakeedhu Island and across the Vattaru Channel is Mulaku Atoll. Mulaku has nine fishing islands and 24 uninhabited islands. The atoll is distinctive in that all the inhabited islands – some of which are very large – are located on the east side. The total population is approximately 4800. The capital island of the atoll is Muli, though Dhiggaru in the north of the atoll is the most populated. Kolhuvaariyaafushi and Boli Mulah islands are known for growing yams.

Until a short time ago, this atoll was closed to tourists, but in 1997 the government agreed to the development of two uninhabited islands in its southeast, Medhufushi and Hakuraahuraa, as tourist resorts. It is only recently, therefore, that the diving of Mulaku Atoll has been brought into the tourist zone.

Along the northern fringing reef of the atoll are five channels, the best of which is the westernmost one known as Mulaku Kandu. The underwater topography of all five of these sites is very similar to the narrow and spectacular channels of Felidhoo Atoll. They are best dived when the ocean current flows into the atoll, and divers should follow a familiar plan of descending to the atoll plate and crossing the channel to the opposite side, following the edge of the dropoff. Mulaku Kandu has the unusual feature of a large submerged pinnacle rising from very deep water in the centre of the channel. This pinnacle is covered with beautifully coloured soft corals and a great concentration of marine life.

It appears that the many narrow channels on the western side of the atoll will also make fantastic dives; although obviously exposed, they are likely to be at their best during the southwest season.

Below: *The sharp, beak-like mouth and generally bright colouration of the parrotfish lend it its name.*

MULAKU RESORTS

Two islands are due to be opened for tourism in Mulaku Atoll in 1999:

Hakuraahuraa Island Resort, Mulaku Atoll
approx. 60 rooms; 120km (76 miles) from airport
This small uninhabited island, in the southeast corner of Mulaku Atoll, sits in the middle of the broad fringing reef.

Medhufushi Island Resort, Mulaku Atoll
approx. 100 rooms; 120km (74 miles) from airport
Medhufushi is a large, narrow island in the southeast corner of the atoll, close to the capital island, Muli.

*Markings that at a distance camouflage creatures such as the marbled shrimp (**above**) and pixy hawkfish (**below**) often prove striking on closer inspection.* **Opposite:** *The lionfish has poisonous dorsal spines.*

ADDU (SEENU)

Addu Atoll has a long and interesting history. Despite its isolation, over 450km (280 miles) from Malé, it has always held an important place in Maldivian politics, particularly so in recent times. At the start of World War II the British built an airstrip on the island of Gan. As the war effort escalated this base became a key hub for British troop movements in the Indian subcontinent. Before long over 1200 Addu locals were employed by the Royal Air Force, and the whole nature of the atoll changed. The population of Gan was moved to Feydhoo, and the four principal inhabited islands, including Gan, were joined by causeways to make the longest island in the Maldives.

When the lease of Gan was terminated in the mid-1970s and the British left, unrest spread through the atoll and the population demanded independence from Malé. For a short while they achieved this but, without foreign investment or natural resources, the Addu people could not sustain an economy, and soon they were forced to rejoin the republic. Today the influence of the British is evident throughout the Maldives, as many of the staff who were trained and worked on the RAF base on Gan have jobs at the tourist resorts.

There are seven locally inhabited islands in Addu Atoll, which has a population of over 17,000. Hithadhoo, the capital island of the atoll, with about 10,000 inhabitants, is second only to Malé in population. This bustling town has its own hospital and a number of secondary schools. In recent times, Addu has grown to be relatively self-sufficient, and the wide main street of Hithadhoo is lined with shops and houses.

There are about 20 uninhabited islands dotted all around the atoll; some of them are no more than tiny sandspits.

The Ocean Reef Club on Gan is the only resort in the atoll. Opened in 1996, it is simply the old British base redeveloped, with the main accommodation in what used to be the officers' quarters. The resort offers inexpensive accommodation and is popular with British ex-servicemen revisiting their old station.

Opposite: *Addu Atoll is comparatively remote and usually only reached by aeroplane.*
Above: *A ribbon sweetlips rests beside a whip coral at night.*

Diving in Addu (Seenu) Atoll

When the British built the coral causeways that link the four main islands of Addu Atoll the effect on the reef environment was dramatic. The causeways have altered the natural tidal flow of oceanic water into and out of the atoll, and have led to a huge change in the nature of the reefs. Water is held inside the atoll, and some of the coral life has suffered greatly. Nevertheless, the big-fish diving in Addu Atoll is impressive, with good sightings of grey reef sharks, eagle rays and barracuda, plus a good manta site. Although the smaller reef fish are not as plentiful as in other tourist atolls, there is still a good variety of sites, and the diving is enhanced by the large wreck of the *British Loyalty* and other legacies of the British presence.

The best diving and snorkelling is on the long outer fringing reefs of the atoll, where the reeftop is between 5m (16ft) and 10m (33ft), and the reef slopes down to the depths of the ocean. Caves and overhangs provide the perfect habitat for turtles and nurse sharks. Out in the blue, grey sharks, tuna and eagle rays glide by.

Below: *Corals and encrusting sponges adorn a wonderful opening in the wall of a cave .*

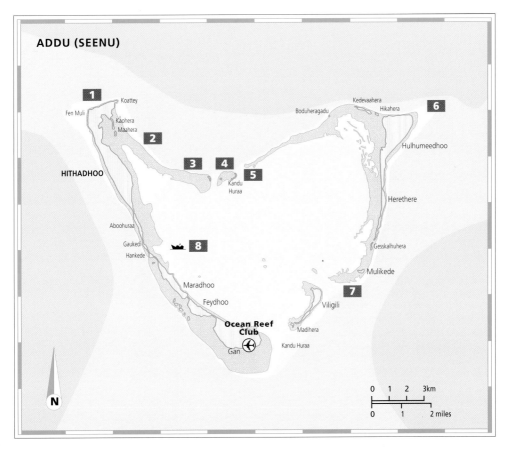

ADDU (SEENU)

Koattey
Fen Muli
Kaohera
Maahera
Kedevaahera
Boduheragadu   Hikahera
Hulhumeedhoo
HITHADHOO
Kandu
Huraa
Herethere
Aboohuraa
Gaukedi
Hankede
Gesskalhuhera
Mulikede
Maradhoo
Feydhoo
Viligili
Ocean Reef
Club
Madihera
Gan   Kandu Huraa

N

| 0 | 1 | 2 | 3km |

| 0 | 1 | | 2 miles |

1 KOATTEY (DEMON POINT)
★★ ★★

Location: The outer reef between Fen Muli and Koattey.
Access: Ocean Reef Club (70min).
Conditions: The site is exposed. There can sometimes be a large swell.
Average visibility: 15m (50ft).
Average depth: 15m (50ft).
Maximum depth: 30m (100ft).
The top of this broad fringing reef is at 5–10m (16–33ft). From here it slopes down to the depths. The best part of the dive is on the plateau, where there are some massive coral formations; on the face of the plateau are overhangs covered in brightly coloured soft coral, foliaceous corals and sea fans of different colours and sizes. On the reeftop you can find green turtles, and in the nooks and crannies of the reef are honeycomb morays and an abundance of reef fish. Keep an eye open in the blue water for eagle rays, barracuda and tuna; on the shoulder of the reef there are often large napoleon wrasse.

2 GULDA LAMAGO
★★ ★★

Location: The outer reef southeast of Koattey.
Access: Ocean Reef Club (55min).
Conditions: This is an exposed site. There can sometimes be a swell.
Average visibility: 15m (50ft).
Average depth: 15m (50ft).
Maximum depth: 40m (130ft).
With its reeftop at 5–10m (16–33ft), Gulda Lamago drops away steeply to the ocean plateau at 40m (130ft). All along this section of the reef are large overhangs and small caves. On the reeftop you can often find green turtles. Sleeping in the sand on the floor of the caves are tawny nurse sharks, and taking refuge in the backs of the caves are colonies of lobsters. On the point of the current you can usually see lots of schooling fish jockeying for position. Manta rays and eagle rays glide by in the blue water, so keep your eyes open.

NAUTILUS

Nautilus (*Nautilus pompilius*) are often washed up on the beach of Maldivian islands but are rarely seen underwater – this is because they live in deep waters of around 240m (800ft). A fascinating creature, the nautilus is the only living cephalopod to have an external shell. The shell contains a number of gas-filled chambers: by adjusting the amount of gas in each chamber the nautilus is able to maintain neutral buoyancy, rise or sink in the water. Only the last chamber in the shell is occupied by the creature. As the nautilus grows it moves forward in its shell and secretes a hard chamber wall across the area it has vacated. It feeds on crabs and small invertebrates.

3 KUDA KANDU BEYRA

★★ ★★

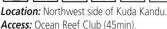

Location: Northwest side of Kuda Kandu.
Access: Ocean Reef Club (45min).
Conditions: This is an exposed site. There can be a swell in any season. The current can be strong.
Average visibility: 15m (50ft).
Average depth: 15m (50ft).
Maximum depth: 30m (100ft).
The name Kuda Kandu means 'small channel'. Just to the west of the channel corner the reeftop is at 5–10m (16–33ft), and from here it slopes down steeply into the ocean. The reef plateau is the best part of the dive, with massive and foliaceous coral formations and lots of sea fans. Often a great variety of different coloured and sized nudibranchs can be found. At 15–20m (50–65ft) are some small caves that are always bustling with life. Out in the ocean, eagle rays, barracuda and whitetip sharks cruise by.

4 BUSHEY OUTSIDE REEF

★★ ★★

Location: Northwest reef of Kandu Huraa.
Access: Ocean Reef Club (40min).
Conditions: This is an exposed site. There can be a swell in any season. The current can be strong.
Average visibility: 15m (50ft).
Average depth: 15m (50ft).
Maximum depth: 30m (100ft).
On this beautiful site you can see a great range of corals of all colours and sizes. The top of the broad fringing reef lies at 5–10m (16–33ft), sloping down steeply from the reef shoulder. The reeftop is in good condition with lots of branching corals and a mass of fish. There are some very large table corals, massive corals and a number of sea fans. In the small overhangs along the reef slope you can often see large moray eels.

5 MUDAKAN

★★★★★ ★★★★★

Location: Northeast of the channel light.
Access: Ocean Reef Club (45min).
Conditions: Usually good.
Average visibility: 15m (50ft).
Average depth: 15m (50ft).
Maximum depth: 30m (100ft).
At this site the ringing reef is very wide on the outside corner. The reeftop, at 5–7m (16–23ft), is good, with many different forms of *Acropora* corals and some colourful reef fish. About 200m (220yd) into the channel the reef slopes down from 12m (40ft) to a sandy bottom that lies at 25–30m (80ft–100ft). You often see some very large manta rays at this point, plus whitetip reef sharks resting on the sand floor.

6 MEEDHOO BEYRA MIYARU

★★★★

Location: Northeast point of Hulhumeedhoo.
Access: Ocean Reef Club (60min).
Conditions: An exposed site, so can be rough.
Average visibility: 15m (50ft).
Average depth: 15m (50ft).
Maximum depth: 30m (100ft).
Any dive-site name which includes *miyaru* ('shark') gives a clue as to what you can expect – and sure enough this is a great place to see lots of grey and whitetip reef sharks. On this outer part of the reef the top is at 5–10m (16–33ft), dropping down to a wide sandy plateau at 30m (100ft). It is here, on the plateau, that the sharks can be seen – the whitetip reef sharks resting in the sand on the bottom and the grey reef sharks swimming above them.

7 MULIKOLHU FARU

★★ ★★

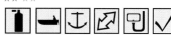

Location: North side of Viligili Kandu.
Access: Ocean Reef Club (35min).
Conditions: Good in most seasons.
Average visibility: 15m (50ft).
Average depth: 20m (65ft).
Maximum depth: 40m (130ft).
When the RAF had its base on Gan Island, a submarine net was placed across this channel. Part of the chains and the buoy that supported the net can still be seen when you dive here. The reeftop, at 8m (25ft), slopes

gently down to 35m (115ft). The top is interesting to explore, as it has lots of reef fish and good corals. Continue into the channel for about 200m (220yd) where, at 14m (45ft), you will find a steel anchor point with, attached, a large linked chain that leads to the bottom of the channel, at 34m (115ft). Close to the chain is a large overhang where you can see sleeping tawny nurse sharks. In all seasons manta rays are often to be found near the sandy bottom of the channel.

8 BRITISH LOYALTY WRECK
★★★★

Location: Inside the atoll, between Hithadhoo and Maradhoo.
Access: Ocean Reef Club (35min).

Conditions: Usually good.
Average visibility: 15m (50ft).
Average depth: 15m (50ft).
Maximum depth: 30m (100ft).
The wreck of the *British Loyalty* has been lying at 34m (100ft) on the sandy floor since she was torpedoed by the Japanese in 1944 during World War II and subsequently scuttled by the British in 1946. The 5583-tonne vessel, about 140m (460ft) long, lies on her starboard side, with her shallowest point being the port side of the hull, at 17m (55ft). You can swim through the torpedo hole in the hull of the ship, although a certain amount of care should be taken. Some of the large propeller blades can still be seen intact on the vessel at a depth of 29m (95ft). The wreck has good coral formations and is home to a great variety of marine life, including a number of large green turtles.

Addu (Seenu)

HOW TO GET THERE

By air: All flights land at the international airport on Hulhule Island in the southern part of North Malé Atoll. From here the only sensible way to get to the resort on Addu Atoll is by the daily Air Maldives (tel 314808/fax 314812) flight on a Dornier or DeHaviland Dash Eight. The flight takes about 90min.

By boat: Cargo vessels run to and from Addu Atoll regularly, but are slow and unreliable. Even in favourable conditions the trip would take at least two days.

WHERE TO STAY AND EAT

Visitors normally stay on Addu's sole registered tourist island, the Ocean Reef Resort, which provides dining facilities.

Ocean Reef Resort
tel 320912/fax 320913; 78 rooms; 480km (298 miles) from airport
Accommodation on Gan is in the old officers' mess. All the rooms are very simply furnished but have AC, ceiling fan, hot and cold water and refrigerator. Outside each room is a small patio area and a beautiful bougainvillaea garden. Facilities include large freshwater swimming pool, floodlit tennis courts, squash courts, catamaran sailing, windsurfing. Pedal bikes can be hired by those wishing to venture to the locally inhabited islands. The dive school, operated by Eurodivers, runs an extensive range of PADI courses. The house reef is accessible.

DIVING EMERGENCIES

There is a hospital on Hithadhoo, which is linked to Gan by a causeway, but facilities are extremely limited. There are no recompression facilities in the atoll; any divers in trouble are carried nearly 450km (300 miles) to the Hyperbaric Centre on Bandos Island Resort (tel 440088/fax 440060).

EXCURSIONS

Several **uninhabited islands** lie close to the Ocean Reef Club Resort and can be explored on an arranged excursion. You can order a picnic lunch from the hotel for the outing. In addition, the Ocean Reef Resort offers **fishing excursions** aboard a *dhoani*.

Below: *Accommodation on Addu Atoll is in the old officers' mess of a former airforce base, with its pleasant gardens.*

SOUTH AND NORTH NILANDHOO (DHAALU AND FAAFU)

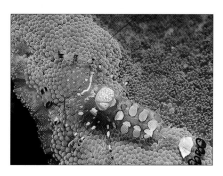

These two atolls, lying just south of Ari Atoll, are recent additions to the tourist zone. In 1997 the Maldivian Government made two uninhabited islands in South Nilandhoo and one uninhabited island in North Nilandhoo available for tourist development. They present an exciting prospect for divers and snorkellers. These areas have never been dived before, and their geology displays many of the characteristics of Ari Atoll, which is well known to offer superb diving.

South Nilandhoo Atoll, 150km (95 miles) from Malé, has eight fishing islands with a total population of over 3500, and over 38 uninhabited islands. The capital island is Kudahuvadhoo, in the very south of the atoll. Here the archaeologist Thor Heyerdahl discovered and excavated a number of sites of historical significance. In the northern centre of the atoll is the island of Ribudhoo, said to be home of the finest jewellers in the Maldives – the reputation of the islanders as skilled craftsmen goes back a long way. Legend has it that hundreds of years ago a sultan banished his chief jeweller to Ribudhoo for stealing gold that had been given to him as material to make jewellery for the sultan. The craftsman from Malé gradually taught the islanders his skills, and his knowledge came to be passed down through the generations. These days jewellery from South Nilandhoo is usually sold in Malé to tourists.

North Nilandhoo is the smaller of the two atolls. It has just five locally inhabited islands with a total population of about 2000, and 18 uninhabited islands. The capital island is Magoodhoo. The fishing island of Nilandhoo is well known to Maldivian historians as a centre for Hindu worship. Heyerdahl excavated a site here in the early 1980s and discovered that, at one stage in its pre-Muslim history, there were probably seven Hindu temples, linked by walls. More importantly to present-day Maldivians, this island is home to one of the oldest and most venerable mosques in the Maldives. Dating back to the 12th century, the mosque was built making use of the stones of the older Hindu temples. Inside, it is decorated with fine Arabic carvings.

Opposite: *Journeying between islands by boat can be a slow business.*
Above: *Almost transparent, the anemoneshrimp is hardly visible against its host anemone.*

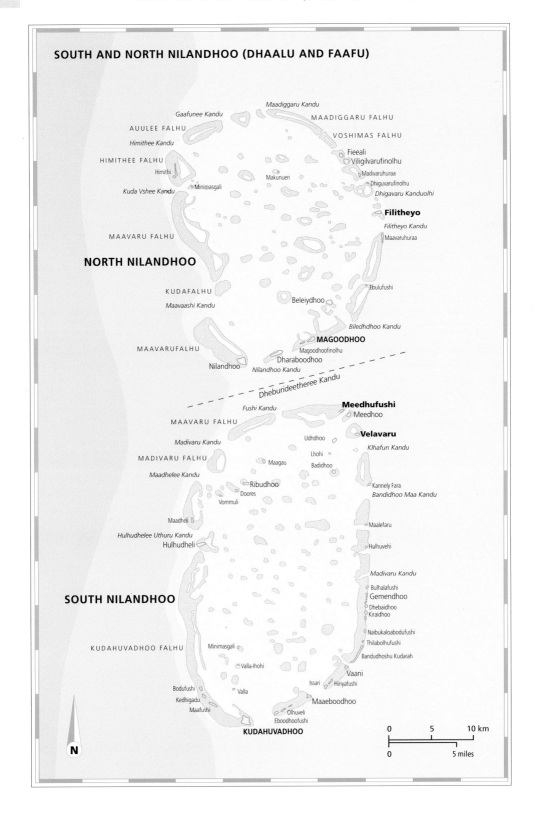

SOUTH AND NORTH NILANDHOO (DHAALU AND FAAFU)

Maadiggaru Kandu

Gaafunee Kandu

MAADIGGARU FALHU

AUULEE FALHU

VOSHIMAS FALHU

Himithee Kandu

Fieeali

HIMITHEE FALHU

Viligilvarufinolhu

Himithi

Madivaruhuraa

Makunueri

Dhiguvarufinolhu

Minimasgali

Kuda Vshee Kandu

Dhigavaru Kanduolhi

Filitheyo

Filitheyo Kandu

MAAVARU FALHU

Maavaruhuraa

NORTH NILANDHOO

KUDAFALHU

Ebulufushi

Beleiydhoo

Maavaashi Kandu

Biledhdhoo Kandu

MAGOODHOO

MAAVARUFALHU

Magoodhoofinolhu

Dharaboodhoo

Nilandhoo

Nilandhoo Kandu

Dheburideetheree Kandu

Fushi Kandu

Meedhufushi

MAAVARU FALHU

Meedhoo

Velavaru

Madivaru Kandu

Udhdhoo

Klhafun Kandu

MADIVARU FALHU

Lhohi

Maagau

Badidhoo

Maadhelee Kandu

Ribudhoo

Doores

Kannely Fara

Vommuli

Bandidhoo Maa Kandu

Maadheli

Maalefaru

Hulhudhelee Uthuru Kandu

Hulhuvehi

Hulhudheli

Madivaru Kandu

Bulhalafushi

SOUTH NILANDHOO

Gemendhoo

Dhebaidhoo

Kiraidhoo

Naibukaloabodufushi

Thilabolhufushi

KUDAHUVADHOO FALHU

Minimasgali

Bandudhoshu Kudarah

Valla-lhohi

Vaani

Issari   Hiriyafushi

Bodufushi

Valla

Kedhigadu

Maaeboodhoo

Maafushi

Olhuveli

Eboodhoofushi

KUDAHUVADHOO

| 0 | 5 | 10 km |

| 0 | | 5 miles |

N

DIVING IN SOUTH AND NORTH NILANDHOO
(DHAALU AND FAAFU) ATOLLS

For the moment the reefs in these atolls are unknown, but what they might offer is eagerly anticipated. At first glance, the northeast corners of both South and North Nilandhoo atolls look good. A number of narrow channels in the outer fringing reef offer definite possibilities, and there is no doubt that many of these channels will also have their own *thila* formations at their centres. We also know that at least two vessels have gone aground off the island of Kudahuvadhoo, in South Nilandhoo Atoll; the larger was the iron ship *Liffey*, wrecked in 1879, and the smaller *Utheemu I*, wrecked in 1960.

The geography of the interior of both atolls looks similar to that of Ari Atoll, with many patch reefs and small submerged *thilas*.

NILANDHOO RESORTS

Three islands are due to become open for tourism in South and North Nilandhoo in 1999:

Filitheyo
approx. 125 rooms; 120km (75 miles) from airport
This large island is in the east of the atoll, with a wide channel to its south.

Meedhufushi
approx. 75 rooms; 150km (95 miles) from airport
Meedhufushi lies In the northeastern corner of the atoll.

Velavaru
approx. 75 rooms; 152km (96 miles) from airport
This island in the northeastern corner of the atoll is currently uninhabited.

Below: *Marvellous soft corals,* Tubastrea *and sea fans compete for space on an outcrop.*

Of the many symbiotic relationships in our oceans, none quite matches that of the sea anemone and the brightly coloured clownfish. In shallow waters of tropical oceans around the world these two creatures live in unique harmony.

The tentacles of the anemone are poisonous to most fish, yet the clownfish has somehow found a way of overcoming this danger. Soft and harmless-looking, the anemone has stinging cells, or nematocysts, that can contain toxins strong enough to kill fish and other potential predators. How have the clownfish adapted to survive this environment? After studying the relationship for many years, marine biologists have suggested a number of methods.

ANEMONE AND ANEMONEFISH

In experiments carried out in an aquarium, the anemonefish were separated from the anemone. It was found that the fish lost their protection and, when returned to their host, were stung by the anemone. However, the stung fish would then perform an elaborate dance around the anemone, carefully touching the anemone's tentacles until eventually the fish became able once more to remain inside the anemone's tentacles. Many scientists believe that the fish smears mucus from the anemone onto itself and needs to keep this mucous covering to maintain its protection.

Of the nearly 1000 species of anemones in the world, only ten are host to anemonefish. These species live in shallow, warm waters where there is enough light for photosynthesis. Belonging to the phylum of coelenterates, the anemone does not itself photosynthesize but contains among its cells live algae that provide the anemone with a certain amount of food.

The anemonefish are members of the family *Pomacentridae*, commonly known as damselfish. There are 28 of these species associated with anemones, mostly found in the Indian and Pacific oceans, and of these 27 are of the *Amphiprion* species. In the Maldives the two most common species are Clark's

anemonefish (*Amphiprion clarkii*) and the Maldives anemonefish (*Amphiprion nigripes*).

These fish have a fascinating life history, involving permanent pair bonds that may last for years and a strong social hierarchy occurring within family groups. The *Amphiprion* are sequential hermaphrodites, not an unusual phenomenon in fish; but interestingly in their case they are also protandrous, that is they begin their adult life as male and change to female. The largest and socially dominant fish in the anemone is the female. If this fish dies, the dominant male in the group – the only one to have functioning testes – then develops ovaries and becomes a female. At the same time, the largest of the non-breeding fish in the group develops functioning testes and takes over the role of the dominant male. It appears that the presence of the female and the dominant male inhibits the full growth of the other clownfish in the anemone, who remain as non-breeding males until their turn comes around.

SYMBIOTIC INTERESTS

What are the advantages of this bizarre partnership? The relationship is symbiotic, though it may initially appear that the benefit is heavily weighted towards the fish. Experiments by Fautin and Allen have shown that when the clownfish are removed, the anemone is very quickly eaten by butterflyfish. In addition, the clownfish may eat parasites from the anemone.

Advantages for the clownfish are numerous. Most importantly, it gains protection from its predators by retreating among the poisonous tentacles of the anemone. You never find a clownfish in the ocean without an anemone, something which suggests that they are unable to survive without their protector. The fish also lay their eggs under the mantle of the anemone, where they are protected from being eaten by other fish.

Next time you are snorkelling or scuba diving in tropical waters, keep a careful eye open for the anemones and their clownfish. Just remember that the dominant fish is the female and all the other fish in the pack are males.

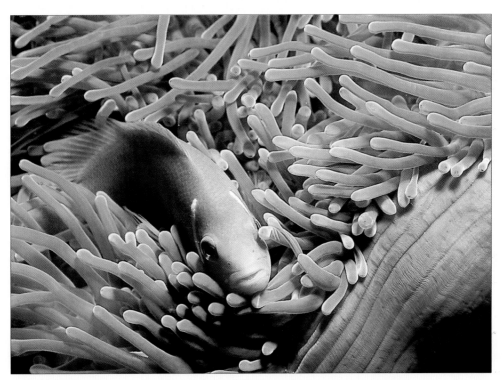

Above: *The Maldives anemonefish gains protection by retreating among its host's tentacles.*
Below: *Only shallow, warm waters are home to anemones that host anemonefish.*

ARI (ALIFU)

A ri Atoll boasts some of the best dive sites in the Maldives. About 60km (37miles) west of Malé, it is separated from North Malé Atoll by the Ariadhoo Channel. It is one of the largest atolls, measuring 80km (50 miles) long and 30km (20 miles) wide.

The region has a total population of over 11,000, spread among the fishing islands. The capital island is Mahibadhoo, on the east side. Three geological atolls make up the administrative atoll of Ari, or Alifu, as it was once known; these are Ari Atoll itself, Rasdhoo Atoll, which is just over 10km (6 miles) to the northeast of Ari and has two resort islands and one fishing island, and the tiny atoll of Thoddoo, located 25km (15 miles) north of the main atoll and with just one fishing island. As there are many resort islands and numerous dive sites in this region we have divided the atolls into two areas: the northern area of Ari Atoll, including Rasdhoo and Thoddoo atolls; and the southern area of Ari Atoll.

Many of the local people rely on tourists for their income, whether through direct employment on the resorts or through the souvenir trade. Tourism has brought great improvements to the infrastructure of the atoll, with the introduction of the telephone network, the development of medical facilities and vastly improved transfer facilities. Nevertheless, a strong fishing tradition still exists, and at times the two elements come into conflict. The shark-fin fisheries of Ari Atoll are driven by market demands and the high profits offered by the Far East, whilst scuba divers come to the Maldives in the hope of seeing the same shark alive in the water.

There are numerous uninhabited islands in Ari Atoll. Although many of those in the northern area are no more than sandbars with a few shrubs, in the southern area there are some large and densely vegetated uninhabited islands. It is unlikely any further tourist development will be allowed in the atoll.

If you visit any of the resort islands in Ari Atoll you are likely to be surprised when someone tells you it is the most highly developed tourist area of the Maldives. Most visitors looking out across the water from their thatched beach cottages quickly forget that the rest

Opposite: *Machchafushi Resort Island in the southern part of Ari Atoll offers great diving.*
Above: *The masked bannerfish is a beautiful inhabitant of the reef.*

Above: *Manta rays frequently glide into cleaning stations all over Ari Atoll.*

of the world exists. Only when you venture from the shore of your tiny island does it become apparent that there are other, widely dispersed resorts in the atoll. These range greatly in size and style, from tiny exclusive places with just 50 beds to the largest resort in the Maldives, Kuramathi, which has 508 beds.

DIVING IN ARI (ALIFU) ATOLL
This is a huge atoll. As you would expect of such a complex area of reef, there is every type of dive site imaginable – for both experienced and inexperienced divers and snorkellers.

Most of the best diving is on *thilas* and outer reefs rather than in channels, which makes the diving a little easier for the less experienced diver. The many *thilas* dotted throughout the atoll are the epitome of the perfect dive site: the reeftop is shallow, providing excellent light for the very best coral growth; the sides are often sheer, dropping down to more than 30m (100ft), and interspersed with caves and overhangs that are fascinating to explore; the sites are usually small enough to swim around in a single dive; and, like an oasis in a desert, the sites attract the full spectrum of pelagic and reef species.

During the northeast season the atoll is well known for its fabulous manta points; here you can sit in shallow water and watch the awesome rays as they glide into the cleaning stations. On the very same points there are often also whale sharks. In the southwest season the grey reef shark populations appear to increase, possibly as a result of the slightly cooler water. Although manta rays are not so common during this season, the encounters with whale sharks continue to impress.

Ari (Alifu): Southern Area

The southern part of Ari Atoll contains ten locally inhabited islands, including the capital of the atoll, Mahibadhoo Island. There are 11 uninhabited islands in this area, and 16 resort islands. There are many excellent dive sites, including a wonderful manta site on the west of the atoll which is good for both snorkelling and diving. Whale sharks are often seen congregating around the southern tip of the atoll at the start of the northeast season.

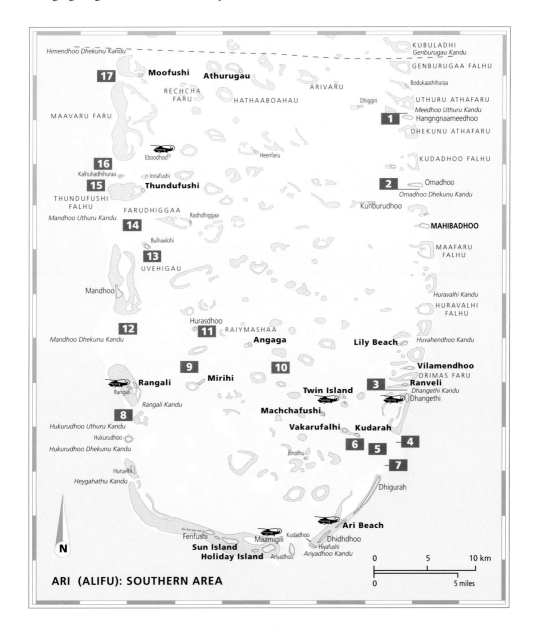

ARI (ALIFU): SOUTHERN AREA

1 HANGNGNAAMEEDHOO THILA (ATHAFARU THILA)
★★★

Location: Northern channel of Hangngnaameedhoo.
Access: Ellaidhoo (60min).
Conditions: Usually good in both seasons. Sometimes choppy if wind is against tide.
Average visibility: 20m (65ft).
Average depth: 20m (65ft).
Maximum depth: 30m (100ft).

The *thila* is set back well inside the narrow channel of this island, whose name is almost unpronounceable! This is a great dive because of the unusual reef topography and the quality and variety of the marine inhabitants, which are many and varied. Lying from east to west, the *thila* is 150m (165yd) long, with its sides sloping off at an angle of 60°. The top of the *thila* forms a ridge just a few metres wide, with three massive corals situated in the middle. At the western point this ridge drops away steeply to the atoll floor at 35m (115ft), forming a large, half-moon-shaped reef which has, over hundreds of years, obstructed the sand-flow into the atoll. Sand has built up against the northern side of the crescent and enormous, brilliantly white dunes have accumulated.

On the outside of the half-moon reef is a large overhang which is well worth exploring; it has an abundance of black coral trees and whip corals, plus a mass of little reef fish.

2 OMADHOO THILA
★★★

Location: 1km (1/2 mile) south of Omadhoo.
Access: Normally by safari boat only. Some resorts may offer day excursions to the *thila*.
Conditions: Good in most conditions.
Average visibility: 20m (65ft).
Average depth: 20m (65ft).
Maximum depth: 35m (115ft).

You can swim around this small *thila* – 120m by 50m (130 by 55yd) – easily in a single dive, but most of the action occurs at the current point. The top of the *thila* is at 10m (33ft); the reef slopes steeply off to the atoll floor. On the northeastern side of the *thila* a big slab of coral, the size of a house's roof, has broken away from the main reef, creating an interesting and unusual feature. The currents are often strong in the channel, and this attracts tuna, jackfish and large schools of fusiliers to the *thila* point. The coral growth is generally good. Note there are areas of fire coral on the reeftop.

3 DHANGETHI BODU THILA
★★★ ★★★

Location: 500m (550yd) north of Dhangethi.
Access: Ranveli (10min), Vilamendhoo (15min), Twin Island (35min), all other resorts in the southwest side of Ari Atoll.
Conditions: Generally good. A swell sometimes develops in the northeast season.
Average visibility: 25m (80ft).
Average depth: 15m (50ft).
Maximum depth: 40m+ (130ft+).

In the middle of the Dhangethi Channel is a huge L-shaped *thila*. Its best section is the reef that faces the ocean, which runs for about 300m (330yd) before turning the corner into the atoll. On the reeftop next to the dropoff, the corals and fish life are excellent, with huge massive and laminar formations and lots of schooling fish. Here the *thila* drops away to the ocean depths in three or more giant steps (leading far beyond a diver's reach); each step has caves and overhangs full of life. Stingrays, whitetip sharks, barracuda and jackfish are common in the channel. If you are lucky you might see a whale shark in the southwest season.

The site is good for snorkellers, assuming conditions are calm.

4 BROKEN ROCK THILA
★★★★

Location: 2.5km (1 1/2 miles) northeast of Dhigurah.
Access: Kudarah (20min), Vakarufalhi (25min). Many other resorts in southern Ari Atoll offer visits to this site.
Conditions: A short, choppy sea can quickly develop in strong winds.
Average visibility: 25m (80ft).
Average depth: 20m (65ft).
Maximum depth: 30m (100ft).

Broken Rock looks like it has been chopped in half by an axe. The site is about 100m (110yd) in length, with a shallowest point at 13m (43ft); a very deep gulley runs across the *thila* from east to west. This gulley, brimming with soft corals and reef fish, is the best part of the dive. Its floor is at 24m (80ft) and its sheer sides have loads of nooks and crannies to explore. On the eastern point of the *thila* are two large coral heads that obstruct the current flow and attract masses of fusiliers, blue-lined snappers and trevallies. This is a superb and colourful dive. Every part of the *thila* has a point of interest and a remarkable array of marine life. Be careful not to go into decompression time, as there is no shallow point at which to make a stop.

5 TINFUSHI THILA

★★★ ★★

Location: Centrally placed in the Dhigurah Channel on the ocean front.
Access: Kudarah (20min), Vakarufalhi (25min), Machchafushi (30min). Many other resorts in this area of South Ari Atoll offer access.
Conditions: Generally good.
Average visibility: 25m (80ft).
Average depth: 20m (65ft).
Maximum depth: 40m+ (130ft+).

Wonderful sea fans grow on the northern side of this long, thin *thila*; they really come alive in the currents that stream in through the Dhigurah Channel from the ocean. The top of the *thila* is at 10m (33ft); the sides slope in steps and ledges down to 40m (130ft). On the western and eastern sides are caves and ledges full of colourful marine life. Look out for the hawkfish nestling in black coral bushes. The *thila* is about 120m (130yd) long and, although you could swim around the site in a single dive, the best parts

are on the eastern and northern sides. Napoleon wrasse, whitetip sharks and eagle rays are among the common visitors you may be lucky enough to find on this lovely reef.

Below: *A reef crab perches delicately on a black coral bush.*

> ### DOLPHINS
>
> The most commonly seen dolphins in the Maldives are spinner dolphins (*Stenella longirostris*) and common dolphins (*Delphinus delphis*). The spinners are easily recognized by their leaping displays as they jump out of the water and spin on their tails. They are always found in schools, varying in number from tens to hundreds of dolphins. The adult spinner dolphin is slender, averaging 2m (6ft) in the male, with a long thin beak.
>
> The common dolphin is a little longer than the spinner, with the male measuring a maximum of 2.6m (8ft). They are often to be found riding in the bow wave, and are also highly vocal creatures. Always listen out for dolphins underwater, since even if you cannot see them it's lovely to hear them.

6 KUDARAH THILA
★★★★★

Location: 1km (1/2 mile) southeast of Kudarah Island Resort.
Access: Kudarah (10min), Vakarufalhi (10min), Machchafushi (20min). Many other resorts in Ari Atoll run trips to here.
Conditions: Spring tides can bring ferocious currents.
Average visibility: 20m (65ft).
Average depth: 20m (65ft).
Maximum depth: 40m (130ft).
The topography here is quite complex. The *thila* is divided into four large coral heads, of varying sizes, that sit on a plateau rising from 40m (130ft) to 12m (40ft). The *thila* is no more than 100m (110yd) in diameter, and you can swim around the whole site in a single dive. Each of the blocks is undercut from 15m (50ft) to 25m (80ft) with superb caves jammed full of soft corals, gorgonians and whip corals. On the southwest corner there is an archway swim-through, and between all four pinnacles there are deep ravines that harbour a stunning amount of marine life. The centre of the *thila* is hollowed out, with a base at 20m (65ft), and thousands of blue-lined snappers school in the gullies that have been created. Watch out for yellow trumpetfish (*Aulostoma chinensis*) shadowing the snappers while hunting on the reef. Grey and whitetip sharks can be seen on the current points. Divers should be careful not to go into decompression on this dive as there are no shallow points available on the reef to carry out stops. This is a Protected Marine Area.

7 DHIGURAH THILA
★★★ ★★★

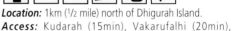

Location: 1km (1/2 mile) north of Dhigurah Island.
Access: Kudarah (15min), Vakarufalhi (20min), Machchafushi (35min), Ari Beach (35min).

Below: *Blue-lined snappers school in their hundreds in a gully, creating a dizzying spectacle.*

Conditions: Quite exposed; a short, choppy sea can sometimes develop quickly if wind is against the direction of tide.
Average visibility: 25m (80ft).
Average depth: 20m (65ft).
Maximum depth: 40m+ (130ft+).
The eastern side of this large *thila* is exposed directly to ocean currents and drops quickly down from 8m (25ft) to the ocean plateau at 45m (150ft). At this point the reef continues in giant steps down into the ocean, far beyond sport-diving depths. The reef wall is about 400m (440yd) long. The whole length of the reef is interspersed with caves and overhangs, and these make this a fascinating and enjoyable dive site. Midway along the *thila* on the eastern side is a fracture in the reef, starting at 15m (50ft) and descending to 40m (130ft). This area is crowded with marine life of all types and sizes. There are a number of coral outcrops along the wall of the *thila*, and each should be explored carefully. If you are diving the site in the southwest season, make a point of watching out for the whale sharks that are commonly sighted on the southeast corner.

The top of the *thila* is good for snorkelling, with leather corals and lots of feeding turtles.

8 HUKURUELHI FARU (MADIVARU)

★★★★★ ★★★

Location: South side of Rangali Channel.
Access: Rangali (10min), Mirihi (35min), Angaga (60min). Many resorts in Ari Atoll offer day excursions to this site during the manta season.
Conditions: Usually good in the northeast season.
Average visibility: 25m (80ft).
Average depth: 10m (33ft).
Maximum depth: 30m (100ft).
Madi means 'ray' in Dhivehi. In the northeast season this is a superb manta cleaning station. As with many good manta points, the reef slopes down gently from its top at 8m (25ft) to the atoll floor at 30m (100ft). Although there are many cleaning stations along this 1km (1/2-mile) reef, the area where the mantas are most active is midway along the northern side. A deep basin almost 100m (110yd) across has formed in the coral and, as the currents flow out of the atoll, the waters eddy in the basin. This attracts the mantas, which hover like great spaceships in the current.

To the east of the basin the reef forms a wall which drops steeply down to the sand floor at 30m (100ft). At a depth of 25m (80ft) there is a large cave running along the reef for 200m (220yd).

Above: *Fusiliers congregate around the hull of a boat.*

Don't swim over the cleaning stations or in the blue water: it is always better to stay low on the reef and to be as quiet as you possibly can. If you are lucky your patience should be rewarded with spectacular manta sightings.

NO GLOVES HERE

Visitors to some of the resort islands may find that they are forced to leave their diving gloves behind in their rooms when they go diving. Many dive centres on the resorts are concerned about reef damage caused by divers hanging onto the corals, so have introduced a policy of no gloves while snorkelling or diving. It is sensible to ask the dive base leader's view before your first dive. Either way, wearing gloves or not, please take care of the precious corals of the Maldives.

Above: *The tassled scorpionfish is well equipped for disguise.*

9 DHEKUNU THILA (STONEFISH REEF)
★★★

Location: 400m (¼ mile) southwest of Dhekunu Faru.
Access: Mirihi (20min), Rangali (25min), Angaga (25min).
Conditions: Good in most conditions.
Average visibility: 20m (65ft).
Average depth: 15m (50ft).
Maximum depth: 35m (115ft).

There are no prizes for guessing what's on the top of this *thila*. This small but fascinating site is home to plenty of the usually elusive stonefish. These are difficult to spot because they bury themselves in the loose sand and broken coral rubble. The *thila* itself is just 60m (200ft) long and 30m (100ft) wide, with the shallowest point of its reeftop at 10m (33ft) and with a second step or ridge at a depth of 14m (45ft). The walls slope off steeply to the atoll plate, at 35m (115ft), and there are a number of small caves and coral outcrops around the *thila* which make very colourful diving. Along with the stonefish on the reeftop, look out for octopus in the small overhangs. This site is also excellent for night diving.

10 ANGAGA THILA
★★★★ ★★

Location: 1km (½ mile) southwest of Angaga.
Access: Angaga (10min), Mirihi (20min), Rangali (50min), Machchafushi (55min), Twin Island (55min).
Conditions: Generally good.
Average visibility: 20m (65ft).
Average depth: 15m (50ft).
Maximum depth: 35m (115ft).

This is a small round *thila* with its top at 8m (25ft) and steeply sloping sides. It does not have stunning coral life, though there is an area of good branching and massive corals where you can find stonefish. There are small caves all around the *thila*, as well as sea fans and black coral trees in the deeper water. It is the fish life on the *thila* that makes this a great dive, particularly the resident family of grey reef and whitetip sharks. You may also see eagle rays and hawksbill turtles and lots of cornetfish (*Fistularia commersonii*). Look out for the unusual nudibranch *Thecacera picta*, often found on the top of the *thila*; this nudibranch is opaque, with black lines running the length of its body and orange-tipped rhinophores.

11 HURASDHOO REEF (PINEAPPLE REEF)
★★★ ☆☆☆☆

Location: The south section of the house reef of Hurasdhoo uninhabited island.
Access: Angaga (20min), Mirihi (25min).
Conditions: Good in most conditions.
Average visibility: 20m (65ft).
Average depth: 10m (33ft).
Maximum depth: 30m (100ft).

Snorkellers as well as divers will enjoy this reef, particularly on a calm sunny day with the backdrop of the beautiful uninhabited island of Hurasdhoo. The reef is centrally located in the atoll and so is protected from any destructive wave action from the ocean. The coral life is excellent, with lots of foliaceous and encrusting hard corals and an abundance of soft corals. The reeftop is shallow – no more than 1m (3ft) in depth – and the sides slope down to the atoll bed at a very gentle gradient. Turtles and a mass of reef fish can be seen on the reef.

12 MANDHOO THILA
★★★

Location: 1km (1/2 mile) due south of the south access channel through Mandhoo Island Reef.
Access: Rangali (25min), Mirihi (45min), Angaga (55min).
Conditions: A big swell can develop on the *thila* in anything more than moderate winds.
Average visibility: 25m (80ft).
Average depth: 20m (65ft).
Maximum depth: 35m (115ft).

This dive is made up of two *thilas* linked together by a saddle of sand and coral. The larger of the two *thilas* is about 60m (66yd) in diameter, with its reeftop at 14m (45ft). The smaller *thila* is 20m (22yd) in diameter with a reeftop a little deeper, at 16m (52ft). Both *thilas* have steeply sloping sides undercut by caves that are full of blue soft corals, squirrelfish and a tremendous variety of other fish life. On the northwest side of the larger *thila* is a huge rock, the size of a double-decker bus, which has broken away to form a gulley 5m (16ft) wide that is packed with marine life. You should first head south to the smaller *thila* and then work your way around to the gulley, making your final ascent from the top of the larger *thila*. Keep an eye open for eagle rays and grey sharks, which are often found cruising in the saddle area. If the current is strong, avoid open-water decompression stops.

13 BULHAALOHI REEF
★★★ ☆☆☆

Location: Northern section of house reef of Bulhaalohi uninhabited island.
Access: Thundufushi (25min), Angaga (70min), Mirihi (70min). Other resort islands may operate full-day excursions to this site.
Conditions: Generally good.
Average visibility: 25m (80ft).
Average depth: 15m (50ft).
Maximum depth: 35m (115ft).

Bulhaalohi is a small uninhabited island. On its northern side the reef extends out some 400m (1/4 mile) to the west. The reeftop is shallow, at 6m (20ft), and the sides drop quickly down to 35m (115ft) before shelving out to the floor of the atoll. The reef wall is interspersed with small caves and overhangs, from 10m (33ft) to 25m (80ft), and makes for a great drift dive. The whole surrounding reef is good for snorkelling, and swimmers, assuming they are fit enough, can go right round the island.

14 BULHAALOHI THILA
★★★ ★

Location: 1km (1/2 mile) northwest of Bulhaalohi Island.
Access: Thundufushi (20min). Other resort islands may operate full-day excursions to this site.
Conditions: A big swell can develop in anything more than moderate winds.
Average visibility: 25m (80ft).
Average depth: 15m (50ft).
Maximum depth: 35m (115ft).

There is little coral growth on top of the *thila*, which is at 8m (25ft), due to the strong wave action that surges through the channel called Mandhoo Uthuru Kandu. But the southwestern corner of the *thila* drops off steeply to the ocean, and here there is a magnificent set of caves and overhangs running at three levels along the reef from 10m (33ft) to 28m (90ft). You jump in on the western point and keep the reef on the left. The first cave, at 18m (60ft), is huge, with a large finger of coral jutting out from its roof. A school of batfish are often to be found around this outcrop, and it is also common to see grey sharks in the area. The cave is full of gorgonians, featherstars, whip corals, sponges and a multitude of reef fish, including schools of oriental sweetlips. Leaving this cave, you descend to the lowest level of caves, at 25m (80ft) to 28m (90ft); these continue for about 150m (165yd) along the reef. At this point it is best to turn around and, slowly ascending, explore the middle level of caves, from 18m (60ft) to 15m (50ft). About halfway along this section of caves there is a tunnel that leads upwards to the shallowest level of caves, at 10m (33ft). The currents can be very strong but, once in the caves, you are sheltered from the flow.

15 KALHUHADHIHURAA FARU
★★★★ ☆☆☆☆

Location: North corner of Kalhuhadhihuraa Reef.
Access: Thundufushi (10min), Moofushi (40min), Athurugau (45min).
Conditions: Very strong currents can run through this channel in both seasons. If the wind is against the tide the water can be choppy.
Average visibility: 30m (100ft).
Average depth: 20m (65ft).
Maximum depth: 40m (130ft).
This is a super dive in both seasons. The topography of the area is interesting and the reef has a remarkable array of caves and overhangs full of hard and soft corals, fish and invertebrates.

With the current running in from the ocean, you jump in at the northwestern point of the reef, which starts at a depth of 6m (20ft) and quickly drops down to the atoll plate at 30m (100ft) or more. Drifting with the reef wall on the right, you quickly come upon the start of a large section of caves and overhangs, from 15m (50ft) to 25m (80ft). At this point there is a huge coral head, the size of a small house, placed 30m (100ft) off the reef; the channel between the block and the reef shallows to 20m (65ft). It is easy to cross to the rock, and here you will see large schools of big-eye trevally, eagle rays, grey sharks and whitetip reef sharks. Back on the reef, the stretch of caves and overhangs continues for another 300m (330yd) before the current slackens into a natural basin, with a sandy bottom at 18m (60ft), and the reeftop at a depth of 6m (20ft). The best shark activity is during the southwest season, but the dive is just as good in the northeast season, when manta rays are often seen in the channel.

The reef can be good for snorkelling if the currents are moderate.

16 KALHUHADHIHURAA THILA
(THUNDUFUSHI THILA)
★★★★ ☆☆☆

Location: In the middle of Kalhuhadhihuraa Kandu.
Access: Thundufushi (10min), Moofushi (40min), Athurugau (45min).
Conditions: Very strong currents can run through this channel in both seasons. If the wind is against the tide the water can be choppy.
Average visibility: 20m (65ft).
Average depth: 18m (60ft).
Maximum depth: 30m (100ft).
The north side of this large round *thila* offers the best diving, as there are caves and overhangs all along the face of the reef between 15m (50ft) and 25m (80ft). On the northwest corner a number of large coral outcrops have fallen away from the reef, and here you can see a mass of fish life. The *thila* is about 200m (220yd) wide, with the reeftop at an average depth of 10m (33ft). Turtles, octopus and grazing fish – such as daisy parrotfish (*Scarus sordidus*) and blue surgeonfish (*Acanthurus leucosternon*) – can be seen on the top of the *thila*, and during the northeast season mantas are often seen feeding on the western side.

If conditions are calm and if the mantas are around, this can be a super place for snorkelling.

17 MOOFUSHI FARU
★★★ ☆☆☆☆

Location: The southern channel between Moofushi Island and Maavaru Faru.
Access: Moofushi (10min), Athurugau (45min), Thundufushi (60min).
Conditions: Can be rough in westerlies but generally protected in moderate conditions.
Average visibility: 25m (80ft).
Average depth: 15m (50ft).
Maximum depth: 35m (115ft).
Set back between Moofushi Island and Maavaru Faru is a reef about 2km (1¼ miles) long. If the current is flowing into the atoll, jump in on the western corner and drift along the colourful wall, keeping the reef on the right. All along the face of the reef, from 15m (50ft) to 25m (80ft), there are large caves and overhangs full of life. Here you can expect to see sea fans and whip corals, napoleon wrasse, sharks and stingrays. If the current is strong, you can take shelter inside the caves, where lobsters and nurse sharks are often seen. A number of large coral outcrops are set along the reef, and at times the water eddies quite strongly in these areas.

The reeftop is at 3m (10ft) so this is an excellent site for snorkellers. Manta rays are frequently seen feeding in this channel during the northeast season, so it is well worth keeping an eye open for them on the surface.

Opposite: *Soft corals cover this reef wall in a true explosion of colour.*

HOW TO GET THERE

By air: There is no airport in Ari Atoll. All international schedule and charter flights land at Hulhule International Airport on North Malé Atoll; transfers to southern Ari Atoll can then be made by either helicopter or seaplane. There are six helipads in this region of Ari Atoll – on the islands of Eboodhoo, Rangali, Maafushivaru, Dhangethi, Ari Beach and Maamigili. The helicopters are operated by Hummingbird Helicopters (tel 325708/9/fax 323161). As an indication, flying time by helicopter from the international airport is about 35min to Eboodhoo and Maafushivaru and 40min to Rangali, Maamigili and Ari Beach.

By boat: Travel to Ari Atoll by speedboat may take up to three hours to some of the furthest resort islands. A *dhoani* transfer could take five hours, and in bad weather can be quite uncomfortable. Be sure to take your seasickness tablets if you think you will need them. Numerous live-aboard dive boats visit this area (see page 29 for contact details).

WHERE TO STAY

Visitors normally stay on registered tourist islands, in other words at a resort. Every resort provides its own dining facilities.

Angaga Island Resort
tel 450012/fax 450520; 51 rooms; 90km (56 miles) from airport
Located well inside the atoll, Angaga is a small island offering a good standard of accommodation and a quiet and exclusive atmosphere. The rooms are individual thatched bungalows, all with AC and hot and cold water. Facilities include windsurfing, waterskiing and catamaran sailing. The house reef is easily accessed. SubAqua Reisen operate the dive school and teach the usual range of PADI and CMAS courses.

Ari Beach Resort (Dhidhdhoofinolhu)
tel 450016/fax 450512; 83 rooms; 95km (60 miles) from airport
This is a long, thin and pretty island with superb beaches and simple accommodation in 120 beachfront rooms. There are two standards of rooms; only the superior rooms have hot and cold water. Facilities include tennis, table tennis, badminton, windsurfing, catamaran sailing, waterskiing, kneeboarding, canoes and pedalo boats. The dive centre is run by Eurodivers. The house reef is too far for shore diving, and the island lagoon is very large, which limits the good boat dive sites available to the resort.

Athurugau Island Resort
tel 450508/fax 450574; 42 rooms; 73km (48 miles) from airport
A small island with good standards of accommodation in semi-detached rooms, each with AC, ceiling fan, hot and cold water, telephone and minibar. There is a small wooden terrace area in front of each room. Facilites include windsurfing, waterskiing, canoeing and catamaran sailing. The house reef is good for diving and snorkelling and is easily accessed from the resort. This is the sister of Thundufushi Island Resort.

Holiday Island (Dhiffushi)
tel 450011/fax 450022; 142 rooms; 93km (58 miles) from airport
A large resort with good beaches and a large lagoon; the sister of Sun Island Resort. The rooms are all bungalows with AC, hot and cold water, IDD and television. Discos, live bands, karaokes and cultural shows are regularly organized. Facilities include tennis, waterskiing, catamaran sailing, windsurfing, table tennis, billiards, gym and sauna. Diving is run by the Calypso Diving Centre, who have excellent training facilities. The house reef can only be reached by boat.

Kudarah Island Resort
tel 450549/fax 450550; 30 rooms; 90km (55 miles) from airport
A very exclusive resort offering accommodation in 25 standard bungalows and five water bungalows. The rooms are of an excellent standard: all have AC, hot and cold water, bath, minibar and telephone. Facilities include seawater swimming pool, floodlit tennis court, windsurfing and canoeing. The dive centre offers a limited range of PADI courses. The house reef is excellent.

Lily Beach Resort (Huvahendhoo)
tel 450013/fax 450646; 84 rooms; 85km (53 miles) from airport
A small island with an excellent house reef, pretty beaches and a high standard of accommodation. There are 68 beachfront rooms and 16 water bungalows, all of which have AC, hot and cold water and minibar. Facilities include freshwater swimming pool, fitness centre, floodlit tennis court and windsurfing. The dive school is run by Ocean Pro, teaching PADI courses in English, German and French.

Machchafushi Island Resort
tel 450615/fax 450618; 58 rooms; 95km (60 miles) from airport
An island offering an excellent standard of diving and a very good house reef. There are 48 standard rooms set on the beach at the water's edge, plus 10 water bungalows sitting on stilts over the ocean. All standard

rooms have AC and hot and cold desalinated water. Facilities include salt-water swimming pool, tennis court, catamaran sailing and windsurfing. E6 processing is available. The dive school is run by Sub Aqua Reisen and offers the usual PADI courses.

Mirihi Marina Resort
tel 450500/fax 450501; 39 rooms; 90km (57 miles) from airport
A tiny, beautiful island offering a high standard of accommodation in a quiet atmosphere. All rooms have hot and cold water, air conditioning, fridge and telephone. There are 31 water villas and 8 bungalows. Facilities include catamaran sailing, windsurfing and a small gym. The dive school offers a range of PADI courses. The house reef is excellent.

Moofushi Island Resort
tel 450517/fax 450509; 60 rooms; 85km (52 miles) from airport
A small exclusive island, with beautiful lagoons and beaches. There are 45 beach bungalows and 15 water bungalows. All rooms have AC, ceiling fan, minibar, telephone and hot and cold water. Facilities include windsurfing, catamaran sailing and canoeing. The Moofushi Dive Centre offers a small range of PADI and CMAS courses. Access to the house reef is limited.

Rangali Hilton
tel 450629/fax 450619; 100 rooms; 95km (61 miles) from airport
This island was purchased by the Hilton group in 1997 and totally renovated. There are 100 AC beachfront bungalows with hot and cold water, bath and minibar. Facilities include good-size swimming pool, tennis court, catamaran sailing and windsurfing. The dive school is run by Sub Aqua Reisen and offers a good range of PADI courses. Diving on the house reef is limited.

Ranveli Beach Resort Island (Viligilivaru)
tel 450570/fax 450523; 56 rooms; 75km (48 miles) from airport
A small, modern island with sophisticated accommodation in two-storey blocks. All the rooms have AC, hot and cold water, bath, minibar and telephone. The bar and restaurant are built on stilts over the water. Facilities include swimming pool, windsurfing and canoeing. The house reef is excellent for snorkelling and diving.

Sun Island Resort (Guraidhoo)
tel 450088/fax 450099; 500 rooms; 93km (58 miles) from airport
This large resort, opened in 1997, has beautiful beaches and a large lagoon. It is the sister of Holiday Island (Dhiffushi). There is a wide range of accommodation in

modern rooms, all with AC, ceiling fan and hot and cold water. Facilities are comprehensive, including a swimming pool and tennis court. A full range of PADI courses is offered. Access to the house reef is limited.

Thundufushi Island Resort

tel 45059/fax 450515; 42 rooms; 90km (54 miles) from airport

This, the sister island to Athurugau, offers similar accommodation in semi-detached bungalows, each with AC, ceiling fan, hot and cold water, telephone and minibar. Facilities include windsurfing, waterskiing, catamaran sailing and canoeing. The island has predominantly Italian clientele and an Italian management. The house reef is good for snorkelling and diving.

Twin Island (Maafushivaru)

tel 450596/fax 450524; 40 rooms; 85km (53 miles) from airport

There is a helipad on this tiny resort island. A good standard of accommodation is provided in 30 beachfront bungalows and 10 water bungalows, all with AC, ceiling fan, hot and cold water, minibar and telephone. Facilities include catamaran sailing, windsurfing and canoeing. The dive centre offers a limited range of PADI dive courses. The house reef is very good for both diving and snorkelling.

Vakarufalhi Island Resort

tel 45000/fax 450007; 50 rooms; 65km (40 miles) from airport

Individual thatched rooms situated around the edge of this tiny island's beach provide a high standard of accommodation. All rooms have AC, ceiling fan, hot and cold water and minibar. Facilities include windsurfing and catamaran sailing. The house reef is excellent, and the beaches and lagoon are beautiful. The dive base is run by Prodivers and offers a full range of PADI courses.

Vilamendhoo Resort

tel 45063/fax 450639; 100 rooms; 85km (53 miles) from airport

This large resort has a simple style and good standard of accommodation. There are 100 detached and semi-detached bungalows, all with AC, ceiling fan, hot and cold water, telephone and minibar. Facilities include windsurfing and catamaran sailing. The house reef is excellent for both diving and snorkelling. The Barrakuda dive base, run by Werner and Lilly Lau, offers a full range of PADI and CMAS courses.

Diving Emergencies

There are no hospitals or recompression chambers in this part of the atoll. Some of the resort islands run general medical surgeries but facilities are extremely limited

and they are mainly for the treatment of ear infections and simple cuts. Divers requiring recompression treatment have to be flown by helicopter or seaplane to the Hyperbaric Centre on Bandos Island Resort in North Malé Atoll.

Excursions

The **fishing islands** of Omadhoo, Mahibadhoo, Dhangethi, Dhigurah, Dhidhdhoo, Maamigili, Fenfushi and Mandhoo are visited by tourists from resort islands in southern Ari Atoll. There are souvenir shops on all these islands. As always, please remember to dress modestly. All the resorts offer excursions to **uninhabited islands** in Ari Atoll. Nearly all resorts also offer **fishing** excursions aboard a *dhoani*. Most resorts offer regular **snorkelling excursions** to their best coral reefs. It is very easy to become sunburnt while in the water, so take a T-shirt to wear while swimming. Also, take plenty of drinking water, plus suntan lotion for the backs of your legs! Be aware that there may be currents: do not lose sight of the cover boat, and try to stay with the group.

Below: *The house reef of Vilamendhoo Resort Island is in excellent condition.*

Ari (Alifu): Northern Area

The northern area of Ari Atoll includes Rasdhoo and Thoddoo atolls to the north. There are seven locally inhabited islands in this region. Thoddoo Island, in the far north, is an important fishing island and is well known for its troupe of girls performing the *bandiyaa* dance. This large but very exposed island is situated in the middle of the ocean pass, and offers no anchorage for anything other than small fishing boats. Most of the other locally inhabited islands, with the exception of Rasdhoo, still have only traditional villages that rely heavily on their fishing fleets. Rasdhoo is located next to the large island of Kuramathi, on which there are three individual resorts; as a result Rasdhoo now has over 30 tourist shops and is the hub of the air transfer services to the resorts on Kuramathi. There are about 13 uninhabited islands in the northern area of the atoll, and 11 resorts in total.

1 UKULHAS THILA
★★★★★

Location: 5km (3 miles) north of Ukulhas Island.
Access: Velidhoo (40min), Nika (50min), Gangehi (55min). Many other resorts in Ari Atoll run full-day excursions to this site in the northeast season.
Conditions: This site is very exposed and should not be visited unless the conditions are good.
Average visibility: 25m (80ft).
Average depth: 20m (65ft).
Maximum depth: 30m (100ft).
The submerged outer reef that forms Ari Atoll extends many kilometres north of the island of Ukulhas and drops away gently into the ocean. Ukulhas Thila rises from this ridge of outer reefs and has become famous in the Maldives for its sightings of manta rays during the northeast season. The *thila* is about 300m (330yd) long and just 30m (33yd) across, with its coral top at an average depth of 20m (65ft). From January to March this is a site where mantas are often seen being cleaned on top of the large *Porites* corals. However, in all seasons, mantas or not, Ukulhas Thila offers a fabulous dive. There is always a huge school of blue-lined snappers, swarms of glassfish in the coral overhangs and every type of moray eel you could imagine. You can usually see grey sharks, whitetip sharks and tuna patrolling in the depths just off the edge of the *thila*. The *thila* is very exposed and quite deep, so take great care not to go into decompression. Blue-water decompression stops should be avoided at all cost as the currents can run across the top of the *thila* very strongly and you can be carried a long way from the cover boat. Be warned – the next stop is Africa!

2 VELIGANDU KANDU
★★★ ★★

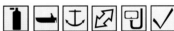

Location: Northernmost channel of Rasdhoo Atoll.
Access: Kuramathi (25min), Veligandu (10min).
Conditions: Usually good surface conditions, although the channel can become a little rough during northeasterly winds.
Average visibility: 20m (65ft).
Average depth: 15m (50ft).
Maximum depth: 25m (80ft).
This shallow channel, about 10m (33ft) deep, is one of the three channels that allow the flow of water into and out of Rasdhoo Atoll. The reef drops away to the north and descends gently to a sand plateau at 25m (80ft); this in turn continues into the depths on a gentle gradient. The best part of the dive is on the massive coral outcrops in the centre of the channel. These have numerous nooks and crannies that harbour all sorts of fish and invertebrate life. During the northeast season you can often see manta rays feeding and cleaning in the channel, and they are sometimes also seen in the area in the southwest season.

GARDEN EELS

There are three species of garden eel found in the Maldives: the white-spotted garden eel (*Gorgasia maculata*), the orange-barred garden eel (*Gorgasia preclara*) and the threespot garden eel (*Heteroconger hassi*). Large colonies of 200–300 garden eels live in burrows in the sand. These creatures are very timid, and as you go near they will disappear into the refuge of their tunnels. It is thought that they have a strict social order – the burrow of each eel in the colony is carefully spaced in the sand, and territories are keenly fought over.

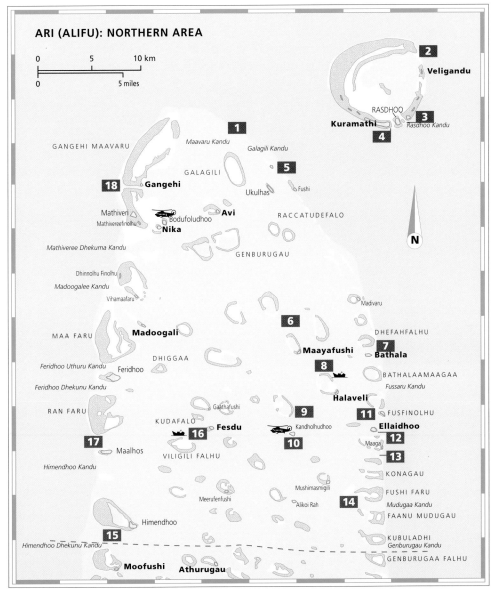

ARI (ALIFU): NORTHERN AREA

0   5   10 km

0   5 miles

2 Veligandu

RASDHOO

3

Kuramathi   Rasdhoo Kandu

4

1

GANGEHI MAAVARU   Maavaru Kandu

Galagili Kandu

GALAGILI   **5**

18 Gangehi

Ukulhas   Fushi

Mathiveri   **Avi**

Mathivereefinolhu   Bodufoludhoo   RACCATUDEFALO

Nika

Mathiveree Dhekuma Kandu

GENBURUGAU

Dhinnolhu Finolhu

Madoogalee Kandu

Vihamaafaru

Madivaru

6

MAA FARU   **Madoogali**

DHEFAHFALHU

7

DHIGGAA   **Maayafushi**   **Bathala**

Feridhoo Uthuru Kandu   Feridhoo   **8**

Feridhoo Dhekunu Kandu   BATHALAAMAAGAA

Fussaru Kandu

Halaveli

Gaathafushi   **9**   FUSFINOLHU   **11**

RAN FARU   KUDAFALO   **Fesdu**   Kandholhudhoo   **Ellaidhoo**

17   **16**   Maaga   **12**

Maalhos   **10**   **13**

VILIGILI FALHU

Himendhoo Kandu   KONAGAU

Mushimasmigili   FUSHI FARU

Meerufenfushi   Alikoi Rah   **14**   Mudugaa Kandu

FAANU MUDUGAU

Himendhoo

KUBULADHI

15   Genburugau Kandu

Himendhoo Dhekunu Kandu   GENBURUGAA FALHU

Moofushi   **Athurugau**

N

---

3 MADIVARU (HAMMERHEAD POINT)

★★★★ ★★★

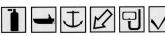

Location: The channel between Madivaru uninhabited island and Rasdhoo Island.

Access: Kuramathi (10min), Veligandu (25min). Some of the other resorts in Ari Atoll run full-day excursions to this site.

Conditions: Usually good in all weathers.

Average visibility: 30m (100ft).

Average depth: 20m (65ft).

Maximum depth: 40m+ (130ft+).

This narrow channel faces the deep ocean and is home to a large school of hammerhead sharks (*Sphyrna lewini*). For the best chance of seeing them the dive should be made at sunrise and when the current is running into the channel. Jump in on the north corner of the channel and swim directly out into blue water, maintaining a depth of 20m (65ft). The experience of seeing schooling hammerheads is very thrilling. Add to this the beautiful reef and *thila* that lie within the channel . . . the dive really is superb. Having enjoyed the

view of the sharks, navigate your way back to the north corner of the complex reef system that lies within the Madivaru Channel. Swimming with the reef on your right hand, you will see a coral ridge stretching out into the ocean. This stunning outcrop extends across the mouth of the channel for about 100m (110yd) and rises gently to a *thila* whose shallowest point is at 8m (25ft). The average depth along the coral ridge is 20m (65ft). On the right-hand side, as you swim along, you see undulating sand populated by hundreds of garden eels. On the left-hand side is the vertical drop to the ocean. Along this dropoff are many caves and overhangs harbouring a huge variety of marine life. As the current flows into the atoll over the ridge, jackfish, tuna, whitetip sharks and eagle rays are regular visitors.

4 KURAMATHI FARU
★★★ ☆☆☆☆

Location: Southernmost point of Kuramathi Resort Island.
Access: Kuramathi (10min), Veligandu (40min).
Conditions: Exposed in southwesterly winds.
Average visibility: 25m (80ft).
Average depth: 20m (65ft).
Maximum depth: 35m (115ft).
The house reef of Kuramathi Resort falls steeply down to a plateau of sand at 25m (80ft) before rising over a ridge of coral with its top at 20m (65ft). The ocean side of this ridge is a sheer wall sporting some enormous sea fans, draped in feather stars, at between 30m (100ft) and 40m (130ft); it is worth taking a torch on the dive to illuminate these spectacular growths. Returning up and over the ridge, you will find garden eels in the sandy gulley, and whitetip sharks and stingrays are common visitors. On top of the reef, hawksbill and green turtles (*Chelonia mydas*) are often seen.

The reeftop lies at just 5m (16ft), making this an excellent site for snorkelling.

5 FUSHI FARU
★★★ ☆☆☆☆

Location: Northeast corner of Fushi Faru, 2km (1¼ miles) east of Ukulhas Island.
Access: Velidhoo (35min), Maayafushi (45min).
Conditions: This site is exposed in both seasons, so good surface conditions are needed if you are to dive comfortably.

Opposite: *Clownfish venture a short way from their host anemones as blue-lined snapper pass overhead.*

Average visibility: 20m (65ft).
Average depth: 15m (50ft).
Maximum depth: 35m (115ft).
The northeastern outer rim of Ari Atoll is broken in many places but most of the rim-reefs have their shallowest points at 10m (33ft). Fushi Faru is one of the few reefs in the area to break the surface, and the site is marked by a small sandbar with a few bushes. The north corner of the reef makes for an interesting and sometimes spectacular dive, for here whale sharks are often seen feeding in the plankton-rich waters. The reef itself consists of some huge *Porites* corals and is home to a colony of thousands of red-toothed triggerfish. Look out for whitetip sharks and turtles.

6 MAAYA THILA
★★★★★

Location: 3km (2 miles) northwest of Maayafushi Resort Island.
Access: Maayafushi (20min), Halaveli (35min), Bathala (40min), Ellaidhoo (50min), Fesdu (50min). Many other resorts in Ari Atoll visit this site on day excursions.
Conditions: Good.
Average visibility: 20m (65ft).
Average depth: 15m (50ft).
Maximum depth: 40m (130ft).
A Protected Marine Area, this offers one of the best-known dives in the Maldives. There is a remarkable variety of marine life on the *thila*, including grey sharks, whitetip sharks, turtles, stonefish, frogfish, zebra morays, batfish and many, many more species. The *thila* is small enough – 30m (33yd) in diameter – that you can swim around it easily in a single dive but, as always, it is the point of the current that concentrates the underwater activity. Jumping onto the top of the *thila*, at 8m (25ft), and swimming due north you come to the edge of the *thila*, where there is a large overhang full of bright orange *Tubastrea* corals. At this point, looking out into the blue, you will see a large satellite rock which is worth exploring. The top of the rock, at 15m (50ft), is covered in colourful hard and soft corals. The vertical sides of the rock drop down to the atoll plate at 40m (130ft). In this channel between the satellite rock and the *thila* grey reef sharks often patrol. On the channel floor whitetip reef sharks can frequently be seen resting on the sand. To the south of the *thila* is another, smaller satellite rock, and this is also an interesting point of the dive – although on this side of the *thila* the coral growth is quite poor. This is an excellent site for night diving.

Although the top of the *thila* is a little deep for snorkelling, you can get a good birdseye view of the action.

7 BATHALA THILA
★★★

Location: In the Bathala Channel, 1km (1/2 mile) due east of Bathala Resort Island.
Access: Bathala (10min), Halaveli (30min), Maayafushi (40min), Ellaidhoo (40min).
Conditions: Sheltered in the southwest season, but can be rough in a strong northeasterly if the current is running out of the atoll.
Average visibility: 20m (65ft).
Average depth: 20m (65ft).
Maximum depth: 40m (130ft).
This *thila* is about 200m (220yd) long and about 50m (55yd) wide. It faces the ocean and runs east–west in the Bathala Channel. In a moderate current you can swim around the *thila* in one dive. However, if the current is running into the atoll, a good dive plan is to jump on the front of the *thila* and stay on the current point watching the action. You can then drift down the *thila* with the current, keeping the reef on the right-hand side. At the western end is a lovely section of caves and overhangs full of sea fans, black coral bushes and abundant fish life. Take care when there is a strong current running as the *thila* is narrow and it is easy to be swept off the site.

8 HALAVELI WRECK
★★★

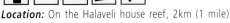

Location: On the Halaveli house reef, 2km (1 mile) northwest of Halaveli Resort Island.
Access: Halaveli (15min), Maayafushi (30min), Bathala (30min), Ellaidhoo (35min), Fesdu (60min).
Conditions: Good, unless winds are very strong.
Average visibility: 15m (50ft).
Average depth: 20m (65ft).
Maximum depth: 28m (60ft).
Sunk in 1991 by the Halaveli Island dive school, this wreck has become home to some interesting marine life and is very popular with divers. The main attractions are the large stingrays (*Taeniura melanospila*) that come in to be fed by the instructors. Although something of a circus, this can be entertaining and provides a great chance to see these beautiful animals at close quarters. There are also some large morays, groupers and a school of batfish that have become accustomed to taking their meals from the visiting divers. The wreck itself lies 50m (55yd) from the main reef and is upright on the sand bed with its keel at a depth of 28m (100ft). The deck is at 20m (65ft) and there is a large mast reaching up to 15m (50ft) which is buoyed to the surface. The main reef is in slightly poor condition so it is better to stay in the area of the wreck. Be careful not to touch the rays, and be aware that at times they can be quite boisterous.

9 KANDHOLHUDHOO THILA
★★★

Location: 1km (1/2 mile) northwest of Kandholhudhoo uninhabited island.
Access: Halaveli (20min), Ellaidhoo (20min), Fesdu (30min), Maayafushi (40min).
Conditions: Good in all seasons.
Average visibility: 20m (65ft).
Average depth: 15m (50ft).
Maximum depth: 30m (100ft).
Some 150m (165yd) long and 70m (77yd) wide, Kandholhudhoo Thila lies well inside the atoll, close to Kandholhudhoo Island, which is uninhabited but has a helipad. The top of the *thila* is at a depth of 8m (25ft) with the sides gently sloping down to the atoll bed at 30m (100ft). This is a shallow, easy dive and at first sight the reef can seem rather mediocre; nevertheless it contains several unusual species of fish. Frogfish and leaf fish can be found on the reef slopes as well as species of gobies with their blind partner shrimps. On the eastern side of the *thila* is a section of caves and overhangs which are home to a variety of reef fish and soft corals.

10 KANDHOLHUDHOO HOUSE REEF
★★ ★★★★

Location: House reef of Kandholhudhoo uninhabited island.
Access: Halaveli (25min), Ellaidhoo (20min), Fesdu (25min), Maayafushi (45min).
Conditions: Good in all seasons.
Average visibility: 20m (65ft).
Average depth: 12m (40ft).
Maximum depth: 30m (100ft).
The western side of the Kandholhudhoo reef has a steeply sloping wall that drops down to the atoll plate at 30m (100ft). This reef is well protected from the destructive action of the ocean and the coral formations here are generally very good. Some parts of the reef were destroyed by crown-of-thorns starfish in the 1980s, but the coral is recovering quickly. It is very common for divers and snorkellers to see hawksbill turtles feeding on the reeftop.

This is a colourful and easy dive for both snorkellers and divers, with usually very little current. The fish life is relatively tame here and underwater photographers will enjoy the tranquillity of the dive.

Above: *Soldierfish can often be seen congregating in caves during the day.*
Below: *At close quarters, the mouth of this* Tubastrea *coral is clearly visible.*

11 ELLAIDHOO THILA
★★★ ★★

Location: 1km (1/2 mile) northwest of Ellaidhoo Resort Island.
Access: Ellaidhoo (15min), Halaveli (30min), Bathala (40min), Maayafushi (45min).
Conditions: Usually good.
Average visibility: 25m (80ft).
Average depth: 15m (50ft).
Maximum depth: 40m (130ft).
Situated well inside the channel and lying east to west, Ellaidhoo Thila is about 250m (275yd) long and 50m (55yd) wide. The eastern point of the *thila* is a steep dropoff with shallow caves at varying depths starting at 12m (40ft). The southern side of the *thila* is better for its hard and soft corals and there are a number of coral outcrops on this side of the reef. Divers often report sightings of large orange frogfish on one of these outcrops at 18m (60ft), so look carefully as you swim by. Fish life on the *thila* is excellent, with large schools of bannerfish, surgeonfish and fusiliers.

12 ELLAIDHOO HOUSE REEF
★★★ ★★★★★

Location: 40m (130ft) from the shore on the south side of Ellaidhoo Resort Island.
Access: Ellaidhoo.
Conditions: Usually good.
Average visibility: 20m (65ft).
Average depth: 12m (40ft).
Maximum depth: 35m (115ft).
The Ellaidhoo house reef has a vertical section on the south side that starts at 3m (10ft) and descends to 30m (100ft) before the reef begins to plateau out into the ocean channel. It is this wall of the house reef that makes the diving from Ellaidhoo so good. The wall is interspersed with caves which have excellent hard and soft corals, fish and invertebrate life. The island is

CLEANER SHRIMP

The banded coral shrimp (*Stenopus hispidus*) is found on all Maldivian reefs and performs an extremely important function. The shrimp establishes cleaning stations in coral crevices and caves and uses its pincers for picking small lice and other parasites off fish. It has three pairs of legs with the third pair being much larger and longer than the others. This large shrimp, often associated with moray eels, is easily recognized by its red and white striped body and legs. Adult males and females pair together and may inhabit the same cleaning station for several years.

situated on the outer rim of the atoll, which means its reef is exposed to the ocean currents: you can often see pelagic species like whitetip sharks, jackfish and tuna. An added attraction to the dive is a small wreck which was sunk at the end of the jetty by the dive centre. The wreck, which lies upside-down at 32m (104ft), offers an interesting dive and is home to some very large groupers and moray eels.

This is a super reef for snorkelling and a fantastic night dive.

13 ORIMAS THILA (MAAGA THILA)
★★★★ ★★★★

Location: South channel of Maaga uninhabited island.
Access: Ellaidhoo (20min), Halaveli (40min), Bathala (60min), Maayafushi (60min).
Conditions: Usually good, although can be choppy if there is wind against the tide.
Average visibility: 20m (65ft).
Average depth: 12m (40ft).
Maximum depth: 40m (130ft).
Orimas Thila is a superb site with a remarkable variety of large and small species of marine life in a confined area. The topography is unusual, with caves, gulleys, crevices and large coral outcrops all contributing to the enjoyment. From the middle of the *thila* on the northern side, you descend over the reeftop and into a large cave which runs along the north face of the *thila* for about 40m (44yd). A shaft of sunlight sometimes streams into the overhang through a small, narrow crevice dropping down from the surface of the reef at 6m (20ft) to the roof of the cave at 12m (40ft). From the cave, you can explore a number of coral outcrops, and one very large coral head that sits at the easternmost point of the *thila* at 28m (92ft). Returning to the reeftop, you pass through a gulley which forms a continuation of the crevice first seen in the cave. Of particular note on the top of the *thila* are the huge numbers of anemones (with attendant clownfish) and stunning table corals.

This is a good site for snorkellers as the reeftop is shallow and there is a great deal of marine activity. Divers and snorkellers should take care if the current is strong as the cave and crevice can cause the waters to eddy.

14 MUSHIMASMIGILI (FISH HEAD)
★★★★★

Location: 4km (2 1/2 miles) south of Mushimasmigili uninhabited island.
Access: Ellaidhoo (40min), Halaveli (60min), Fesdu (60min). Other resorts in Ari Atoll and some resorts in North and South Malé atolls run day excursions.

Above: *The wreck of a large fishing boat (Site 16) lies southwest of Fesdu Resort Island.*

Conditions: Usually good.
Average visibility: 20m (65ft).
Average depth: 15m (50ft).
Maximum depth: 42m (138ft).

Mushimasmigili is named after the small brown fusilier that is found in huge numbers on the *thila*. This is a Protected Marine Area and home to grey reef sharks, napoleon wrasse and great schools of fusiliers and yellow grunts. The small oval *thila* is about 100m (110yd) long and 60m (67yd) wide with its reeftop at 10m (33ft). The southern side of the *thila* drops down steeply in two steps from 8m (25ft) to 20m (65ft) and then from 20m (65ft) to the atoll plate at 42m (138ft). At the southeastern corner of the step, projecting out from the *thila*, is a large overhang commonly known as The Fish Head. In the overhang you will find a huge school of thousands of blue-lined snapper. The north and western sides of the *thila* drop down more steeply, and at 20m (65ft) the reef is undercut with an overhang around a large portion of the *thila*. In this overhang there are many large sea fans and black coral trees decorated with featherstars. This is a great dive site with a huge amount to see; it is most famous for its resident school of grey reef sharks, which often pass just a few metres from you.

15 HIMENDHOO THILA

★★★ ★★★

Location: 1.5km (1 mile) south of Himendhoo Faru.
Access: Fesdu (50min), Moofushi (50min).
Conditions: Usually good in the northeast season.
Average visibility: 20m (65ft).
Average depth: 15m (50ft).
Maximum depth: 30m (100ft).

This *thila* is usually dived from December to April, when the currents predominantly flow out of the channel and large schools of manta rays feed on the surface. The *thila* is long and narrow, 300m (330yd) by 50m (55yd), with its reeftop at a depth of 10m (33ft) and with gently sloping sides. On the south side there are some interesting caves and overhangs between 20m (65ft) and 30m (100ft) that are worth exploring in the absence of manta rays. However, the main reason to dive here is to watch the mantas as they come in from the ocean to feed on the plankton-rich waters that flow out of the atoll. Take care on the reeftop as there are large areas of fire coral which can be very painful if touched.

If the mantas are congregating around the *thila* it is

often better to snorkel with them than use scuba. However, the *thila* is only a good site for snorkellers if the mantas are feeding on the surface.

16 FESDU WRECK
★★★★

Location: 1km (¹/₂ mile) southwest of Fesdu Resort Island on the north side of Viligili Falhu.
Access: Fesdu (15min), Maayafushi (30min), Madoogali (40min), Ellaidhoo (45min). Other resort islands in Ari Atoll run day trips to the site.
Conditions: Usually good, although visibility may be reduced in unsettled weather.
Average visibility: 20m (65ft).
Average depth: 20m (65ft).
Maximum depth: 30m (100ft).
Fesdu wreck sits on a sand slope alongside a small *thila*. The wreck is a large fishing boat about 30m (100ft) in length. It lies north to south with its bow facing northwards at a depth of 30m (100ft) and the stern of the vessel with its propeller still in place at a depth of 27m (80ft). There is a large wheelhouse centrally placed on the wreck which is home to a great swarm of glassfish, giant moray eels and red-mouthed grouper. The wreck is covered in beautiful, delicate soft corals and is an excellent dive for both novice and experienced divers. To the west of the vessel the small *thila*, about 30m (33yd) in diameter, lies 50m (165ft) away from the main reef. In good conditions, it is possible to enter on top of the wreck and end the dive by swimming on to the *thila* and then to the main reef. Otherwise you can enter on the *thila* and swim east to the wreck, returning to the *thila* at the end of the dive.

17 MAALHOS THILA
★★★★ ★★★

Location: North channel of Maalhos fishing island.
Access: Fesdu (45min), Moofushi (50min), Madoogali (50min). Other resort islands on the eastern side of the atoll run day trips to the site.
Conditions: Exposed in the southwest season, when conditions can be very difficult. Very strong currents can flow over this *thila* in both seasons.
Average visibility: 30m (100ft).
Average depth: 25m (80ft).
Maximum depth: 40m+ (130ft+).
Lying in the Maalhos Channel close to the northern corner of Ran Faru, Maalhos Thila is 200m (220yd) long and just 50m (55yd) wide. This is one of the most beautiful and colourful *thilas* in the Maldives, with

superb hard corals and stunning soft corals adorning the many caves and overhangs that run the length of the site. The reef fish life is intense with great schools of blue-lined snapper, soldierfish, moorish idols and sweetlips swimming against a backdrop of sea fans, whip corals and black coral trees. There are several large coral heads on the ocean side of the *thila* and here you can see barracuda, eagle rays and whitetip sharks. One of the reasons the *thila* is so alive with colour is that the currents flowing around and over it are very strong; be aware of this before you jump into the water. The shallowest point of the *thila* is 10m (33ft) so decompression diving should be avoided.

18 GANGEHI KANDU
★★★ ★★★

Location: Southern reef of the Gangehi Channel.
Access: Gangehi (10min), Nika (20min), Avi (30min).
Conditions: Exposed in westerlies, but otherwise usually good. Currents can be strong in the channel. If wind is against tide, the conditions here can quickly become choppy.
Average visibility: 20m (65ft).
Average depth: 15m (50ft).
Maximum depth: 40m (130ft).
This is a classic Maldivian drift dive through one of the many breaks in the atoll rim where the movement of plankton-rich oceanic water into and out of the atoll is colossal. The site is best dived with the current flowing into the atoll, when you can jump into the water on either the north or south corner of the channel. The current carries you along the reef past swarms of red-toothed triggerfish and a great variety of colourful reef fish. Look out for hawksbill turtles as they graze on the reeftop.

During the northeast season, when the current runs out of the channel, large schools of manta rays are often seen feeding on the surface during the out-running tide. Divers' bubbles will scare the mantas in a situation like this so it is better to snorkel than to use scuba equipment.

NUDIBRANCHS

Nudibranch means 'naked gills' – these molluscs have no shell. There are a huge number of brightly coloured nudibranchs in the Maldives, usually found on the reeftop feeding on sponges and bryozoans. No more than 10cm (4 inches) in length, many of them have rhinophores (tentacles) that can be retracted, gills, a body or mantle and a foot. Nudibranchs often lay their eggs in bright coloured rings, which delicately adorn the reef.

HOW TO GET THERE

By air: All international schedule and charter flights land at Hulhule International Airport in North Malé Atoll; transfers to the northern part of Ari Atoll can then be made by either helicopter or seaplane. The seaplanes are operated by Maldivian Air Taxi (tel 315201/fax 315203). There are three helipads in this area of Ari Atoll, on the islands of Rasdhoo, Bodufolodhoo and Kandolodhoo. The helicopters are operated by Hummingbird Helicopters (tel 325708/9/fax 323161). As an indication, flying time by helicopter from the international airport is about 25min to Rasdhoo and 30min to Bodufolodhu and Kandolodhu.

By boat: Travel to the northern area of Ari Atoll by speedboat may take up to three hours to some of the furthest resort islands. A *dhoani* transfer could take five hours and in bad weather can be quite uncomfortable. Numerous live-aboards visit this area (see page 29 for contact addresses).

WHERE TO STAY

Visitors normally stay on registered tourist islands, in other words at a resort. Every resort provides its own dining facilities.

Avi Island Resort (Velidhoo)

tel 450595/fax 450595; 30 rooms; 65km (40 miles) from airport
This is a small island with beautiful beaches and a large, sheltered lagoon. Accommodation is of a good standard, in bungalows. Facilities include waterskiing, canoeing and a tennis court. The dive centre offers a range of PADI courses and there is good access to the house reef on the north side of the island. Visa, American Express, MasterCard.

Bathala Island Resort

tel 450587/fax 450558; 36 rooms; 55km (36 miles) from airport
This beautiful island, just 300m (330yd) by 150m (165yd), has simple accommodation in 36 individual thatched cottages. Some rooms have AC and minibar. Facilities are limited, with scuba diving being the main activity. The PADI school runs a range of courses; the house reef is easily accessible, just 10m (11yd) from the beach, and offers very good diving. Visa, American Express, MasterCard.

Ellaidhoo Tourist Resort

tel 450514/fax 450586; 50 rooms; 55km (36 miles) from airport
A small simple island with accommodation in traditional bungalows. This resort – the first in the Maldives to offer Nitrox – is great for divers: Sub Aqua dive school provides an excellent standard of training. Facilities include windsurfers and a catamaran.

Excellent house reef with a small wreck lying at 30m (100ft) at the end of the jetty.

Fesdu Fun Island

tel 450541/fax 450547; 55 rooms; 65km (40 miles) from airport
A small island, with an informal atmosphere and individual cottages and water bungalows. All rooms have hot and cold water and some have AC. Facilities include windsurfing, catamaran sailing and waterskiing. The dive school offers PADI courses. The house reef has easy access and is good for both diving and snorkelling. Visa, American Express, MasterCard, Diners' Club, JCB.

Gangehi Resort

tel 450505/fax 450506; 25 rooms; 75km (48 miles) from airport
A small, exclusive Italian-managed resort with 25 well equipped bungalows. Eight of these are deluxe water bungalows. Rooms have AC, hot and cold water, bath, minibar and telephone. Facilities include windsurfing. The dive centre offers PADI courses and there is a good house reef. Visa, American Express, MasterCard.

Halaveli Holiday Village

tel 450559/fax 450564; 50 rooms; 61km (38 miles) from airport
A small, pretty island, with simple accommodation in detached cottages at the water's edge. All rooms have AC, hot and cold water. Facilities include windsurfing, catamaran sailing and canoeing. The dive centre is run by Tropical Gangsters Inc who are a PADI 5-star IDC. The house reef on the east and southeast sides of the island is excellent. Visa, American Express, MasterCard, Diners' Club.

Kuramathi Tourist Resorts

55km (36 miles) from airport
There are three resorts on this island: Kuramathi Village (tel 450527/fax 450556), Kuramathi Cottage Club (tel 450532/fax 450642) and Kuramathi Blue Lagoon (tel 450579/fax 450531). The Village is the largest, with over 200 rooms; the Cottage Club has 30 standard rooms and 50 water bungalows; Blue Lagoon is more exclusive, with 20 water bungalows and 30 standard rooms. A bus service runs between the resorts. There is limited access to the house reef on the southern side of the island.

Maayafushi Tourist Resort

tel 450588/fax 450568; 60 rooms; 61km (38 miles) from airport
Small and round with beautiful beaches and lagoon, this island is renowned for its excellent diving. Accommodation is in very simple terraced bungalows; some rooms have AC, all have ceiling fan. Facilities include windsurfing and catamaran sailing.

The dive centre runs a good range of PADI courses and the house reef is good. Visa, American Express, MasterCard.

Madoogali Resort

tel 45058/fax 450554; 50 rooms; 70km (46 miles) from airport
A small Italian-run resort with good-sized thatched, single-storey rooms on the water's edge, each with AC, hot and cold water, telephone and fridge. Facilities include catamaran sailing, windsurfing, waterskiing and parasailing. The dive school offers PADI courses and the house reef is good for snorkelling and diving. Visa, American Express, MasterCard, Diners' Club.

Nika Hotel

tel 450516/fax 450577; 27 rooms; 70km (46 miles) from airport
One of the most expensive and exclusive islands in the Maldives, with predominantly Italian guests. Accommodation is in large individual thatched bungalows, each with a secluded beach area. Facilities include tennis, badminton, windsurfing and catamaran sailing. The dive school offers PADI courses and the house reef is good.

Veligandu Island

tel 450594/fax 450519; 55 rooms; 50km (32 miles) from airport
A small, tranquil island with a beautiful sandbank. Accommodation is in single beach bungalows; there are also several water bungalows and suites. Some rooms have AC, hot water, minibar and telephone. Facilities include catamaran sailing and windsurfing. The dive centre offers PADI courses and the house reef is good for snorkelling and diving. Visa, American Express, MasterCard.

DIVING EMERGENCIES

Some of the resort islands in this part of the atoll have established relationships with European doctors, who provide basic medical services in exchange for free holidays. However, facilities are extremely limited and any problem considered to be serious will require evacuation to the main hospital or private clinic in Malé (AMDC Clinic tel 325979/ADK Medical Centre tel 324332). There are no recompression facilities in North Ari Atoll; any emergency cases have to be flown by helicopter or carried by speedboat to the Hyperbaric Centre on Bandos Island Resort in North Malé Atoll (tel 440088/ fax: 440060).

EXCURSIONS

The **locally inhabited islands** of Rasdhoo, Mathiveri, Bodufoludhoo, Feridhoo, Maalhos and Himendhoo can be visited. There are souvenir shops on all these islands. Please dress modestly. All resorts offer excursions to **uninhabited islands**. Most resorts offer **fishing** excursions aboard a *dhoani*.

A night dive can be a thrilling and fascinating experience. Numerous species not easily visible during the day come out to feed at night, and often the reef is alive with activity. Some fish do hide on the reef at night, but many display very interesting behaviour and a night dive is an ideal opportunity to watch.

During the day, colours are progressively filtered out of the water with descending depth, with reds being the first to go and only blue light reaching the deep water. On a night dive, things are different. The only light source, your torch, is close to the reef and the objects of interest, making the full spectrum of light available to illuminate the subject. Instead of the blue-green colours that you see on a dive during the day, the artificial light from your torch brings bright colours to the reef and allows you to see the colours as they really are. In addition, your attention is held within the beam of your torch, encouraging you to look more carefully and, hopefully, notice more of the tiny creatures on the reef.

Below: *A torch helps focus the attention.*

CREATURES OF THE NIGHT

At the beginning of the food chain, plankton makes its presence felt far more noticeably at night: tiny shrimps and invertebrates that usually live in the sandy bottom during the day swim out in numbers to feed on the plankton. Direct your torch out into the open water off the reef, and hundreds of wriggling plankton will swim into the beam, the perfect meal for nocturnal feeders. Small and large invertebrates such as starfish are also noticeably active on the reef at night.

Most nocturnal fish are carnivores that are looking to feed on invertebrates on the reef. Bright schools of fish that normally stick closely together for protection during the day, such as the blue-lined snapper (*Lutjanus kasmira*), break away at night and spend their evenings hunting for small crustaceans on the reef.

The squirrelfish (*Sargocentron* spp) and soldierfish (*Myripristis* spp), with their large eyes, may be seen on night dives, while larger animals such as moray eels, stingrays and whitetip reef sharks will certainly be busy on the reef at night. Morays are often seen out of their usual craggy holes, as they chase prey across the reef.

THE LUNAR CYCLE

The phase of the moon has a strong influence on nocturnal reef life, and the reproductive cycle and behaviour of many species of fish and invertebrates is affected by the lunar cycle. When there is a full moon and the reef is brightly lit, you may see corals spawning, clownfish laying their eggs on the rocky substrate beneath their host anemone and a distinct lack of predatory fish hunting on the reef.

If you dive when there is no moon, you should see a greater number of fish out of their burrows as they hunt for prey under the cover of the dark night. You are also more likely to see invertebrates such as crabs and octopus scuttling across the reef top.

Bear in mind a number of points before leaping into the water for a night dive. First of

Above: *A tailspot squirrelfish is joined at night by a vermilion rock cod and oriental sweetlips.*

all, it is essential to have at least two torches, one to be used all the time and one kept as a back up in the event that the first one should fail. Care should be taken when kitting up not to shine the torch into the boat captain's face – this will ruin his night vision and, if he is navigating through narrow reefs to reach the site, could be disastrous! The same rule applies underwater with your dive buddy.

Many night divers attach a chemical dive stick to their tanks which glows throughout the dive. Left on constantly, these can be very irritating as they ruin the underwater night vision; personally I believe it better to keep the chemical stick in your pocket in the event that you need it for emergency purposes. You should also pay extra attention to your depth gauges as it is often difficult to gauge depth without a wide visual reference and all too easy to stray too deep on a night dive. If you

are staying at a resort and night diving from the shore, do make sure you tell someone that you are going on a night dive and, equally, make sure you sign yourself back in after the dive.

Night diving in the Maldives is not always easy as there are no navigational lights – the best diving, of course, is on those very reefs which may be difficult for a boat to navigate. Consequently, night diving is not always available from resorts so, if it is important to you, check the policy of the dive centre with your tour operator prior to making a booking. Some of the resort islands offer excellent night diving from the shore on their house reef, as well as night diving from boats. However, by far and away the best night diving is from live-aboard dive boats, which can anchor close to remote outer reefs that are difficult to get to by night from the resorts.

SOUTH AND NORTH MAALHOSMADULU (BAA AND RAA)

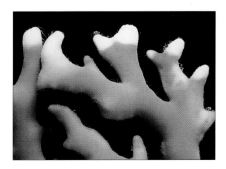

Although designated part of the tourist zone, South Maalhosmadulu Atoll for many years remained undeveloped and was visited only by tourists on the larger live-aboard boats. However, in late 1995 the exclusive resort island of Sonevafushi was opened and the government has since made further islands available for development. The first resort in North Maalhosmadulu Atoll is due to be opened at the same time.

The majority of the islands of South Maalhosmadulu Atoll are on the eastern side, with a large number concentrated in the northeastern corner. Many make lovely anchorages as they are densely vegetated with tall palm trees and surrounded by beautiful turquoise lagoons. All the locally inhabited islands rely heavily on their fishing industry, and the atoll has a large collective fishing fleet. Small cargo *dhoanis* travel once a week from the capital island of Eydafushi to Malé to trade dried tuna for food and building materials. In the south of the atoll, the island of Thulaadhoo is known for its *lielaa jehun* black lacquer boxes and vases, made from coconut wood turned on a hand lathe and then carved decoratively and coloured with resins. The small fishing island of Kamadhoo is one of the few islands to have a troupe of *bandiyaa* dancing girls, who travel all over the Maldives performing to tourists and for national festivals. Three of the locally inhabited islands are in Goidhoo Atoll, which lies just 12km (7 miles) to the south of South Maalhosmadulu Atoll but falls under the same administrative area. The French explorer François Pyrard was wrecked on the reef off Fulhadhoo in 1602, and was held prisoner here for a number of years. During his captivity he wrote an account of his experiences in his book *The Voyages of François Pyrard of Laval to the East Indies, the Maldives, the Moluccas and Brazil*.

Many of the uninhabited islands in South Maalhosmadulu Atoll are used to sustain the atoll's small agricultural trade. As well as coconuts, bananas, water melon and papaya are cultivated and taken to Malé throughout the year.

At present there is just one resort in South Maalhosmadulu, Sonevafushi on Kunfunadhoo Island, but the government has announced that a further four

Opposite: *Dharavandhoo is one of the locally inhabited islands in South Maalhosmadulu Atoll.*
Above: *This rare pink coral with white tips is found at Bathalaa Kandu (Site 11).*

uninhabited islands are now available for tourist development. These are the islands of Fonimagoodhoo, Kihaadhufaru, Horubadhoo and Dhunikolhu.

To the north of South Maalhosmadulu Atoll, separated by the 3km (2-mile) wide Moresby Channel, is the atoll known as North Maalhosmadulu. It is only recently that the government has included this atoll in the tourist zone with the development of the uninhabited island of Meedhupparu as a resort.

DIVING AND SNORKELLING IN SOUTH AND NORTH MAALHOSMADULU (BAA AND RAA) ATOLLS

The best diving in South Maalhosmadulu is on the many *thilas* situated just inside the fringing reefs of the atoll. Drift diving and snorkelling on the outer reefs can be very enjoyable, with good hard-coral formations and the opportunity to see large pelagic species cruising by. However, the channels are generally very wide and as a result do not concentrate the marine life in the same way as *thilas* in the middle of the channels.

The northeast season is a time of calm water and generally very good visibility throughout the atoll. Most of the dive sites here are in excellent condition, as there are few resorts in the atoll and many sites lie inside the protective atoll reef.

In the southwest season the atoll is known for superb manta ray and whale shark encounters. Bear in mind, however, that this is a time when seas can be rough and the visibility may be reduced.

Generally, the currents in South Maalhosmadulu Atoll are not as strong as those experienced elsewhere. One reason for this is that during the northeast season, from December to April, the atoll is in the lee of Faadhippolhu and South Miladhunmadulu atolls to the west. In the southwest season, from May to November, the unusual width of the channels helps to dissipate the currents.

The diving of North Maalhosmadulu Atoll, only recently brought into the tourist zone, is still to be discovered, but is expected to share similarities with South Maalhosmadulu Atoll.

Below: *The current brings sites alive, attracting pelagic species and adding movement to the reef.*

South Maalhosmadulu (Baa)

There are ten fishing islands in South Maalhosmadulu Atoll, with a total population in the region of 10,000. The capital island is Eydafushi, which has a large man-made harbour. The atoll has over 38 uninhabited islands and one resort, though a further four resorts are under construction.

In many areas the reefs are pristine, and whether you are a diver or snokeller, the natural beauty of this unspoiled atoll is readily apparent both above and below water. One of the secrets of South Maalhosmadulu Atoll is the large number of mantas and whale sharks that can be seen during the southwest monsoon months of May, June and July. The weather is not at its best at this time, but for a tremendous opportunity to see these pelagic species, South Maalhosmadulu is certainly a place to visit.

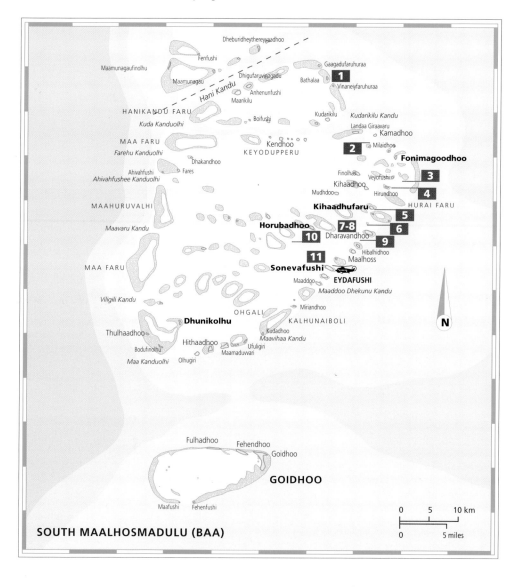

FORGOTTEN SPONGES

Often brightly coloured and attractive, sponges are nevertheless easily overlooked. They may be encrusting, growing over a rock face or they may grow upright – but whatever form they take, they are always attached. The body is usually perforated with numerous holes through which water is taken in (to supply the sponge with oxygen) and suspended fragments of food are ingested. The water carries waste carbon dioxide away. Sponges are thought of as the first multicellular animals; their fossil remains have been traced back 650 million years.

1 BATHALAA KANDU

★★★ ★★★

Location: Southern reef of Bathalaa Kandu.
Access: Live-aboard only.
Conditions: Usually calm, but can become choppy if wind is against tide.
Average visibility: 25m (80ft).
Average depth: 20m (65ft).
Maximum depth: 35m (115ft).

The star of this dive is the beautiful and now rare coral *Distichopora violacea*, which protrudes at right angles from the sheer reef wall. The coral grows in crown-like clusters and is a bright pink colour with tipped edges. For years this species of coral has been plundered for the jewellery trade and it is now, sadly, only occasionally found on deeper reefs away from inhabited islands.

The site is at its best when the current is running into the atoll. Jump in on the northeast corner of the Bathalaa Island reef and follow into the channel keeping the reef on the left-hand side. The reeftop is at 6m (20ft), with the sides sloping gently down to a shoulder at 15m (50ft). At this point it drops vertically away to the atoll floor at 35m (115ft). The pink coral is found on the lower section between 20m (65ft) and 35m (115ft).

The reeftop is excellent for snorkelling, with a mass of healthy hard corals and fish life.

2 MILAIDHOO HOUSE REEF

★★★ ★★★★

Location: House reef of Milaidhoo uninhabited island.
Access: Live-aboard only.
Conditions: Usually calm, unless winds are very strong.
Average visibility: 25m (80ft).
Average depth: 20m (65ft).
Maximum depth: 40m (130ft).

The tiny island of Milaidhoo is situated about 2km (1 mile) inside the atoll; its reef is washed by the very strong currents that flow through Kamadhoo Kandu. The best area of this 500m (550yd) long reef is the northwest side, where there is a sheer wall that drops from the reeftop at 2m (7ft) down to 35m (115ft) and is interspersed with caves and overhangs, full of brightly coloured soft corals, sponges, sea fans and whip corals. The south side, a gentle slope with mixed sand and coral, is not so good. If there is a strong current, take care to stay close to the reef to avoid being swept off. Shelter can always be found in one of the many caves, so don't be put off by the strong currents.

3 VEYOFUSHI BODU GIRI

★★★ ★★★★

Location: 500m (550yd) southeast of Veyofushi uninhabited island.
Access: Live-aboard only.
Conditions: Usually calm, unless winds are very strong.
Average visibility: 25m (80ft).
Average depth: 20m (65ft).
Maximum depth: 40m (130ft).

This is a long *giri* that runs north to south, situated inside the atoll and facing the ocean currents. The reef does not break the surface but the centre is always awash with white water, as the swell breaks over it in all but the calmest of conditions. The northeast corner is the most interesting part of the dive. Here a large part of the reef has fallen away, creating a basin scattered with huge coral heads which teem with fish life. On the very point of the *giri* one of these large coral heads rises from 30m (100ft) to 12m (40ft), standing bolt upright. Between this rock and the reef, at 15m (50ft), is a narrow gulley just 3m (10ft) wide and 10m (33ft) long. In the centre of the basin, among the coral outcrops, stands a second pinnacle that rises from 40m (130ft) to within 15m (50ft) of the surface. At 30m (100ft) between this pinnacle and the reef there is a fabulous 5m (16ft) long tunnel which pulsates with life. The area of the rocks and the shallow caves on the reef are covered by orange *Dendronephthya* soft coral.

The reeftop is excellent for snorkelling with many beautiful corals and an abundance of fish life.

4 HIRUNDHOO HOUSE REEF

★★★ ★★★★

Location: Eastern point of Hirundhoo house reef.
Access: Live-aboard only.
Conditions: Usually calm, unless winds are very strong.
Average visibility: 25m (80ft).
Average depth: 15m (50ft).
Maximum depth: 30m (100ft).

This is a beautiful and usually easy dive, good for both experienced and inexperienced divers. The best section of the reef is 100m (110yd) long and is on the eastern point of the island. Here the reef descends from 6m (19ft) to 30m (100ft) with two levels of caves; one from 12m (40ft) to 20m (65ft) and the second between 20m (65ft) and 25m (80ft). The caves are decorated with a variety of fine yellow and orange soft corals and sponges, black coral bushes, whip corals and sea fans. Exploring the caves is fascinating as they are home to a host of colourful fish and invertebrate life.

The reeftop is in fabulous condition, and the snorkelling is very good on this site.

5 KAKANI THILA
★★★★

Location: 500m (550yd) northeast of Kihaadhufaru.
Access: Sonevafushi (60min).
Conditions: Usually calm, unless winds are very strong.
Average visibility: 25m (80ft).
Average depth: 20m (65ft).
Maximum depth: 40m (130ft).
The *thila* is 150m (165yd) long and 50m (55yd) wide with its reeftop at 10m (33ft). Midway along the reef on the north side, the sea bed plunges over a step from 30m (100ft) to more than 60m (200ft). At 30m (33yd)

Below: *This remarkable mollusc has a tube-like shell which is cemented to the coral.*

along the ridge of the dropoff there are caves and overhangs and a number of huge coral heads stacked upon each other. The whole area is covered in the orange and yellow soft corals common in the atoll, and large schools of oriental sweetlips, jackfish, barracuda and napoleon wrasse live here. Continuing along the *thila* there are a number of large caves on the vertical face. This is a wonderful dive with good fish life and stunning topography.

6 DHONISU THILA
★★★★

Location: 1km (1/2 mile) north of Dharavandhoo fishing island.
Access: Sonevafushi (40min).
Conditions: Usually calm, but a short, choppy sea may develop in strong winds.
Average visibility: 25m (80ft).
Average depth: 20m (65ft).
Maximum depth: 40m+ (130ft+).
This *thila* is about 100m (110yd) in diameter, with the reeftop at about 12m (40ft). The southern side slopes gently down to the atoll floor at 35m (115ft), but there are many large coral heads scattered around the base of the slope rising up to 20m (65ft). All these blocks are decorated with soft and hard corals and provide refuge for many species of colourful reef fish. The north and east sides of the *thila* are sheer, dropping to a depth of 45m (150ft). On the northeastern point you can descend down the face of the *thila* to 30m (100ft) where there is a narrow crevice in the reef. This opens into a broad tunnel, which leads back up to the reeftop. Both the crevice and the tunnel are densely packed with life. Schools of sabre squirrelfish (*Sargocentron spiniferum*), moorish idols and large red rock cod are to be found inside. The top of the *thila* has above-average coral formations with some areas of broken coral.
Generally the site is too deep for snorkelling.

7 FAIMINI BODU THILA
★★★★ ★★★★

Location: 2km (1 1/2 miles) to the northwest of Dharavandhoo fishing island.
Access: Sonevafushi (40min).
Conditions: Usually calm.
Average visibility: 25m (80ft).
Average depth: 15m (50ft).
Maximum depth: 35m (115ft).
Faimini Bodu Thila ('Faimini's big *thila*') is an extraordinary ridge of coral, just 5m (5yd) wide and 500m (550yd) long, rising dramatically from a depth of 35m (115ft) to 10m (33ft). The narrow top that forms

the ridge undulates along the whole length of the reef, varying in depth from 8m (25ft) to 18m (60ft). The reef runs northeast–southwest; you can begin the dive on the northeastern point where the ridge drops sharply down to the ocean floor and where a huge cavernous overhang can be explored. From here the best course is keeping the reef on the right-hand side. The southeastern side of the ridge is a sheer wall with numerous nooks and crannies, sea fans and whip corals. The reeftop is densely populated by hard and soft corals.
This is an excellent site for snorkelling.

8 FAIMINI KUDA THILA
★★★★ ★★★

Location: 50m (55yd) from the southwestern point of Faimini Bodu Thila (Site 7).
Access: Sonevafushi (40min).
Conditions: Usually calm.
Average visibility: 25m (80ft).
Average depth: 20m (65ft).
Maximum depth: 35m (115ft).
Just across the channel from Faimini Bodu Thila lies Faimini Kuda Thila ('Faimini's small *thila*'). You can enjoy this dive on its own or in combination with its bigger brother (Site 7). The *thila* is a fabulous stack, 20m (22yd) wide and 30m (33yd) long, with its reeftop at 15m (50ft) and with huge caves and overhangs packed full of life around most of the reef. Often the most exciting plan for the dive is to jump in on the southwestern point of the larger *thila* and descend to 35m (115ft) to the sand floor. Crossing the sandy channel to Site 8, you can often enjoy thrilling displays of pelagic fish.

9 DHARAVANDHOO THILA
★★★ ★★★

Location: 1km (1/2 mile) north of Dharavandhoo fishing island.
Access: Sonevafushi Island Resort (30min).
Conditions: Usually calm, but a short, choppy sea may develop in strong winds.
Average visibility: 25m (80ft).
Average depth: 20m (65ft).
Maximum depth: 35m (115ft).
Dharavandhoo Thila forms part of a large submerged reef complex which is about 400m (440yd) in length. The *thila* is shaped like a teardrop with a curl on the bottom. The northern point has a diameter of 60m (67yd); the *thila* tapers off to the southern point which is just 10m (11yd) wide. The top of the *thila* is shallower in the north with its reef at 8m (25ft), gently sloping down to the southern end which is at a depth

Above: *This tiered coral head may be hundreds, if not thousands, of years old.*
Below: *A group of oriental sweetlips circles the reef.*

WHY DO FISH SCHOOL?

There are four main reasons why it is thought that fish school. With so many eyes keeping guard it is difficult for a predator to successfully attack a school of fish, so the risk of predation is greatly reduced. Fish do not swim directly behind each other, but at 45° from the fish in front, so that there is increased hydrodynamic efficiency to be gained by swimming in a large group. It is also thought that fish in schools have increased reproductive success and, lastly, that they have an increased efficiency at finding food.

of 15m (50ft). The best dive plan is to jump in on the northeast point and follow with the reef on the right-hand side. In the first section of the dive the reef is steep with caves and overhangs full of black coral bushes, sea fans and bright orange *Tubastrea* and sponges. On the sea bed at 40m (130ft) a number of large coral heads concentrate the fish life. Towards the middle and southern end of the reef the caves are slightly smaller and the reef wall is covered in yellow and blue soft corals. On the reeftop there are many massive *Porites* and in the southwest season it is common to see manta rays being cleaned here.

10 HORUBADHOO THILA
★★★★

Location: 1km (1/2 mile) south of Horubadhoo Resort Island.
Access: Sonevafushi (25min).
Conditions: Usually good, but a short, choppy sea can develop with wind against tide.
Average visibility: 20m (65ft).
Average depth: 20m (65ft).
Maximum depth: 40m+ (130ft+).
A classic Maldivian *thila* site, this is situated in a wide channel and rises from the atoll plate at 45m (150ft) to within 10m (33ft) of the surface. It is the isolation of the *thila* from any other reefs that ensures it is crowded with fish seeking shelter and predators seeking food. The *thila* is oval, 80m (88yd) in length and 30m (33yd) wide, so you can comfortably swim around it in a single dive. On the northeastern side, the reef drops down from 10m (33ft) to 40m (130ft) in a series of steps. Under each of the ledges from 25m (80ft) downwards there are shallow caves and overhangs. During the northeast season the current strikes the *thila* on the east side and here you can often sea large schools of grey sharks and eagle rays. Schools of big-eye trevally, yellowfin fusiliers and batfish mingle off the reef. Dogtooth tuna, barracuda and trevally circle in the currents. The reef walls of the remaining parts of the *thila* slope steeply to 30m (100ft) and there are many large caves and overhangs

around the entire perimeter. There are two large crevices that bisect the *thila* from north to south. These gullies, at a depth of 15m (50ft), are festooned with soft corals and fish life. Brightly coloured yellow trumpetfish (*Aulostoma chinensis*) can be seen on top of the reef, hunting behind the black-saddled coral trout (*Plectropomus laevis*).

11 KUNFUNADHOO THILA
★★★ ★★

Location: 500m (550yd) north of Sonevafushi Resort Island.
Access: Sonevafushi (10min).
Conditions: Usually calm, but a short, choppy sea may develop in strong winds.
Average visibility: 25m (80ft).
Average depth: 20m (65ft).
Maximum depth: 40m+ (130ft+).
Oval in shape and about 100m (110yd) by 60m (66yd), this compact *thila* makes for an enjoyable and exhilarating dive. The top of the *thila* is shallow, at about 3m (10ft), while the eastern and southern sides plunge vertically down to the atoll floor at 40m (130ft). The *thila* is located in the centre of a channel that faces the ocean and as a result is densely populated with marine life feeding on the plankton-rich waters. The eastern face is undercut by a huge section of caves that run the entire length of the *thila*. Brightly coloured whip corals and huge black coral bushes sway in the currents. On the southern point of the *thila*, there is a huge pinnacle of rock rising from the atoll floor at 40m (130ft) to a depth of 18m (60ft). The channel created between the pinnacle and the *thila* is a favourite haunt for whitetip sharks and eagle rays that like to glide in the currents which funnel through. The reeftop, although shallow, is fascinating and there are many stonefish, scorpionfish and octopus hiding among the corals.

In calm seas the site is good for snorkelling but, if there is a swell, conditions generally become too difficult.

FEATHERSTARS

The echinoderms or spiny-skinned invertebrates include the featherstars. The arms of all featherstars are arranged in multiples of five and they feed by trapping plankton and suspended detritus in tiny filaments on their arms.
During the day many species curl themselves around sea fans or corals, but at night they emerge and crawl to suitable vantage points such as the tops of rocks or corals where they spread their arms and feed on plankton. Be careful not to touch the crinoids as the hooks in the arms can get caught up and are very difficult to remove.

How to Get There

By air: All international flights land at the airport on Hulhule Island in the southern part of North Malé Atoll. Most transfers to South Maalhosmadulu Atoll are made either by helicopter to the helipad on Sonevafushi Island Resort or by seaplane to the lagoon of the resort. The seaplanes are operated by Maldivian Air Taxi (tel 315201/fax 315203) and their Twin Otters can land at most of the tourist resorts. The helicopters are operated by Hummingbird Helicopters (tel 325708/fax 323161). As an indication, flying time by helicopter from the international airport to Sonevafushi Island Resort is 1 hour.

By boat: There are no boat transfers to South Maalhosmadulu Atoll. It is too far from Malé to transfer comfortably by boat.

Where to Stay

Visitors normally stay on registered tourist islands, in other words at a resort. Every resort provides its own dining facilities. There is currently just one resort open in South Maalhosmadulu Atoll, Sonevafushi. However, resorts on the islands of Fonimagoodhoo, Kihaadhufaru, Horubadhoo and Dhunikolhu are under construction.

Sonevafushi Island Resort (Kunfunadhoo)
tel 230304/fax 230374; 60 rooms; 120km (75 miles) from airport
This is one of the most exclusive resorts in the Maldives. It is a large island with beautiful beaches and a spectacular house reef. There is a range of room types including the Rehendi rooms, which are thatched, semi-detached beach cottages each with a king size bed and private beach area. The Crusoe villas are larger

with galleried bedrooms and a downstairs living area. Facilities on the island are simple and include a spa, massage and beauty centre. Watersports available are windsurfing, catamaran sailing and waterskiing. The Soleni Dive Centre offers a small range of PADI courses. The island's house reef is excellent for snorkelling and diving.

Dhunikolhu Island Resort
Due to open in 1999; 100 rooms; 125km (80 miles) from airport
In the southwest part of South Maalhosmadulu, this medium-size island is set inside the atoll and has a beautiful deep-water lagoon on the south side. The beaches on the island are stunning and the centre of the island is densely vegetated with many coconut palms. The house reef can only be reached by boat.

Fonimagoodhoo Island Resort
Due to open in 1999; 100 rooms; 140km (90 miles) from airport
This is a boomerang-shaped island lying inside the northeast part of the atoll. The beaches are beautiful and the centre densely vegetated. There is access to the house reef on the western side and a deep water lagoon on the east side.

Horubadhoo Island Resort
Due to open in 1999; 100 rooms; 120km (75 miles) from airport
With an excellent house reef, easily accessed and within just 20m (65ft) of the shore line, the island of Horubadhoo will make an excellent resort. The beaches are stunning and there are some very good dive sites accessed by boat that are close to the island.

Kihaadhufaru Island Resort
Due to open in 1999; 100 rooms; 130km (80 miles) from airport

This is quite a small island set inside the atoll on the east side. There is a large lagoon on the eastern side of the island and access to the house reef is good on the north and west sides. The centre of the island is densely vegetated.

Diving Emergencies

There is no hospital in South Maalhosmadulu Atoll and guests requiring any kind of medical assistance would need to transfer by speedboat, helicopter or seaplane to the main hospital or private clinic in Malé (AMDC Clinic tel 325979/ADK Medical Centre tel 324332). There are no recompression facilities in the atoll and any diving emergencies are carried by speedboat to the Hyperbaric Centre on Bandos Island Resort (tel 440088/fax 440060) Both these atolls are extremely remote and divers should bear in mind that they are a long way from the recompression facilities.

Excursions

The **uninhabited islands** of South Maalhosmadulu Atoll are particularly beautiful, some of them large, others tiny beaches with just a handful of palm trees. The resorts usually offer a picnic or half-day snorkelling expedition to an uninhabited island. Sonevafushi Resort offers a **cocktail party** on a small sandspit near to the resort – this is a wonderful way to watch the sun going down. In addition, all the atoll's **locally inhabited islands** can be visited by tourists from resort islands. Do remember, as always, to dress modestly. Finally, most resorts offer **fishing** excursions aboard a *dhoani*.

Below: *Most resorts offer excursions to an uninhabited island.*

North Maalhosmadulu (Raa)

North Maalhosmadulu Atoll is 65km (42 miles) long and encompasses the Powell Islands to the north. This is an enormous atoll with 16 locally inhabited fishing islands and a population of more than 12,500. As is the case in many atolls in the Maldives, the majority of the locally inhabited islands in North Maalhosmadulu are located on the eastern side.

The capital island is Ugoofaaru, which has a very big fishing fleet, reputedly the largest in the country. Many of the islands in this atoll have a strong boat-building tradition. The large island of Alifushi to the north has become a centre for

Below: *At night the featherstar climbs up the reef to a prominent position, where it clings to an available surface such as this hermit crab and spreads its arms in the current.*

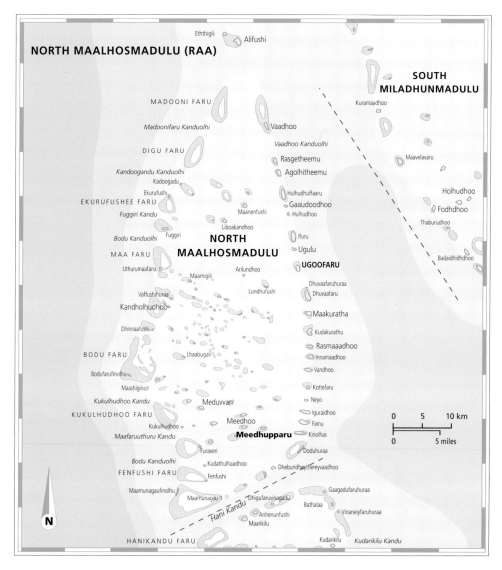

NORTH MAALHOSMADULU (RAA)

Eththigili
Alifushi

SOUTH
MILADHUNMADULU

MADOONI FARU

Kuramaadhoo

Madoonifaru Kanduolhi

Vaadhoo

Vaadhoo Kanduolhi

DIGU FARU

Rasgetheemu

Maavelavaru

Agolhitheemu

Kandoogandu Kanduolhi

Kadoogadu

Hulhudhuffaaru

Holhudhoo

Ekurufushi

Gaaudoodhoo

Fodhdhoo

EKURUFUSHEE FARU

Hulhudhoo

Fuggiri Kandu

Maanenfushi

Thaburudhoo

Liboakandhoo

Bodu Kanduolhi   Fuggiri

NORTH

Ifuru

MAA FARU

MAALHOSMADULU

Ugulu

Badaidhidhdhoo

Uthurumaafaru

Arilundhoo

UGOOFARU

Maamigili

Dhuvaafaruhuraa

Lundhufushi

Dhuvaafaru

Vaffushihuraa

Kandholhudhoo

Maakuratha

Dhinnaafushi

Kudakurathu

Rasmaaadhoo

BODU FARU   Lhaabugali

Innamaadhoo

Bodufarufinolhu

Vandhoo

Maashigiri

Kottefaru

Kukulhudhoo Kandu   Meduvvari

Neyo

KUKULHUDHOO FARU

Iguraidhoo

Kukulhudhoo   Meedhoo

Fainu

Maafaruuthuru Kandu   **Meedhupparu** Kinolhas

Bodu Kanduolhi   Kudathulhaadhoo

Doduhuraa

FENFUSHI FARU

Dheburidhoytherreyvaadhoo

Fenfushi

Maamunagaufinolhu

Gaagadufaruhuraa

Maamunagau   Dhigufaruvinagadu

Bathalaa

Vinaneiyfaruhuraa

Hani Kandu   Anhenunfushi

Maarikilu

N

HANIKANDU FARU

Kudarikilu   Kudarikilu Kandu

0   5   10 km

0   5 miles

teaching the traditional skills of boat building, and may produce several dozen fishing boats a year.

There are 76 uninhabited islands in the region, and one new resort island in the process of being developed. It is likely that more uninhabited islands will be developed as tourist resorts in the near future.

North Maalhosmadulu Atoll has particularly complex reef formations at its centre. There are numerous wide channels on both the western and eastern sides of the atoll, several of which have *thilas* in the middle. In keeping with the nature of South Maalhosmadulu, it is to be expected that many of these *thilas* will provide excellent diving.

NORTH MAALHOSMADULU RESORTS

The first island to be developed for tourism in North Maalhosmadulu is due to open in 1999:

Meedhupparu Island Resort
approx. 215 rooms; 145km (90 miles) from airport
Located well inside the southern part of the atoll, this is a medium-sized island with a house reef.

*Reef life need not be brightly coloured: some nudibranchs (**above left** and **below**) and anemones (**above right**) have more muted colouration.* **Opposite:** *Sweepers school above whip corals and sea fans.*

FAADHIPPOLHU (LHAVIYANI)

Faadhippolhu Atoll has a unique claim – it is the only atoll in the Maldives where a crocodile has been caught! On the west side, the long thin island of Felivaru is home to the country's single tuna-fish canning factory. Here a misplaced crocodile was found feeding on the factory scraps, having been carried over from India or Sri Lanka on the strong ocean currents of the northeast monsoon.

Faadhippolhu Atoll lies 120km (75 miles) from Malé and is just 37km (23 miles) wide and 35km (22 miles) long, with a total population of about 8000. The Felivaru Tuna Fish Canning Factory is an important source of employment and one of the largest contributors to the Maldivian economy. Opened as a joint venture between a Japanese company and the Maldivian Government in the late 1970s, Felivaru now produces about 90,000 tonnes of canned tuna per year and employs some 2000 staff. All the tuna is caught using traditional rod-and-line methods, which has proved a great advantage since Western consumers began demanding dolphin-friendly tuna.

To the northeast of Felivaru is the locally inhabited island of Hinnavaru, with a population of 2500, while to the south is the atoll's capital island, Naifaru, with a population of over 3000. These two islands house the majority of the staff that work in the fish factory. However, because of overcrowding, the government is currently implementing a number of schemes to relocate some of the population. The most significant of these schemes aims to encourage inhabitants of both islands to move to the island of Madivaru, which is already a National Security Service base. There are three more locally inhabited islands elsewhere in Faadhippolhu Atoll: Maafilaafushi and Kurendhoo, on the west side of the atoll, and Olhuvelifushi, in the east.

Faadhippolhu is full of large, densely vegetated uninhabited islands, and unusually all of these are situated on the outer rim of the atoll. In total there are 54 uninhabited islands, four of which have recently been chosen by the government for new resort development. These are the islands of Kanuhuraa, Komandhoo, Madhiriguraidhoo and Hudhufushi. As demand from tourism increases, it seems likely that some of the other

Opposite: *Wood bleaches in the sun on the beach of Dhidhdhoo uninhabited island.*
Above: *A delicate white soft coral feeds with its polyps extended.*

uninhabited islands in the atoll will be also be chosen for development.

There is one long-established resort in Faadhippolhu Atoll, Kuredu Island Resort, which was opened in the late 1970s. This is the northernmost tourist island in the Maldives and also one of the largest, measuring 1.5km (1 mile) in length; it has beautiful beaches and a huge shallow lagoon on the southern side.

Diving in Faadhippolhu (Lhaviyani) Atoll

Faadhippolhu Atoll has a superb variety of dive sites, from pristine coral reefs to exciting narrow channels; in addition there are the wrecks of Felivaru (Site 11). The fringing reef that runs south from Selhlhifushi around to Aligau is very long, which has an important effect on the flow of water through the atoll. The water in the southeastern part of the atoll flows less freely than the waters of the northern part of the atoll. As a result, there is little destructive wave action and many of the *giris* and patch reefs inside the southern area are in perfect condition. However, without the current flow, this part of the atoll has less in the way of opportunities to see large schools of pelagic fish – for this, you need to explore the reefs and narrow passes on the northeastern and northwestern sides of the atoll. Generally most of the channels in Faadhippolhu Atoll are deeper than those in the southern atolls.

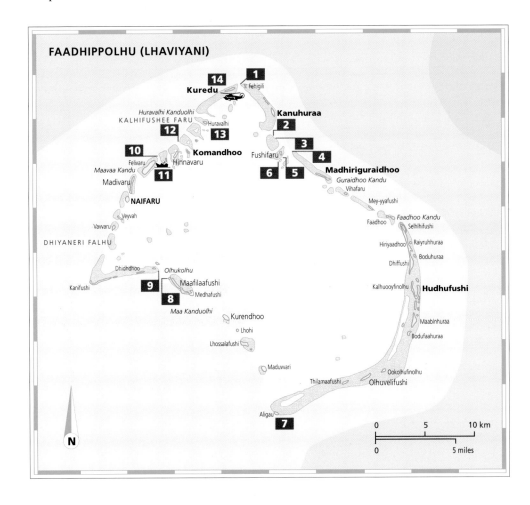

1 FEHIGILI

Location: Eastern side of the Fehigili Channel.
Access: Kuredu (10min).
Conditions: Currents can be very strong, creating a choppy sea at times.
Average visibility: 25m (80ft).
Average depth: 20m (65ft)
Maximum depth: 30m+ (100ft+)
The inside reef of the Fehigili channel drops down in a series of steps until it reaches the ocean dropoff at 40m (130ft). The steps, which team with life, radiate from the corner of the channel like a spiral staircase with each ledge descending in 10m (33ft) increments. Where the steps meet the corner of the reef, there are large caves and overhangs between 15m (50ft) and 30m (100ft) full of *Dendronephthya* soft corals, densely schooling soldierfish, squirrelfish and harlequin sweetlips to name but a few. Divers wishing to venture a little deeper can descend to the atoll plate at 35m (115ft) where there is a huge overhang with its ceiling and walls adorned with blue and yellow soft coral and bright orange *Tubastrea*. Back at the corner on the ocean side, the reef forms a small basin marked by two huge rocks at either end. This basin is packed with schooling fish which appear to be larger and friendlier than usual, making this a fabulous site for photography. This is also a great place for grey sharks, schooling barracuda, trevally, tuna and who knows what else that may come in from the ocean.

2 KANUHURAA KANDU
★★★ ☆☆☆☆☆

Location: South corner of the Kanuhuraa Channel.
Access: Kuredu (35min).
Conditions: Currents can be strong, leading to a choppy sea if there is wind over tide.
Average visibility: 30m (100ft).
Average depth: 20m (65ft).
Maximum depth: 40m (130ft).
The southern corner of this wide, deep channel is an excellent drift dive with good reef and pelagic life. You descend on the outer ocean reef to the corner where the atoll plate meets the ocean dropoff at 35m (115ft). Here there are a number of large caves with bright white sand floors and decorated with yellow soft corals, sea fans and whip corals. For an opportunity to see sharks and other pelagic species you can venture out along the channel dropoff, but should keep the reef within sight, returning to ascend in shallower water. 100m (110yd) from the ocean corner the reef forms a sheer wall from 5m (16ft) to 25m (80ft), with schooling fish and very

good reef and coral life. The reeftop has many *Porites* corals and you should look out for the beautiful regal tang which is common in this atoll.

3 FUSHIFARU INSIDE REEF (TABLE REEF)
★★★★ ☆☆☆☆☆

Location: The south reef of Boamandhipper Kandu.
Access: Kuredu (50min).
Conditions: There can be a strong current across the reeftop which may lead to a choppy sea.
Average visibility: 20m (65ft).
Average depth: 10m (33ft).
Maximum depth: 40m (130ft).
There is no doubt that this is one of the most beautiful table coral reefs in the Maldives. The corals are in pristine condition; some of them are huge, reaching up to 3m (10ft) in diameter. The corals display a fantastic variety of colour and provide shelter for a myriad of fish. The north side of Fushifaru island has a broad fringing reef, with gardens beginning midway along the reef and extending westwards for about 200m (660ft). The start of the best area is marked by a huge *Porites* coral that rises to just below the surface from the shoulder of the reef at 15m (50ft). This big coral outcrop has a great variety of fish life living in and around it, including a large school of glassfish (*Parapriacanthus ransonneti*) and a number of vermilion rock cod (*Cephalopolis miniata*), as well as black-saddled coral trout (*Plectropomus laevis*). On the same section of the reef, just over the dropoff, are caves and overhangs between 15m (50ft) and 35m (115ft).

A superb site for snorkellers.

4 FUSHIFARU KANDU
★★★★

Location: Southern channel of Fushifaru Island.
Access: Kuredu (40min).
Conditions: Currents can be very strong in the channel and a choppy sea can develop.
Average visibility: 30m (100ft).
Average depth: 30m (100ft).
Maximum depth: 40m (130ft).
The channel between Fushifaru and the fringing reef of Guraidhoo Island is a spectacular and challenging dive. The reef of Fushifaru island slopes gently down and extends out 350m (390yd), before meeting the vertical dropoff which spans across the 400m (440yd) wide channel. This channel is best dived when the current is flowing into the atoll from the ocean. Experienced divers should jump into the blue water on

FISH EYE VIEW

Fish have large lenses in their eyes and, rather than changing the shape of the lens as we humans would do, most fish move the entire lens backwards to view objects that are near and forwards to view objects that are far away. Some nocturnal reef fish such as squirrelfish (*Sargocentron tiereoides*) and goggle eyes (*Priacanthus hamrur*) have extremely large eyes so as to maximize the amount of light available. Most fish have their eyes set wide apart: this monocular vision means that each eye sees something different.

the ocean side and make a rapid descent to 35m (115ft), allowing the current to take them into the face of the channel. At the top of the dropoff is a ledge and a set of caves which extend across the mouth of the channel. Grey sharks and eagle rays hunt in the currents that sweep along this vertical wall; huge schools of jackfish circle above and barracuda are frequently seen along with giant yellowfin and dogtooth tuna. Leaving the wall and drifting inside the atoll, the channel quickly shallows to 20m (65ft) and you can either drift over the *thila* that lies in the middle of the channel or make your way to the north or south fringing reefs.

5 FUSHIFARU THILA

★★★★★ ★★★★★

Location: 1km (1/2 mile) east of Fushifaru Island.
Access: Kuredu (40min).
Conditions: Currents can be very strong in the channel and a choppy sea can develop.
Average visibility: 25m (80ft).
Average depth: 12m (40ft).
Maximum depth: 25m (80ft).
This is a stunning site with fabulous coral and fish life. The *thila* is about 250m (275yd) long and 30m (33yd) wide, with the reef sides sloping gently from the reeftop at between 10m (33ft) and 15m (50ft) to the atoll bed at 30m (100ft). The pass to the north of the *thila* is very narrow, and here there is a saddle of sand that rises to 15m (50ft). The easternmost point of the *thila* slopes towards the ocean dropoff. The top of the *thila* is the best part of the dive with excellent hard and soft coral formations. Watch out for the family of napoleon wrasse and the schools of humpback and blue-striped snapper. Along the length of the *thila* are large *Porites* corals where large numbers of cleaner wrasse are found, and mantas can often be seen on the *thila* from May through to November. The natural beauty of this site is remarkable, and as a result it has been designated a Protected Marine Area. As always, you should be very careful of your buoyancy.

6 FUSHIFARU GIRI

★★★ ★★★

Location: 500m (550yd) southwest of Fushifaru uninhabited island.
Access: Kuredu (40min).
Conditions: Protected from swell, but a strong current can lead to choppy surface conditions.
Average visibility: 20m (65ft).
Average depth: 15m (50ft).
Maximum depth: 30m (100ft).
This is a small submerged reef just 200m (220yd) by 100m (110yd), set inside the atoll. The top of the *giri* is at 8m (25ft) and has good coral life and an abundance of reef fish, but the best diving is on the northern side. Here are caves and overhangs dropping down in a series of ledges from 8m (25ft) to 35m (115ft), before the reef plateaus out to the sandy atoll floor alive with garden eels at 30m (100ft). Watch out for regal tangs, turtles and napoleon wrasse. Mantas are often seen in this area of the atoll in both northeast and southwest seasons as they come inside the atoll to feed.

7 ALIGAU

★★★

Location: Southern point of Aligau Island reef.
Access: Live-aboard only.
Conditions: Very exposed. A large swell may be present in either season if winds are strong.
Average visibility: 30m (100ft).
Average depth: 30m (100ft).
Maximum depth: 40m+ (130ft+)
Aligau is the southernmost point of Faadhippolhu Atoll. Here the reef drops steeply to 600m (2000ft) and beyond, and is completely open to the ocean currents traversing the Karshidhoo Bodu Channel. The dive can be thrilling, with sightings of large pelagic species such as silvertip sharks, huge tuna and giant trevally. As may be expected at such an exposed site, the reef is healthy with a good variety of hard corals, but not pretty. The reeftop is at 8m (25ft) and shelves quickly to 35m (115ft) before becoming a vertical wall that disappears to the depths below. On the southwest point at the top of the dropoff at 35m (115ft) there is a large coral outcrop, and a fault in the reef where you will find an array of fish life.

Opposite: *The vermilion rock cod is usually quite reclusive and may be found lurking between corals.*

8 OLHUKOLHU FARU
★★★ ☆☆☆

Location: Eastern side of Olhukolhu Kandu.
Access: Live-aboard only.
Conditions: Usually calm; although a swell can be present during strong winds in the southwest season.
Average visibility: 20m (65ft).
Average depth: 10m (33ft).
Maximum depth: 40m (130ft).
During the northeast season, when the currents flow predominantly out of the atoll to the west, it is very common to see manta rays feeding at this site. The Olhukolhu Channel is narrow and shallow with its reeftop at 10m (33ft) and its side dropping steeply into the ocean. The best coral and fish life are seen on the top and shoulder of the reef, and divers should particularly look out for leaf fish camouflaged on the reef.

This is an excellent site for snorkellers, particularly when the mantas are feeding. In fact, divers may be better off leaving scuba tanks behind if they want to have the best opportunity to get close to the mantas.

9 DHIDHDHOO FARU
★★★ ☆☆☆

Location: South side of Dhidhdhoo Island reef.
Access: Live-aboard only.
Conditions: Sheltered in the northeast season; can be a large swell in the southwest season if winds are strong.
Average visibility: 20m (65ft).
Average depth: 15m (50ft).
Maximum depth: 30m (100ft).
This is a broad reef that extends out from the island for 300m (330yd) before shelving off steeply to a sandy plateau at 35m (115ft). The best part of the dive is the top and shoulder of the reef at a depth of 15m (50ft). On the reeftop there are lots of massive corals, the largest of which are about 6m (20ft) in diameter, all crowded with life seeking refuge. Nurse sharks are often found sleeping wedged beneath a coral head. The reef appears frantic with fish life; schools of dark-banded fusiliers swim in lines, daisy parrotfish (*Scarus sordidus*) graze the reef and huge harlequin sweetlips lurk under coral ledges. This is a very good site for night diving.

Fishing remains the backbone of Maldivian society. Although tourism has had a dramatic effect on the economy, most Maldivians still live a life of subsistence based on the sea.

The fishing techniques used in the Maldives are remarkably unsophisticated and have not changed for hundreds of years. Trolling, bait fishing and pole-and-line fishing are the main methods in use, although recently there has been a dramatic increase in long-line shark fishing and live grouper fishing.

Bait fishing and pole-and-line fishing are the most interesting methods. Bait fishing is carried out early in the morning, with the aim of stocking up on bait for later pole-and-line fishing. The fish are caught by snorkellers chasing them into small nets, and may be any one of a number of species, though most often the slender sweeper (*Parapriacanthus ransonneti*). The baitfish are generally found on shallow reefs and once caught are stored live in the flooded central compartment of the fishermen's boat, or *mas dhoani*, ready for the pole-and-line fishing.

Pole-and-line fishing accounted for a total fish catch of 97,400 tonnes in 1995. Most of the fish caught by this method are either skipjack or yellowfin tuna. The captain of the boat first looks for signs of a shoal of tuna. A giveaway may be a flock of birds flying close to the water or perhaps the bubbling surface where fish are seen feeding. Once a shoal has been located, handfuls of baitfish are thrown into the sea and one or two of the crew splash the water at the side of the boat. The baitfish, feeling vulnerable in the open ocean, immediately swim under the boat for shelter, which helps to bring the tuna fish in close. The fishermen use barbless hooks attached to long bamboo or fibreglass poles and, as the fish bite, they repeatedly swing them on board at great speed.

TUNA

Most of the fish eaten in the Maldives is tuna. Notwithstanding the great quantity and variety of reef fish, tuna is plentiful and has traditionally been the staple diet of the Maldivians.

Tuna is a sleek fusiform fish, torpedo-like in shape and adapted to reach maximum possible speed underwater. While swimming, its dorsal fins are retracted into grooves, the eyes form a smooth surface with the head and the tail is lunate to provide maximum forward thrust. As fast-swimming fish, tuna have a fascinating physiology. They need a large supply of oxygen for which they have developed a sizeable gill area; instead of a pumping mechanism to pass water through the gills, they need to swim constantly with their mouths open. This adaptation has led in turn to the development of a relatively small swim bladder, which means that tuna also need to swim to avoid sinking.

There are 13 species of tuna fish, with five main species found in the Maldives. These are the skipjack tuna (*Katsuwonus pelamis*), called *godhaa* in Dhivehi, yellowfin tuna (*Thunnus albacares*) or *kanneli*, dogtooth tuna (*Gymnosarda unicolor*) or *voshimas*, frigate tuna (*Auxis thazard*) or *raagodi,* and eastern little tuna (*Euthynnus affinis*) or *latti.*

PROCESSING THE CATCH

Their fish caught, the fishermen of Malé Atoll will make a daily journey to the fish market in Malé. Here, the tuna are laid out on the floor and prices are negotiated. Those too far from the capital may either sell their fish to collector boats from the Felivaru Canning Factory, or will return to their home island with the catch, where some of it will be sold to locals and the remainder will be dried.

Methods of drying vary according to the season. In the wet southwest season the fish are usually smoked. This is a job that fishermen's wives usually take on. The fish are cooked in a large pan for a short time and then laid out for smoking inside the kitchen. In the drier northeast season, the fish are laid out on tables to dry in the sun. Once dried the tuna is called *hikki mas* and may be kept for the family's own consumption, or taken to be sold in the dried fish market in Malé.

10 FELIVARU KANDU
★★★

Location: The channel between Felivaru factory island and Gaaerifaru.
Access: Kuredu (60min).
Conditions: Exposed in the southwest season and can be rough if wind is strong.
Average visibility: 30m (100ft).
Average depth: 25m (80ft).
Maximum depth: 30m (100ft).
During the southwest season the currents flow into the atoll from the north through this narrow channel. You can jump in on either the east or the west side of the channel, descending to the point where the atoll floor meets the ocean dropoff at the corner of the reef. From here, it is possible to cross the 200m (220yd) wide channel from one side to the other, staying on the lip of the dropoff which is at 30m (100ft). In the channel you can see squadrons of eagle rays, whitetip and grey reef sharks, tuna and rainbow runners cruising on the currents. On the western corner of the reef there are schooling bannerfish (*Heniochus diphreutes*) in their thousands, as well as a great diversity of other marine life. Only experienced divers should attempt to cross the channel.

11 THE GRAVEYARD
★★★★

Location: 1km (1/2 mile) northeast of Felivaru Island on the Gaaerifaru reef.
Access: Kuredu (60min).
Conditions: Currents can be very strong across the top of the wreck; at times there are overfalls.
Average visibility: 20m (65ft).
Average depth: 16m (52ft).
Maximum depth: 32m (105ft).
Not just one but two wrecks lie in this channel within 60m (66yd) of each other. The larger of the two vessels, the *Skipjack*, can be seen from miles away as its rusting bow stands 6m (20ft) proud of the surface. The ship was once owned by the Felivaru Canning factory, which was intending to scrap it, but while Maldivians were working on board, it caught fire and some days later sank. The *Skipjack* rests vertically against the reef with its stern on the sandy sea floor at 30m (100ft). There are two open holds and it is possible to swim into the holds and up through the bow of the vessel. At 15m (50ft) is a huge submerged gantry: this area of the wreck is very pretty, with a heavy encrustation

---

SOFT CORALS

Among the most beautiful and commonly seen invertebrates on the reefs of the Maldives are soft corals. There are a huge number of species, often brightly coloured and translucent. Soft corals are actually colonies of polyps, differing from hard corals in that they do not have a solid skeleton. Spicules of calcium carbonate are found instead in the fleshy body of the coral.

---

of bright-coloured hard and soft corals. On the foredeck there are swarms of orange butterfly perch (*Anthias squamipinnis*) and hundreds of sergeant major fish (*Abudefduf vaigiensis*) ferociously guarding their territories. Friendly schools of batfish (*Platax tiera*) swim from one wreck to the other, while map pufferfish (*Arothron mappa*) bumble along the reef.

The second wreck, the *Gaafaru*, is 60m (66yd) to the southeast of the first and lies on its port side on sand at 30m (100ft). The vessel is intact and you can explore the wheelhouse and some of the holds.

As with all wreck diving, be very careful when entering the wrecks. Very strong currents run over both these wrecks but particular care should be taken when swimming underneath the hull of the *Skipjack*, as divers can sometimes be washed through the gap between the hull and the reef. Although there is no immediate danger if this happens, it can be very unnerving.

12 HINNAVARU KANDU
★★★

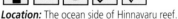

Location: The ocean side of Hinnavaru reef.
Access: Kuredu (50min).
Conditions: Exposed in southwest to northerly winds but sheltered in the northeast season.
Average visibility: 30m (100ft).
Average depth: 25m (80ft).
Maximum depth: 30m+ (100ft+).
Hinnavaru is a heavily populated island which houses the workforce of Felivaru Canning Factory. The dive site is the northeast corner of the island's reef where it meets Hinnavaru Kandu. All along this section of the atoll, the outer reef plummets to depths of about 850m (2800ft), and the narrow channels where oceanic water funnels into the atoll provide tremendously exciting diving. You jump in on the northeast corner of the reef and descend down to the point where the atoll plate meets the dropoff at 30m (100ft). For the best viewing, swim out for about 50m (55yd) into the middle of the channel along the lip of the dropoff. Here you can see grey reef sharks, plus

Above: *Friendly batfish swim beside the wreck of the* Skipjack *(Site 11).*

large schools of jackfish and rainbow runners cruising the rim of the atoll. The channel is too wide to cross, so you should retrace your steps and return to the reef corner before ascending to shallow water. Inside the channel, the reef is very broken so it is best to stay on the outer section.

TITAN TRIGGERFISH

When nesting, titan triggerfish (*Balistoides viridescens*) can be extremely aggressive, often chasing divers up to the surface if they approach a nest too closely. These large fish may grow up to 75cm (30in) in length and feed on a variety of invertebrates including sea urchins and molluscs. They generally lay their eggs in a shallow crater which they then cover with small pieces of dead coral. Triggerfish possess large teeth and they can inflict a very painful bite, so take care not to go too near a nest.

---

13 NARCOLA GIRI
★★★ ★★★★

Location: 1.5km (1 mile) south of Huravalhi uninhabited island.
Access: Kuredu (35min).
Conditions: Usually good, but there can be a choppy sea at times.
Average visibility: 20m (65ft).
Average depth: 15m (50ft).
Maximum depth: 30m (100ft).

The northern side of this long, narrow reef, 100m (110yd) by 30m (33yd), offers the best diving. At the western end of the *giri*, one-third of the way along the reef, a deep crevice in the coral harbours a mass of reef life; next to it is a large coral outcrop. All around the *giri*, the reef wall slopes steeply and there are several caves and overhangs on the eastern point. Variegated sharks (*Stegostoma fasciatum*) are sometimes to be seen resting on the sand slope at 30m (100ft), and here also a field of garden eels waves in the current.

The reeftop, which is at 3m (10ft), is very healthy with plenty of good coral life; there is plenty to see here for snorkellers.

14 KUREDU OCEAN REEF
★★★ ★★★

Location: The north reef of Kuredu Resort Island, 150m (165yd) from the beach.
Access: Kuredu Resort Island (15min).
Conditions: Usually calm, but can be rough in strong northeasterlies.
Average visibility: 30m (100ft).
Average depth: 20m (65ft).
Maximum depth: 40m (130ft).

This northwest reef faces the deep Baraveli Kandu, which separates Faadhippolhu Atoll from South Miladhunmadulu Atoll. The reef drops steeply down to 40m (130ft), where the gradient changes to become a sandy slope. The reeftop, at 5m (15ft), is principally populated with massive corals. The reef wall is washed by oceanic waters and is home to many, many species of reef fish. There are some excellent shallow caves and overhangs along the length of this 10km (6 mile) reef. Divers should always stay alert in the blue water as they may be rewarded with sightings of unusual pelagic species.

This is a very good drift dive, and also excellent for snorkelling.

HOW TO GET THERE

By air: All international flights land at the airport on Hulhule Island in the southern part of North Malé Atoll. Most transfers to Faadhippolhu Atoll are made by air, either by helicopter to the helipad on Kuredu Island Resort or by seaplane to the lagoon of the destination resort. The seaplanes are operated by Maldivian Air Taxi (tel 315201/fax 315203). The helicopters are operated by Hummingbird Helicopters (tel 325708/fax 323161). As an indication, flying time by helicopter from the international airport to Kuredu Island Resort is 1 hour.

By boat: Kuredu Island has a speedboat operating reasonably regular transfers to the resort, depending on guest arrivals. This transfer takes at least 4 hours and can be rough at times, so make sure you take some seasickness tablets if you think you might need them.

WHERE TO STAY

Visitors normally stay on registered tourist islands, in other words at a resort. Every resort provides its own dining facilities. There is currently just one open resort in Faadhippolhu Atoll, Kuredu. However, the government has recently announced that a further four islands are to be developed: Hudhufushi, Kanuhuraa, Komandhoo and Madhiriguraidhoo.

Kuredu Island Resort
tel 230337/fax 230332; 300 rooms; 125km (80 miles) from airport
This is one of the largest resort islands in the Maldives, with beautiful beaches and a large, shallow lagoon that is excellent for watersports. Accommodation is in individual, thatched bungalows set around the edge of the island close to the water's edge. The rooms are simply furnished and all have ceiling fan, double or twin bed, open-air bathroom and a terrace. There are two room types: standard rooms with shower and unheated water, and superior rooms with AC, small fridge and hot and cold water. There are four restaurants, two cafés and two bars. Sports facilities include tennis, gym, aerobics, windsurfing and catamaran sailing. The 5-star PADI dive school is run by the Swedish company Prodivers who offer a large range of PADI and CMAS courses including IDC courses. Access to the house reef is limited to the northern side.

Hudhufushi Island Resort
Due to open in 1999; approx. 200 rooms; 100km (62 miles) from airport
Located on the east side of the atoll, Hudhufushi is a large island shaped like a horseshoe. It forms part of a very broad fringing reef and has many tiny uninhabited islands to the south. Access to the house reef is limited.

Kanuhuraa Island Resort
Due to open in 1999; approx. 100 rooms; 120km (75 miles) from airport
In the northeast of the atoll, this is a beautiful island with superb beaches and a large lagoon to the west. The centre of the island is heavily vegetated with coconut trees. Access to the house reef is limited.

Komandhoo Island Resort
Due to open in 1999; approx. 45 rooms; 120km (75 miles) from airport
A long thin island, set 1km (1/2 mile) inside the atoll. There are very beautiful beaches and a small shallow lagoon. Access to the house reef is easy and the reef is excellent for diving and snorkelling.

Madhiriguraidhoo Island Resort
Due to open in 1999; approx. 100 rooms; 110km (70 miles) from airport
Another large, long and narrow island located on the outer rim of the atoll. There is a beautiful lagoon on the western side and stunning beaches all around the island.

DIVING EMERGENCIES

There is no hospital in Faadhippolhu Atoll and guests requiring any kind of medical assistance need to transfer by speedboat, helicopter or seaplane to the main hospital or private clinic in Malé (AMDC Clinic tel 325979/ADK Medical Centre tel 324332). Nor are there recompression facilities in Faadhippolhu Atoll and any diving emergencies are carried by speedboat to the Hyperbaric Centre on Bandos Island Resort (tel 440088/fax 440060). Faadhippolhu Atoll is one of the more remote atolls: divers should bear in mind that they are a long way from the recompression facilities.

EXCURSIONS

There are over 50 **uninhabited islands** in Faadhippolhu Atoll, some of them large and very beautiful, others tiny beaches with just a handful of palm trees. The resorts usually offer a picnic or half-day snorkelling expedition to one of these uninhabited islands. The **fishing islands** of Hinnavaru, Naifaru, Kurendhoo, Maafilaafushi and Olhuvelifushi can be visited by tourists from resort islands. There are souvenir shops on all these, plus small supply shops stocking a limited quantity of fresh and tinned foods. Please remember to dress modestly. Finally, most resorts offer **fishing** excursions aboard a *dhoani*.

Below: *Four uninhabited islands in Faadhippolhu Atoll have been designated as new tourist resorts.*

The Marine Environment

THE NATURE OF CORALS AND REEFS

Tropical reefs are built mainly from corals, primitive animals closely related to sea anemones. Most of the coral types that contribute to reef construction are colonial; that is, numerous individuals, called polyps, come together to create what is essentially a single compound organism. The polyps produce calcareous skeletons; when thousands of millions of them are present in a single colony they form large, stony (in fact, limestone) structures, which build up as reefs.

What happens is that, when corals die, some of the skeleton remains intact, thus adding to the reef. Cracks and holes then fill with sand and the calcareous remains of other reef plants and animals, and gradually the whole becomes consolidated, with new corals growing on the surface of the mass. Thus only the outermost layer of the growing reef is alive.

Corals grow slowly, adding about 1–10cm (0.4–4in) growth in a year, though more in some branching *Acropora*. After a few years they begin to reproduce, releasing tiny forms that float freely among the plankton for days or weeks. Eventually they settle, to continue the growth of the reef. The forms corals create as they grow vary enormously according to the species and to the place on the reef where the colony is growing.

Colonies range in size from a few centimetres in diameter to giants several metres across. Some colonies are many hundreds of years old. Some are branched or bushy, others tree-like; some take the form of plates, tables or delicate leafy fronds, and yet others are encrusting, lobed, rounded or massive.

Microscopic plants called zooxanthellae are of great importance to the growth and health of corals. These are packed in their millions into the living tissues of reef-building corals (and of various other reef animals, such as giant clams). Although reef corals capture planktonic organisms from the water, a significant amount of their food comes directly from the zooxanthellae. It is for this reason that the most prolific coral growths are in the shallow, well lit waters that the zooxanthellae prefer.

Types of Reef

In most regions with plentiful coral communities, the calcareous skeletons of coral polyps have built up to form a variety of different types of reef. The reefs of the Maldives take the form of atolls. There are 26 atolls in total, arranged for the most part in two parallel columns running north–south, with further atolls at the northern and southern ends arranged in a single column. They range in size from approximately 74km (45 miles) by 65km (40 miles) (Huvadhoo Atoll in the south) to 2km (1 mile) in diameter (Thoddoo, north of Ari Atoll).

Atolls are structures of ancient origin, having formed millions of years ago. They are ring-shaped reefs enclosing a shallow lagoon of a depth of between 35m (115ft) and 85m (280ft), while dropping away to deep water on the outside – about 2500m (8250ft) deep on the eastern side of the Maldives chain, and 4000m (13,200ft) on the western side. The atolls began as fringing reefs round a volcanic ridge and, as this base gradually subsided beneath the water level, the top kept growing. Research so far indicates that in the Maldives there is a limestone 'cap' over 2000m (6600ft) thick lying over the submerged volcanic rock.

REEF LIFE
Reef Zones and Habitats

Reefs can be divided into a number of zones reflecting differences in features such as depth, profile, distance from the shore, amount of wave action, and type of seabed. Associated with each zone are characteristic types of marine life.

The Back Reef and Lagoon

The back reef and lagoon fill the area between the shore and the seaward reef. Here the seabed is usually a mixture of sand, coral rubble, limestone slabs and living coral colonies. The water depth varies from a few metres to 50m (165ft) or more, and the size of the lagoon can be anywhere from a few hundred to thousands of square metres. The larger lagoons may be dotted with islands and smaller reefs, each with their own smaller lagoon.

Sites within lagoons are obviously more sheltered than those on the seaward reef, and they are also more affected by sedimentation. On lagoon sites you find many attractive seaweeds. Most of the corals are delicate, branching types. Large sand-dwelling anemones are often found, and in places soft corals and false corals are likely to form mats over the seabed. Especially where there is a current you may encounter extensive beds of sea-grasses, the only flowering plants to occur in the sea. Among the many animal species that make these pastures their home are the longest sea cucumbers you will find anywhere on the reef.

Opposite: *These stunning sea fans are fragile and need to be treated with care and respect.*

Although some typical reef fishes are absent from this environment, there is no shortage of interesting species. On the one hand there are roving predators – snappers, wrasse, triggerfish, emperors and others – on the lookout for worms, crustaceans, gastropods, sea urchins and small fish. Then there are the bottom-dwelling fishes that burrow into the sand until they are completely hidden, emerging only when they need to feed. There are also a number of fish that live in lagoons as juveniles and move to the reef as adults.

Most entertaining to watch, if you spot them, are the small gobies that live in association with pistol shrimps. In this partnership the shrimp is the digger and the goby, stationed at the entrance to the burrow, is the sentry. The small fish remains ever on the alert, ready to retreat hurriedly into the burrow at the first sign of disturbance. The shrimp has very poor eyesight, so it keeps its antennae in close touch with the goby in order to pick up the danger signal and, likewise, retire swiftly to the safety of the burrow.

Faros

The Maldives atolls are unusual because they contain numerous ring-shaped reefs (faros) within the main lagoons. Faros also occur on the atoll rim, in which case they tend to be horseshoe-shaped or elongated. The larger ones have their own lagoon, but smaller ones may be almost filled with sand. The origin and formation of faros is not entirely understood, neither is it known why most are in the north and central atolls rather than in southern ones.

Within the atolls are submerged reefs generally referred to in the Maldives as thilas and giris. A thila is usually situated in the middle of a channel on the atoll rim and rises to within 10m (33ft) of the surface. A giri is a small patch reef that rises almost to the surface.

The Reef Flat

Reef flats are formed as their associated reefs push steadily seaward, leaving behind limestone areas that are eroded and planed almost flat by the action of the sea. The reef flat may be partly exposed at low tide, but at high tide it can provide interesting areas for snorkelling.

The inner part of the reef flat is the area most sheltered from the waves, and here you may find beautiful pools full of corals and small fish. Among the common sights are micro-atolls of the coral genus Porites. They have a distinctive doughnut (toroidal) shape, with a ring of coral surrounding a small, sandy-bottomed pool, which is a result of low water level and hot sun inhibiting the upward growth of the coral. In deeper water, as on the reef rim, the same coral forms huge, rounded colonies.

Toward the outer edge of the reef flat, where wave action is much more significant, surfaces are often encrusted with calcareous red algae, and elsewhere you will usually find a fine mat of filamentous algae that serves as grazing pasture for fish, sea urchins, gastropods, molluscs and other animals. Some fish are permanent inhabitants of the reef-flat area, retreating to pools if necessary at low tide. Others, like parrotfish and surgeonfish, spend a great deal of their time in deeper water, crowding over to the reef flat with the rising tide.

The Seaward Reef Front

Most divers ignore the shoreward zones of the reef and head straight for sites on the reef front, on the basis that here they are most likely to see spectacular features and impressive displays of marine life. Brightly lit, clean, plankton-rich water provides ideal growing conditions for corals, and the colonies they form help create habitats of considerable complexity. There is infinite variety, from shallow gardens of delicate branching corals to walls festooned with soft corals and sea fans.

The top 20m (66ft) or so of the seaward reef is especially full of life. Here small, brilliantly coloured damselfish and butterfly perch swarm around the coral, darting into open water to feed on plankton. Butterflyfish show their dazzling arrays of spots, stripes and intricate patterns as they probe into crevices or pick at coral polyps. Many have elongated snouts especially adapted for this delicate task. By contrast, you can see parrotfish biting and scraping at the coral and leaving characteristic white scars.

Open-water species, such as fusiliers, snappers and sharks, cover quite large areas when feeding, and wrasse often forage far and wide over the reef. But many species are more localized and can be highly territorial, on occasions even being prepared to take on a trespassing diver. Clownfishes (Amphiprion species and Premnas biaculeatus) are among the boldest, dashing out from the safety of the anemone tentacles in which they hide to give chase. In the Maldives the jewel damsel (Plectroglyphidodon lacrymatus) is well known to divers as it will readily nip at any part of your anatomy that strays into its territory.

Fish-watching can give endless pleasure but there is much else to see besides. Any bare spaces created on the reef are soon colonized, and in some places the surface is covered with large organisms that may be tens or even hundreds of years old. These sedentary reef-dwellers primarily rely on, aside from the omnipresent symbiotic algae, water-borne food. Corals and their close relatives – anemones, sea fans and black corals – capture planktonic organisms using their tiny stinging cells. Sea squirts and sponges strain the plankton as seawater passes through specially adapted canals in their body walls. Other organisms have rather different techniques. The Christmas-tree worm, for example, filters out food with the aid of its beautiful, feathery crown of tentacles.

Apart from the fishes and the sedentary organisms there is a huge array of other life forms to observe on the reef. Tiny crabs live among the coral branches and larger ones wedge themselves into nooks and crannies, often emerging to feed at night. Spiny lobsters hide in caverns, coming out to hunt under cover of darkness. Gastropod molluscs are another type of marine creature seldom seen during the day, but they are, in fact, present in very large numbers, especially on the shallower parts of the reef. Many of them are small, but on occasion you might come across one of the larger species, like the giant triton (*Charonia tritonis*).

Some of the most easily spotted of the mobile invertebrates are the echinoderms. The most primitive of these are the featherstars, sporting long, delicate arms in all colours from bright yellow to green, red and black. The best-known of their relatives, the sea urchins, is the black, spiny variety that lives in shallow reef areas and is a potential hazard to anyone walking onto the reef.

Many of the small, brightly coloured starfish that wander over the reef face feed on the surface film of detritus and microorganisms. Others are carnivorous, browsing on sponges and sea mats, and a few feed on living coral polyps. The damage they cause depends on their size, their appetite and, collectively, their population density. Potentially the most damaging of all is the large predator *Acanthaster planci*, the crown-of-thorns starfish.

Whether brilliantly attractive or frankly plain, whether swiftly darting or sessile, all the life forms you find on the reef are part of its finely balanced ecosystem. You are not. You are an intruder, albeit a friendly one. You are under obligation to cause as little disturbance and destruction as possible among these creatures.

MARINE CONSERVATION

Reefs are valuable to local people as fishing grounds and as sources of other important natural products, including shells. But in the past few decades they have come under increasing pressure from human activities. As a result they are, in places, showing signs of wear and tear.

Corals are slow-growing. If damaged or removed they may require years to recover or to be replaced. In the natural course of events, storm-driven waves create havoc from time to time on coral reefs, especially in the typhoon belt. But some human activities are similarly destructive, especially blast-fishing (which fortunately does not occur in the Maldives) and the indiscriminate collection of corals to sell as marine curios.

Overfishing is a further hazard to reef environments and has already led to a perilous decline in populations of target species in some areas. Overfishing can also damage reefs by altering the balance of local ecosystems. For example, decreasing the populations of herbivorous fish can lead to an explosive increase in the algae on which those species feed, so the corals of the reef may suffer by becoming overgrown.

Some areas are being damaged by pollution, especially where reefs occur close to large centres of human population. Corals and other reef creatures are sensitive to dirty, sediment-laden water, and are at risk of being smothered when silt settles on the bottom. Sewage, nutrients from agricultural fertilizers and other organic materials washed into the sea encourage the growth of algae, sometimes to the extent that, again, the corals of the reef suffer by becoming overgrown.

Although, like other visitors to the reef, divers wish simply to enjoy themselves, and although most divers are conscious of conservation issues and take steps to reduce any damage their presence could cause, tourism and development in general have created many problems for the reefs. In the Maldives, mining of coral for use as a building material has damaged a number of reefs. Harbours, jetties and sea walls are on occasion built so close to reefs – sometimes on top of them – that the environment is drastically altered and the populations of reef organisms decline. Boats may damage the corals through inadvertent grounding or careless anchoring. And, once divers enter the water, they may unintentionally cause damage as they move about on the reef.

Growing awareness of environmental issues has given rise to ecotourism. The main underlying principle of this activity is often summarized as 'take nothing but photographs, leave nothing but footprints'. But even footprints can, like any form of touching, cause damage to creatures living in fragile environments, particularly to corals and the species that live among them. A better way to think of ecotourism is in terms of managing tourism and tourists in such a way as to make the industry ecologically sustainable. Tourism brings much-needed employment, and if carefully planned can bring economic and environmental benefits, with profits exceeding those derived from such activities as fishing. For example, in the Maldives the humphead wrasse is protected: it is understood that it is more important to conserve stocks on the reef than to export them for short-term gain.

Although divers, as well as many dive operators and resorts, have been at the forefront in protecting reefs and marine ecosystems, we all need somewhere to eat and sleep. If a small resort is built without a waste-treatment system, the nearby reefs may not be irreparably damaged. But if those same reefs start to attract increasing numbers of divers, and spawn more resorts, strict controls become necessary.

In such discussions of ecotourism we are looking at the larger scale. It is too easy to forget that tourists and divers are not amorphous groups but collections of individuals, with individual responsibilities and capable of making individual decisions. Keeping reefs ecologically sustainable depends as much on each of us as it does on the dive and resort operators. Here are just some of the ways in which you, as a diver, can help preserve the reefs that give you so much:

- Try not to touch living marine organisms with your body or your diving equipment. Be particularly careful to control your fins, since their size and the force of kicking can damage large areas of coral. Don't use deep fin-strokes next to the reef, since the surge of water these cause can disturb delicate organisms.
- Learn the skills of buoyancy control. Too much damage is caused by divers descending too rapidly or crashing into corals while trying to adjust their buoyancy. Make sure you are properly weighted, and learn to achieve neutral buoyancy. If you have not dived for a while, practise somewhere you will not cause damage.
- Avoid kicking up sand. Clouds of sand settling on the reef can smother corals. Snorkellers should be careful not to kick up sand when treading water in shallow reef areas.

- Never stand on corals, however robust they may seem. Living polyps are easily damaged by the slightest touch. Never pose for pictures or stand inside giant basket or barrel sponges.
- If you are out of control and about to collide with the reef, steady yourself with your fingertips on a part of the reef that is already dead or covered in algae. If you need to adjust your diving equipment or mask, try to do so in a sandy area well away from the reef.
- Don't collect or buy shells, corals, starfish or any other marine souvenirs.
- On any excursion, whether with an operator or privately organized, make sure you take your garbage back for proper disposal on land.
- Take great care in underwater caverns and caves. People cause damage when they crowd into caves, so if possible go in when there are no crowds. Do not stay too long: your air bubbles collect in pockets on the roof of the cave, and delicate creatures living there can 'drown' in air.
- If booking a live-aboard dive trip, ask about the company's environmental policy, particularly on the discharge of sewage and anchoring. Do not book boats that cause unnecessary anchor damage, have bad oil leaks, or discharge untreated sewage near reefs or in enclosed lagoons close to shore.
- Do not participate in spearfishing for sport – spearfishing is illegal in the Maldives.
- Do not feed fish. It may seem harmless but it can upset their normal feeding patterns and provoke aggressive behaviour. It can also be unhealthy for them if you give them food that is not part of their normal diet.
- Do not move marine organisms around to photograph or play with them. In particular, do not hitch rides on turtles: it causes them considerable stress.

COMMON REEF FISH AND INVERTEBRATES

Butterflyfish (family Chaetodontidae)
Butterflyfish are among the most colourful of reef inhabitants. They have thin, compressed bodies, usually with a stripe near the eye and often with a dark blotch near the tail. This blotch serves to confuse predators, who mistake it for an eye and attack the wrong end of the fish. Butterflyfish can also swim backward to escape danger. Many species live as mated pairs with clearly defined territories, while others occur in small groups .or school in large numbers.

Chevroned butterflyfish (*Chaetodon trifascialis*)

Cuttlefish (family Sepiidae)
Cuttlefish are relatives of the squid but have an internal shell of 'bone'. They have a remarkable ability to change their body colours, patterns and textures in order to blend in with their background, or make threatening or other displays. They often use a pulsating colour to mesmerise prey. Cuttlefish are common in all habitats but are often missed because of their superb camouflage.

Cuttlefish (*Sepia* sp.)

Damselfish and clownfish (family Pomacentridae)
These fish often farm their own patch of algae, aggressively driving away other herbivores. Found almost everywhere on the reef, they also sometimes form large groups to feed on plankton. Clownfish (*Amphiprion* sp.), which live among the stinging tentacles of sea anemones, are also members of this family.

Maldives anemonefish (*Amphiprion nigripes*)

Goatfish (family Mullidae)
Easily recognized by their chin whiskers – a pair of long barbels which they use to hunt for food – goatfish are often seen moving along sandflats, stirring up small clouds of sand as they feel beneath the surface for prey. They sometimes forage in small groups or large schools. Goatfish are bottom-dwellers, which is the term for fish that feed or lie camouflaged on the ocean floor.

Yellow-saddled goatfish (*Parupeneus cyclostomus*)

Goby (family Gobiidae)
The goby is a bottom-dweller, with the ability to remain stationary and undetected on the sea bed for long periods of time. They have large protruding eyes which are raised above the level of the head and powerful jaws which enable them to snatch prey and dart back to safety. Gobies are among the most successful reef families, with literally hundreds of species. In fact new species of these small, secretive fish are being discovered all the time.

Dawn goby (*Amblyeleotris aurora*)

Hawkfish (family Cirrhitidae)

The pretty hawkfish is territorial and is usually seen resting on the coral waiting for its prey of crustaceans and small fish. There are five species in the Maldives with the most common being the arc-eye hawkfish (*Paracirrhites arcatus*), blackside hawkfish (*Paracirrhites forsteri*) and the long-nosed hawkfish (*Oxycirrhites typus*) that lives in black coral bushes.

Long-nosed hawkfish (*Oxycirrhites typus*)

Moray eel (family Muraenidae)

These ancient species of fish have gained their undeserved reputation for ferocity largely because, as they breathe, they open and close their mouth to reveal their numerous sharp teeth. Although they are generally not aggressive, the larger species can inflict serious and painful wounds. Moray eels hide the rear portion of their bodies in a selected coral crevice and stay in shelter during the day, emerging at night to feed on shrimps, octopus and mussels. They do not have fins or scales.

Yellow-margined moray (*Gymnothorax flavimarginatus*)

Parrotfish (family Scaridae)

So called because of their sharp, parrot-like beaks and bright colours, the parrotfishes are among the most important herbivores on the reef. Many change colour and sex as they grow, the terminal-phase males developing striking coloration by comparison with the drabness of the initial-phase males and females. Many build transparent cocoons of mucus to sleep in at night, the mucus acting as a scent barrier against predators.

Parrotfish (*Scarus* sp.)

Pipefish and seahorse (family Syngathidae)

The long thin pipefish swim with their bodies vertical, which is not very efficient. Like seahorses, which are also poor swimmers, they tend to lurk in seagrass beds away from currents. Seahorses use their tails to wrap themselves around corals and seagrasses to stop themselves being swept away. Their vulnerability has forced them to become masters of disguise, sometimes mimicking a blade of grass or a gorgonian.

Pipefish (*Corythoichthys* sp.)

Pufferfish (family Tetraodontidae)

These small to medium-size omnivores feed on algae, worms, molluscs, and crustaceans. Pufferfish are found all the way down the reef to depths of about 30m (100ft). They are slow-moving, but when threatened they inflate themselves into big, round balls by sucking water into the abdomen, so that it becomes almost impossible for predators to swallow them. Many species, such as the porcupinefish, are prickly and are even more difficult to attack when inflated.

Black-spotted pufferfish (*Arothron nigropunctatus*)

Lionfish (family Scorpaenidae)
These remarkable fish, also known as 'firefish', are commonly found in the Maldives. They inhabit the reef slope and are often seen hunting on coral ledges for small fish and crustaceans. In the same family as scorpionfish and stonefish, lionfish can inflict a very painful sting from their dorsal spines, so divers should be wary of them.

Lionfish (*Pterois miles*)

Snapper (family Lutjanidae)
Snappers are important carnivores on the reef, feeding mostly at night. Many are inshore-dwellers, although the yellowtail snapper is a midwater fish, and the commercially exploited red snapper dwells at all depths. Snappers are becoming much rarer on some reefs because they are long-lived and slow-growing, which means that, once populations are drastically reduced by fishing, they take a long time to replenish their numbers.

Blue-lined snapper (*Lutjanus kasmira*)

Soldierfish and squirrelfish (family Holocentridae)
Both soldierfish and squirrelfish are nocturnal species and are often confused with each other. Squirrelfish are distinguished by a long spine on the gill cover. Soldierfish have a rounder, bulkier body and are more evenly coloured than squirrelfish. The red or reddish-orange coloration and large eyes are common also among other nocturnal fish, such as bigeyes. Dozing in caves or under rocks or corals by day, they emerge by night to feed. They have serrated, spiny scales and sharp, defensive fins.

Long-jawed squirrelfish (*Sargocentron spiniferum*)

Triggerfish (family Balistidae)
Medium-to-large fish with flattened bodies and often striking markings. Most species are distinctinctly coloured and easily recognizable. They have powerful teeth and feed on crustaceans and echinoderms on the mid-reef. When a triggerfish is threatened it squeezes itself into a crevice and erects its first dorsal spine, locking it into place with a second, smaller spine, which stays wedged until the 'trigger' is released.

Clown triggerfish (*Balistoides conspicillum*)

Wrasse (family Labridae)
Wrasse vary enormously in size, from the tiny cleaner wrasse (*Labroides* sp.) to the giant humphead wrasse (*Cheilinus undulatus*), which can reach nearly 2m (6½ft) in length. Wrasse are usually brightly coloured and go through various colour and sex changes as they mature. Their distinctive buck teeth are well adapted to pulling molluscs from rocks or picking off crustaceans. Most live in shallow reef areas, although some are frequently found at greater depths.

Humphead wrasse (*Cheilinus undulatus*)

Underwater Photography

Photography has become one of the most popular underwater pastimes. Being able to capture on film some of the amazing creatures we see underwater is highly rewarding. However, it can also be extremely frustrating, as the real difficulties of underwater photography – backscatter, fish that refuse to stay still, flooded camera housings, and so on – become apparent. You need a lot of perseverance and luck to get really good results, but if you are prepared to persist you will find you have developed a passion that will last for a lifetime of diving.

Shallow-Water Cameras

Several cameras on the market are suitable for snorkelling. Kodak and Fuji both offer cheap, single-use cameras that are waterproof down to about 2m (6ft), and work well enough in clear, sunlit waters. If you object to disposables, Minolta and Canon make slightly more expensive cameras that can be used down to depths of about 5m (16ft).

Submersible Cameras and Housings

You have essentially two main options for serious underwater photography. The first is to lash out on a purpose-built waterproof camera; the second is to buy a waterproof housing for your normal SLR land camera. Each system has its pros and cons.

The submersible camera used by most professionals is the Nikonos, a 35mm non-reflex camera with a TTL (through-the-lens) automatic exposure system and dedicated flashguns. (A popular alternative is the Sea & Sea Motor Marine II.) The specially designed Nikonos lenses give sharper results underwater than any housed lenses, but the lack of reflex focusing makes it difficult to compose pictures, and you can easily cut off part of a subject. They range from 15mm to 80mm in focal length, but must be changed in air. Underwater, the 35mm lens is of real use only with extension tubes or close-up outfits, although it can be used in air. The 28mm lens should be considered the standard.

Other companies supply accessories for the Nikonos: lenses, lens converters, extension tubes and housings to accommodate fisheye and superwide land-camera lenses. Lens converters are convenient because they can be changed underwater. The Motor Marine II makes good use of these, with converters for wide-angle and macro. The Nikonos close-up kit can be changed underwater.

Land cameras can be used underwater in specialist metal or Plexiglas housings. Housings without controls, as used for fully automatic cameras, require fast films to obtain reasonable shutter speeds and lens apertures in

the low ambient light underwater. Housings are available for all top-grade reflex cameras, but there are advantages and disadvantages to each system:

- Metal housings are strong, reliable, work well at depth, and last a long time if properly maintained. They are heavier to carry, but are buoyant in water. Their higher cost is justified if your camera is expensive and deserves the extra protection.
- Plexiglas housings are fragile and need very careful handling in and out of the water. They are available for a wide range of cameras. They are lightweight, which is convenient on land, but in water are often too buoyant, so that you have to attach extra weights to them. Some models compress at depth, so the control rods miss the camera controls . . . but, if you adjust the rods to work at depths, they do not function properly near the surface. However, since most underwater photographs are taken near the surface, in practice this drawback is not usually a serious one.

'O' Rings

Underwater cameras, housings, flashguns and cables have 'O' ring seals. These and their mating surfaces or grooves must be kept scrupulously clean. 'O' rings should be lightly greased with silicone grease in order to prevent flooding; too much grease will attract grit

E6 PUSH/PULL PROCESSING

If you have been on holiday or on a longer trip, there is always a possibility that, unknown to you, your cameras, flashguns or meters may not have been performing correctly. The exposures may be wrong: while colour negative films allow an exposure latitude of four f-stops (black-and-white films even more), colour transparency films are sensitive to within a quarter of an f-stop. Your problems do not end there: the processor himself can suffer from power cuts or machinery failures.

In the light of these considerations, professional photographers never have all their exposed film processed at the same time. Instead, they have it done in small batches.

This way you can review the results of the film processed so far. If all is not right, the processing of an E6 film can be adjusted by a professional laboratory so that, in effect, the exposure is made faster by up to two f-stops or slower by up to one f-stop. Some changes in colour and contrast result, but they are not significant.

Kodachrome films can likewise be adjusted in the processing, although not to the same extent. This can be done by various laboratories in the USA or, in the UK, by the Kodak Professional Laboratory at Wimbledon.

If you suspect a particular film, have a clip test done. This involves the initial few frames being cut off and processed first so that you can have a look at the results.

and hairs. Silicone spray should not be used, as the cooling can crack the 'O' ring.

Removable 'O' rings should be stored off the unit to stop them becoming flat, and the unit should be sealed in a plastic bag to keep out moisture. User-removable 'O' rings on Nikonos cameras and flash-synchronization cables are best replaced every 12 months; non-removable 'O' rings should be serviced every 12–18 months. The 'O' rings on housings usually last the life of the housing.

Lighting

Sunlight can give spectacular effects underwater, especially in silhouette shots. When the sun is at a low angle, or in choppy seas, much of the light fails to penetrate the surface. To get the best of it, photograph for two hours either side of the sun's highest point. Generally you should have the sun behind you and on your subject.

Water acts as a cyan (blue–green) filter, cutting back red, so photographs taken with colour film have a blue–green cast. Different filters can correct this in either cold or tropical waters, but they reduce the already limited amount of light available. The answer is flash, which will put back the colour and increase apparent sharpness.

Modern flashguns have TTL automatic-exposure systems. Underwater, large flashguns give good wide-angle performance up to 1.5m (5ft). Smaller flashguns have a narrower angle and work up to only 1m (40in); diffusers widen the angle of cover, but you lose at least one f-stop in output. Some land flashguns can be housed for underwater use.

Flashguns used on or near the camera make suspended particles in the water light up like white stars in a black sky (backscatter); the closer these are to the camera, the larger they appear. The solution is to keep the flash as far as possible above and to one side of the camera. Two narrow-angle flashguns, one on each side of the camera, often produce a better result than a single wide-angle flashgun. In a multiple-flash set-up the prime flashgun will meter by TTL (if available). Any other flashgun connected will give its pre-programmed output, so should be set low to achieve modelling light.

When you are photographing divers you must remember that the eyes within the mask must be lit. Flashguns with a colour temperature of 4500K give more accurate skin tones and colour.

Fish scales reflect light in different ways depending on the angle of the fish to the camera. Silver fish reflect more light than coloured fish, and black fish almost none at all, so to make sure you get a good result you should bracket exposures. If using an automatic flashgun, do this by altering the film-speed setting. At distances under 1m (40in) most automatic flashguns tend to overexpose, so allow for this. The easiest way to balance flash with available light is to use TTL flash with a camera set on aperture-priority metering. Take a reading of the

FILM AND CAMERA TIPS

• If you have to buy film locally, do so from a top photography outlet or a major hotel, where the turnover of stock will be reasonably swift and where the film will have spent most of its storage life in cool conditions.

• If you keep film refrigerated, give it at least two hours to defrost before putting it in a camera.

• Do not assemble underwater cameras in cool, air-conditioned rooms or cabins. Condensation is likely to form inside them when you take them into the water.

• Normal cameras that have been in an air-conditioned environment will mist up when you take them out into the warm atmosphere. You need to wait at least ten minutes for the condensation to dissipate before you can take clear photographs.

mid-water background that agrees with your chosen flash-synchronization speed, and set the aperture one number higher to give a deeper blue. Set your flash to TTL and it will correctly light your subject.

Once you have learnt the correct exposures for different situations you can begin experimenting aesthetically with manual exposure.

Film

For black-and-white photography, fast 400 ISO film is best. For beginners wishing to use colour, negative print film is best as it has plenty of exposure latitude. (Reversal film is better for reproduction, but requires very accurate exposure.) Kodachrome films are ideal for close work but can give mid-water shots a blue–green water background; although this is accurate, people are conditioned to see a blue sea. Ektachrome and Fujichrome produce blue water backgrounds; 50–100 ISO films present the best compromise between exposure and grain, and pale yellow filters can be used to cut down the blue.

Subjects

What you photograph depends on your personal interests. Macro photography, with extension tubes and fixed frames, is easiest to get right: the lens-to-subject and flash-to-subject distances are fixed, and the effects of silting in the water are minimized. Expose a test film at a variety of exposures with a fixed set-up; the best result tells you the exposure to use in future for this particular setting and film. Some fish are strongly territorial. Surgeonfish, triggerfish and sharks may make mock attacks and you can get strong pictures if you are brave enough to stand your ground. Manta rays are curious and will keep coming back if you react quietly and do not chase them. Angelfish and butterflyfish swim off when you first enter their territory, but if you remain quiet they will usually return and allow you to photograph them.

Diver and wreck photography are the most difficult. Even with apparently clear water and wide-angle lenses there will be backscatter, and you need to use flash if you are going to get a diver's mask lit up.

Underwater night photography introduces you to another world. Many creatures appear only at night, and some fish are more approachable because they are half-asleep. However, focusing quickly in dim light is difficult, and many subjects disappear almost as soon as they are lit up, so you need to preset the controls.

On the Shoot – Tips

- Underwater photography starts before you enter the water. If you have a clear idea of what you wish to photograph, you are likely to get better results. And, remember, you can't change films or prime lenses underwater.
- Autofocus systems that work on contrast (not infrared) are good underwater but only for high-contrast subjects.
- When you are balancing flash with daylight, cameras with faster flash-synchronization speeds – 1/125sec or 1/250sec – give sharper results with fast-moving fish. The lens aperture will be smaller, so you must be accurate in your focusing.
- Masks keep your eyes distant from the viewfinder. Buy the smallest-volume mask you can wear.
- Cameras fitted with optical action finders or eye-piece magnifiers are useful in housings but not so important with autofocus systems.
- Coloured filters can give surrealistic results, as do starburst filters when photographing divers with shiny equipment, lit torches, or flashguns set to slave.
- Entering the water overweight makes it easier to steady yourself. Wearing an adjustable buoyancy lifejacket enables you to maintain neutral buoyancy.
- Remember not to touch coral and do not wear fins over sandy bottoms – they stir up the sand.

- Wear a wetsuit for warmth.
- Refraction through your mask and the camera lens makes objects appear one-third closer and larger than in air. Reflex focusing and visual estimates of distances are unaffected but, if you measure a distance, compensate by reducing the resultant figure by one-third when setting the lens focus.
- When there is a flat port (window) in front of the lens, the focal length is increased and the image sharpness decreased due to differential refraction. Most pronounced with wide-angle lenses, this should be compensated for using a convex dome port. Dome ports need lenses that can focus on a virtual image at about 30cm (12in), so you may have to fit supplementary +1 or +2 dioptre lenses.

A problem for travelling photographers and videographers is battery charging. Most towns have stockists for AA and D cell batteries, though they may be old or have been badly stored – if the weight does not preclude this, it is best to carry your own spares. Despite their memory problems, rechargeable nickel–cadmium batteries have advantages in cold weather, recharge flashguns much more quickly and, even if flooded, can usually be used again. Make sure you carry spares and that your chargers are of the appropriate voltage for your destination. Quick chargers are useful so long as the electric current available is strong enough. Most video cameras and many flashguns have dedicated battery packs, so carry at least one spare and keep it charged.

Video

Underwater video photography is easier. Macro subjects require extra lighting but other shots can be taken using available light with, if necessary, electronic improvement afterwards. Backscatter is much less of a problem. You can play the results back on site and, if unhappy, have another try – or, at the very least, use the tape again somewhere else.

Health and Safety for Divers

The information on first aid and safety in this part of the book is intended as a guide only. It is based on currently accepted health and safety guidelines, but it is merely a summary and is no substitute for a comprehensive manual on the subject – or, even better, for first aid training. We strongly advise you to buy a recognized manual on diving safety and medicine before setting off on a diving trip, to read it through during the journey, and to carry it with you to refer to during the trip. It would also be sensible to take a short course in first aid.

We urge anyone in need of advice on emergency treatment to see a doctor as soon as possible.

WHAT TO DO IN AN EMERGENCY
- Divers who have suffered any injury or symptom of an injury, no matter how minor, related to diving, should consult a doctor, preferably a specialist in diving medicine, as soon as possible after the symptom or injury occurs.
- No matter how confident you are in making a diagnosis, remember that you are an amateur diver and an unqualified medical practitioner.
- If you are the victim of a diving injury do not let fear of ridicule prevent you from revealing your symptoms. Apparently minor symptoms can mask or even develop into a life-threatening illness. It is better to be honest with yourself and live to dive another day.
- Always err on the conservative side when treating an illness or an injury. If you find that the condition is only minor you – and the doctor – will both be relieved.

FIRST AID
The basic principles of first aid are to:
- do no harm
- sustain life
- prevent deterioration
- promote recovery.

If you have to treat an ill or injured person:
- First try to secure the safety of yourself and the ill or injured person by getting the two of you out of the threatening environment: the water.
- Think before you act: do not do anything that will further endanger either of you.
- Then follow a simple sequence of patient assessment and management:
  1 Assess whether you are dealing with a life-threatening condition.
  2 If so try to define which one.
  3 Then try to manage the condition.

Assessing the ABCs:
Learn the basic checks – the ABCs:
A: for AIRWAY (with care of the neck)
B : for BREATHING
C: for CIRCULATION
D: for DECREASED level of consciousness
E: for EXPOSURE (a patient must be exposed enough for a proper examination to be made).

- **Airway (with attention to the neck):** check whether the patient has a neck injury. Are the mouth and nose free from obstruction? Noisy breathing is a sign of airway obstruction.

- **Breathing:** look at the chest to see if it is rising and falling. Listen for air movement at the nose and mouth. Feel for the movement of air against your cheek.

- **Circulation:** feel for a pulse (the carotid artery) next to the windpipe.

- **Decreased level of consciousness:** does the patient respond in any of the following ways?
  A - Awake, aware, spontaneous speech.
  V - Verbal Stimuli: does he or she answer to 'Wake up?'
  P - Painful Stimuli: does he or she respond to a pinch?
  U - Unresponsive.

- **Exposure:** preserve the dignity of the patient as much as you can, but remove clothes as necessary to carry out your treatment.

Now, send for help
If, after your assessment, you think the condition of the patient is serious, you must send or call for help from the nearest emergency services (ambulance, paramedics). Tell whoever you send for help to come back and let you know whether help is on the way.

Recovery position
If the patient is unconscious but breathing normally there is a risk that he or he she may vomit and choke on the vomit. It is therefore critical that the patient be turned on one side with arms outstretched in front of the body. This is called the recovery position and it is illustrated in all first aid manuals.

If you suspect injury to the spine or neck, immobilize the patient in a straight line before you turn him or her on one side.

If the patient is unconscious, does not seem to be breathing, and you cannot feel a pulse, do not try to turn him or her into the recovery position.

If you cannot feel a pulse

If your patient has no pulse you will have to carry out CPR (Cardiopulmonary Resuscitation). This consists of techniques to:
- ventilate the patient's lungs (expired air resuscitation)
- pump the patient's heart (external cardiac compression).

CPR (Cardiopulmonary Resuscitation)

Airway

Open the patient's airway by gently extending the head (head tilt) and lifting the chin with two fingers (chin lift). This lifts the patient's tongue away from the back of the throat and opens the airway. If the patient is unconscious and you think something may be blocking the airway, sweep your finger across the back of the tongue from one side to the other. If you find anything, remove it. Do not try this if the patient is conscious or semi-conscious because he or she may bite your finger or vomit.

Breathing: EAR (Expired Air Resuscitation)

If the patient is not breathing you need to give the 'kiss off life', or expired air resuscitation (EAR) – you breathe into his or her lungs. The 16 per cent of oxygen in the air you expire is enough to keep your patient alive.

1 Pinch the patient's nose to close the nostrils.
2 Place your open mouth fully over the patient's mouth, making as good a seal as possible.
3 Exhale into the patient's mouth hard enough to make the chest rise and fall. Give two long slow breaths.
4 If the patient's chest fails to rise, try adjusting the position of the airway.
5 Check the patient's pulse. If you cannot feel one, follow the instructions under 'Circulation' below. If you can, continue breathing for the patient once every five seconds, checking the pulse after every ten breaths.
- If the patient begins breathing, turn him or her into the recovery position (see page 165).

Circulation

If, after giving expired air resuscitation, you cannot feel a pulse, you should try external cardiac compression:

1 Kneel next to the patient's chest.
2 Measure two finger breadths above the notch where the ribs meet the lower end of the breast bone.
3 Place the heel of your left hand just above your two fingers in the centre of the breast bone.
4 Place the heel of your right hand on your left hand.
5 Straighten your elbows.
6 Place your shoulders perpendicularly above the patient's breast bone.
7 Compress the breast bone 4–5cm (1½–2in) to a rhythm of 'one, two, three . . .'
8 Carry out 15 compressions.

Continue giving cycles of 2 breaths and 15 compressions, checking for a pulse after every 5 cycles. The aim of CPR

is to keep the patient alive until paramedics or a doctor arrive with the necessary equipment.

Check before you dive that you and your buddy are both trained in CPR. If not, get some training – it could mean the difference between life and death for either of you or for someone else.

DIVING DISEASES AND ILLNESSES
Acute decompression illness

Acute decompression illness is any illness arising from the decompression of a diver – in other words, by the diver moving from an area of high ambient pressure to an area of low pressure. There are two types of acute decompression illness:
- decompression sickness ('the bends')
- barotrauma with arterial gas embolism.

It is not important for the diver or first aider to be able to differentiate between the two conditions because both are serious, life-threatening illnesses, and both require the same emergency treatment. The important thing is to be able to recognize acute decompression illness and to initiate emergency treatment. The box on page 167 outlines the signs and symptoms to look out for.

The bends (decompression sickness)

Decompression sickness or 'the bends' occurs when a diver has not been adequately decompressed. Exposure to higher ambient pressure underwater causes nitrogen to dissolve in increasing amounts in the body tissues. If this pressure is released gradually during correct and adequate decompression procedures, the nitrogen escapes naturally into the blood and is exhaled through the lungs. If the release of pressure is too rapid, the nitrogen cannot escape quickly enough and bubbles of nitrogen gas form in the tissues. The symptoms and signs of the disease are related to the tissues in which the bubbles form and it is described by the tissues affected – joint bend, for example.

Symptoms and signs include:
- nausea and vomiting
- dizziness
- malaise
- weakness
- pains in the joints
- paralysis
- numbness
- itching of skin
- incontinence.

Barotrauma with arterial gas embolism

Barotrauma is the damage that occurs when the tissue surrounding a gaseous space is injured following a change in the volume of air in that space. An arterial gas embolism is a gas bubble that moves in a blood vessel; this usually leads to the obstruction of that blood vessel or a vessel further downstream.

Barotrauma can occur in any tissue surrounding a gas-filled space. Common sites and types of barotrauma are:
- ears (middle ear squeeze) → burst ear drum
- sinuses (sinus squeeze) → sinus pain/nose bleeds
- lungs (lung squeeze) → burst lung
- face (mask squeeze) → swollen, bloodshot eyes
- teeth (tooth squeeze) → toothache.

Burst lung is the most serious of these since it can result in arterial gas embolism. It occurs following a rapid ascent during which the diver does not exhale adequately. The rising pressure of expanding air in the lungs bursts the delicate alveoli – air sacs in the lungs – and forces air into the blood vessels that carry blood back to the heart and, ultimately, the brain. In the brain these air bubbles block blood vessels and obstruct the supply of blood and oxygen to the brain. This causes brain damage.

ROUGH AND READY NONSPECIALIST TESTS FOR THE BENDS

If you suspect a diver may be suffering from the bends, carry out these tests. If the results of your checks do not seem normal, the diver may be suffering from the bends and you must take emergency action. Take the appropriate action outlined on page 166 even if you are not sure of your assessment – the bends is a life-threatening illness.

1 Does the diver know:
   who he/she is?
   where he/she is?
   what the time is?
2 Can the diver see and count the number of fingers you hold up? Hold your hand 50cm (20in) in front of the diver's face and ask him/her to follow your hand with his/her eyes as you move it from side to side and up and down. Be sure that both eyes follow in each direction, and look out for any rapid oscillation or jerky movements of the eyeballs.
3 Ask the diver to smile, and check that both sides of the face have the same expression. Run the back of a finger across each side of the diver's forehead, cheeks and chin, and ask whether he/she can feel it.
4 Check that the diver can hear you whisper when his/her eyes are closed.
5 Ask the diver to shrug his/her shoulders. Both should move equally.
6 Ask the diver to swallow. Check that the adam's apple moves up and down.
7 Ask the diver to stick out his/her tongue at the centre of the mouth – deviation to either side indicates a problem.
8 Check the diver has equal muscle strength on both sides of the body. You do this by pulling/pushing each of the diver's arms and legs away from and back toward the body, asking him/her to resist you.
9 Run your finger lightly across the diver's shoulders, down the back, across the chest and abdomen, and along the arms and legs, feeling upper and underside surfaces. Check that the diver can feel your finger moving along each surface.
10 On firm ground (not on a boat) check that the diver can walk in a straight line and, with eyes closed, stand upright with feet together and arms outstretched.

The symptoms and signs of lung barotrauma and arterial gas embolism include:
- shortness of breath
- chest pain
- unconsciousness.

Treatment of acute decompression Illness:
- ABCs and CPR (see pages 165-6) as necessary
- position the patient in the recovery position (see page 165) with no tilt or raising of the legs
- give 100 per cent oxygen by mask or demand valve
- keep the patient warm
- remove to the nearest hospital as soon as possible. The hospital or emergency services will arrange for recompression treatment.

Carbon dioxide or carbon monoxide poisoning
Carbon dioxide poisoning can occur as a result of skip breathing (diver holds breath on SCUBA), heavy exercise on SCUBA or malfunctioning rebreather systems. Carbon monoxide poisoning occurs as a result of: exhaust gases being pumped into cylinders; hookah systems; air intake too close to exhaust fumes.

Symptoms and signs of carbon monoxide poisoning:
- blue colour of the skin
- shortness of breath
- loss of consciousness.

Treatment of carbon monoxide poisoning:
- get the patient to a safe environment
- ABCs and CPR (see pages 165-6) as necessary
- 100 per cent oxygen through a mask or demand valve
- get the patient to hospital.

Head injury
Any head injury should be treated as serious.

Treatment of a head injury:
- the diver must surface and do no more diving until a doctor has been consulted
- disinfect the wound
- if the diver is unconscious, contact the emergency services
- if breathing and/or pulse have stopped, administer CPR (see page 166)
- if the diver is breathing and has a pulse, check for bleeding and other injuries, and treat for shock
- if the wounds permit, put the injured person into the recovery position and, if possible, give 100 per cent oxygen
- keep the patient warm and comfortable and monitor pulse and respiration constantly.

Do **NOT** give fluids to unconscious or semi-conscious divers.

Hyperthermia (raised body temperature)

A rise in body temperature results from a combination of overheating, normally due to exercise, and inadequate fluid intake. A person with hyperthermia will progress through heat exhaustion to heat stroke, with eventual collapse. Heat stroke is an emergency: if the diver is not cooled and rehydrated he or she will die.

Treatment of hyperthermia:
- move the diver as quickly as possible into a cooler place and remove all clothes
- call the emergency services
- sponge the diver's body with a damp cloth and fan him or her manually or with an electric fan.
- if the patient is unconscious, put him or her into the recovery position (see page 165) and monitor the ABCs as necessary
- if the patient is conscious you can give him or her a cold drink.

Hypothermia (low body temperature)

Normal internal body temperature is just under 37°C (98.4°F). If for any reason it falls much below this – usually, in diving, because of inadequate protective clothing – progressively more serious symptoms may follow, and the person will eventually die if the condition is not treated rapidly. A drop of 1C° (2F°) causes shivering and dis- comfort. A 2C° (3F°) drop induces the body's self-heating mechanisms to react: blood flow to the hands and feet is reduced and shivering becomes extreme. A 3C° (5F°) drop results in memory loss, confusion, disorientation, irregular heartbeat and breathing.and eventually death.

Treatment of hypothermia:
- move the diver as quickly as possible into a sheltered and warm place; *or:*
- prevent further heat loss: use an exposure bag; surround the diver with buddies' bodies; cover his or her head and neck with a woolly hat, warm towels or anything else suitable
- if you have managed to get the diver into sheltered warmth, remove wet clothing, dress your patient in warm, dry clothing and wrap him or her in an exposure bag or heat blanket; however, if you are still in the open, the diver is best left in existing garments
- if the diver is conscious and coherent administer a warm shower or bath and a warm, sweet drink
- if the diver is unconscious, check the ABCs (see page 165), call the emergency services, make the patient as warm as possible, and treat for shock (see page 169).

Near-drowning

Near-drowning is a medical condition in which a diver has inhaled some water – water in the lungs interferes with the normal transport of oxygen from the lungs into the bloodstream. A person in a near-drowning condition may be conscious or unconscious.

Near-drowning victims sometimes develop secondary drowning, a condition in which fluid oozing into the lungs causes the diver to drown in internal secretions, so all near-drowning patients must be monitored in a hospital.

Treatment of near-drowning:
- get the diver out of the water and check the ABCs (see page 165); depending on your findings, begin EAR or CPR (see page 166) as appropriate
- if possible, administer oxygen by mask or demand valve
- call the emergency services and get the diver to a hospital for observation, even if he/she appears to have recovered from the experience.

Nitrogen narcosis

Air contains about 80 per cent nitrogen. Breathing the standard diving mixture under compression can lead to symptoms very much like those of drunkenness (nitrogen narcosis is popularly known as 'rapture of the deep'). Some divers experience nitrogen narcosis at depths of 30–40m (100–130ft). Down to a depth of about 60m (200ft) – which is beyond the legal maximum depth for sport-diving in the UK and the USA – the symptoms are not always serious; but below about 80m (260ft) a diver is likely to lose consciousness. Symptoms can occur very suddenly. Nitrogen narcosis is not a serious condition, but a diver suffering from it may do something dangerous.

Treatment of nitrogen narcosis: the only treatment for this condition is to get the diver to ascend immediately to shallower waters.

TRAVELLING MEDICINE

Many doctors decline to issue drugs, particularly antibiotics, to people who want them 'just in case'; but a diving holiday can be ruined by an ear or sinus infection, especially in a remote area or on a live-aboard boat, where the nearest doctor or pharmacy is a long and difficult journey away.

Many travelling divers therefore carry with them medical kits that could lead the uninitiated to think they are hypochondriacs. Nasal sprays, ear drops, antihistamine creams, anti-diarrhoea medicines, antibiotics, sea-sickness remedies . . . Forearmed, such divers can take immediate action as soon as they realize something is wrong. At the very least, this may minimize their loss of diving time.

Always bear in mind that most decongestants and remedies for sea-sickness can make you drowsy and therefore should NEVER be taken before diving.

Shock

Shock is a medical condition and not just the emotional trauma of a frightening experience. Medical shock results from poor blood and oxygen delivery to the tissues. As a result of oxygen and blood deprivation the tissues cannot carry out their functions. There are many causes; the most common is loss of blood.

Treatment for medical shock:

This is directed at restoring blood and oxygen delivery to the tissues:

- check the ABCs (see page 165)
- give 100 per cent oxygen
- control any external bleeding by pressing hard on the wound and/or pressure points (the location of the pressure points is illustrated in first-aid manuals); raise the injured limb or other part of the body
- use a tourniquet only as a last resort and only on the arms and legs
- if the diver is conscious, lay him/her on the back with the legs raised and the head to one side; if unconscious, turn him or her on the left side in the recovery position (see page 165).

MARINE-RELATED AILMENTS

Sunburn, coral cuts, fire-coral stings, swimmers' ear, sea-sickness and bites from various insects are perhaps the most common divers' complaints – but there are more serious marine-related illnesses you should know about.

Cuts and abrasions

Divers should wear appropriate abrasive protection for the undersea environment. Hands, knees, elbows and feet are the areas most commonly affected. The danger with abrasions is that they become infected, so all wounds must be thoroughly washed and rinsed with water and an antiseptic as soon as possible after the injury. Infection may progress to a stage where antibiotics are necessary. If the site of an apparently minor injury becomes inflamed, and the inflammation spreads, consult a doctor immediately – you may need antibiotics to prevent the infection spreading to the bloodstream.

Swimmers' ear

Swimmers' ear is an infection of the external ear canal caused by constantly wet ears. The condition is often a combined fungal and bacterial infection. To prevent it, always dry your ears thoroughly after diving. If you know you are susceptible to the condition, insert alcohol drops after diving. If an infection occurs, the best treatment is to stop diving or swimming for a few days and apply ear drops such as:

- 5 per cent acetic acid in isopropyl alcohol; *or*
- aluminium acetate/acetic acid solution.

FIRST-AID KIT

Your first-aid kit should be waterproof, compartmentalized and sealable, and, as a minimum, should contain the following items:

- a full first-aid manual – the information in this appendix is for general guidance only
- contact numbers for the emergency services
- coins for telephone
- pencil and notebook
- tweezers
- scissors
- 6 large standard sterile dressings
- 1 large Elastoplast/Band-Aid fabric dressing strip
- 2 triangular bandages
- 3 medium-size safety pins
- 1 pack sterile cotton wool
- 2 50mm (2in) crepe bandages
- eyedrops
- antiseptic fluid/cream
- bottle of vinegar
- sachets of rehydration salts
- sea-sickness tablets
- decongestants
- painkillers
- anti-AIDS pack (syringes/needles/drip needle)

Sea or motion sickness

Motion sickness can be an annoying complication on a diving holiday involving boat dives. If you suffer from motion sickness, discuss the problem with a doctor before your holiday – or at least before boarding the boat. But bear in mind that many medicines formulated to prevent travel sickness contain antihistamines, which make you drowsy and will impair your ability to think quickly while you are diving.

Biting insects

Some regions are notorious for biting insects. Take a good insect repellent and some antihistamine cream to relieve the effects.

Sunburn

Be sure to take plenty of precautions against sunburn, which can cause skin cancer. Many people get sunburned on the first day of a holiday and spend a very uncomfortable time afterwards recovering. Pay particular attention to the head, the nose and the backs of the legs. Always use high-protection factor creams, and wear clothes that keep off the sun.

Tropical diseases

Visit the doctor before your trip and make sure you have the appropriate vaccinations for the regions you intend to visit on your trip.

Fish that bite

- **Barracuda** These very rarely bite divers, although they have been known to bite in turbid or murky, shallow water, where sunlight flashing on a knife blade, a camera lens or jewellery has confused the fish into thinking they are attacking their normal prey.

  Treatment: clean the wounds thoroughly and use antiseptic or antibiotic cream. Bad bites will also need antibiotic and anti-tetanus treatment.

- **Moray eels** Probably more divers are bitten by morays than by all other sea creatures added together – usually through putting their hands into holes to collect shells or lobsters, remove anchors, or hide baitfish. Once it bites, a moray often refuses to let go, so you may have to persuade it to by gripping it behind the head and exerting pressure with your finger and thumb until it opens its jaw. You can make the wound worse by tearing your flesh if you pull the fish off.

  Treatment: thorough cleaning and usually stitching. The bites always go septic, so have antibiotics and anti-tetanus available.

- **Sharks** Sharks rarely attack divers, but should always be treated with great respect. Their attacks are usually connected with speared or hooked fish, fish or meat set up as bait, lobsters rattling when picked up, or certain types of vibration, such as that produced by helicopters. The decomposition products of dead fish (even several days old) seem much more attractive to most sharks than fresh blood. The main exception is the great white shark, whose normal prey is the sea lion or seal, and which may mistake a diver for one of these. You are very unlikely to see a great white shark or a tiger shark when diving in the Maldives, but one dangerous species, the silky shark, is sometimes seen. Grey reef sharks can be territorial. They often warn of an attack by arching their backs and pointing their pectoral fins downward. Other sharks often give warning by bumping into you first. If you are frightened, a shark will detect this from the vibrations given off by your body. Calmly back up to the reef or boat and get out of the water.

  Treatment: a person who has been bitten by a shark usually has severe injuries and is suffering from shock (see page 169). If possible, stop any bleeding by applying pressure. The patient will need to be stabilized with blood or plasma transfusions, so call an ambulance or get the diver to hospital. Even minor wounds are likely to become infected, so the diver will need antibiotic and anti-tetanus treatment.

- **Triggerfish** Large triggerfish – usually males guarding eggs in 'nests' – are particularly aggressive and will attack divers who get too close. Their teeth are very strong, and can go through rubber fins and draw blood through a 4mm (⅙in) wet suit.

  Treatment: clean the wound and treat it with antiseptic cream.

Venomous sea creatures

Many venomous sea creatures are bottom-dwellers – they hide among coral or rest on or burrow into sand. If you need to move along the sea bottom, shuffle along, so that you push such creatures out of the way and minimize the risk of stepping directly onto sharp venomous spines, many of which can pierce rubber fins. Antivenins require specialist medical supervision, do not work for all species, and need refrigerated storage, so they are rarely available when they are needed. Most of the venoms are proteins of high molecular weight that break down under heat.

General treatment: tie a broad bandage at a point between the limb and the body and tighten it. Remember to release it every 15 minutes. Immerse the limb in hot water (perhaps the cooling water from an outboard motor if no other supply is available) at 50°C (120°F) for two hours, until the pain stops. Several injections around the wound of local anaesthetic (such as procaine hydrochloride), if available, will ease the pain. Young or weak people may need CPR (see page 166). Remember that venoms may still be active in fish that have been dead for 48 hours.

- **Cone shells** Live cone shells should never be handled without gloves: the animal has a mobile, tubelike organ that shoots a poison dart. This causes numbness at first, followed by local muscular paralysis, which may extend to respiratory paralysis and heart failure.

  Treatment: tie a bandage between the wound and the body, tighten it, and release it every 15 minutes. CPR (see page 166) may be necessary.

- **Crown-of-thorns starfish** This starfish has spines that can pierce gloves and break off under the skin, causing pain and sometimes nausea lasting several days.

  Treatment: the hot-water treatment (30min) helps the pain. Septic wounds require antibotics.

- **Fire coral** Corals of the genus *Millepora* are not true corals but members of the class Hydrozoa – i.e., they are more closely related to the stinging hydroids. Many people react violently from the slightest brush with them – producing blisters sometimes as large as 15cm (6in) across, which can last for as long as several weeks.

  Treatment: bathe the affected part in methylated spirit or vinegar (acetic acid). Local anaesthetic may be required to ease the pain, though antihistamine cream is usually enough.

- **Jellyfish** Most jellyfish sting, but few are dangerous. As a rule, those with the longest tentacles tend to have the most painful stings. Jellyfish are common in inshore waters and they can be difficult to see in murky water. They stick to the skin with their tentacles, causing extreme pain and leaving lasting scars. In extreme cases a victim may stop breathing.

  Treatment: in the event of a sting, the recommended treatment is to pour acetic acid (vinegar) over both animal and wounds and then to remove the animal with forceps or gloves. CPR (see page 166) may be required.

- **Lionfish** These are slow-moving except when swallowing prey. They hang around on reefs and wrecks and have a heavy sting in their beautiful spines.

  Treatment: Clean the wound, bathe it in hot water and follow up with antibiotic and anti-tetanus treatment.

- **Rabbitfish** These have venomous spines in their fins, and should on no account be handled.

  Treatment: use the hot-water treatment.

- **Sea snakes** These have venom ten times more powerful than a cobra's, but are rarely aggressive and their short fangs cannot usually pierce a wetsuit.

  Treatment: apply a broad ligature between the injury and the body, and wash the wound. CPR (see page 166) may be necessary. Antivenins are available but need skilled medical supervision.

- **Sea urchins** The spines of some sea urchins are poisonous and all sea urchin spines can puncture the skin, even through gloves, and break off, leaving painful wounds that often go septic.

  Treatment: for bad cases bathe the affected part of the body in very hot water. This softens the spines, making it easier for the body to reject them. Soothing creams or a magnesium sulphate compress will help reduce the pain, as will the application of the flesh of papaya fruit. Septic wounds need to be treated with antibiotics.

- **Stinging hydroids** Stinging hydroids often go unnoticed on wrecks, old anchor ropes and chains until you put your hand on them, when their nematocysts are fired into your skin. The wounds are not serious but they are very painful, and large blisters can be raised on sensitive skin, which can last for some time.

  Treatment: as for fire coral.

- **Stinging plankton** You cannot see stinging plankton, and so cannot take evasive measures. If there are reports of any in the area, keep as much of your body covered as you can.

  Treatment: as for fire coral.

- **Stingrays** Stingrays vary considerably in size from a few centimetres to several metres across. The sting consists of one or more spines on top of the tail; although these point backward they can sting in any direction. The rays thrash out and sting when they are trodden on or caught. The wounds may be large and severely lacerated.

  Treatment: clean the wound and remove any spines. Bathe or immerse in very hot water and apply a local anaesthetic if one is available; follow up with antibiotics and anti-tetanus.

- **Stonefish** These are the most feared, best camouflaged and most dangerous of the scorpionfish family. The venom is contained in the spines of the dorsal fin, which is raised when the fish is agitated. Wounds generally result in intense pain and swelling.

  Treatment: as for lionfish.

- **Other stinging creatures**
  Venoms can also occur in soft corals, the anemones associated with clownfish and the nudibranchs that feed on stinging hydroids. If you have sensitive skin, do not touch any of them.

Cuts

Underwater cuts and scrapes, especially those caused by coral, barnacles and sharp metal, will usually, if they are not cleaned out and treated quickly, go septic; absorption of the resulting poisons into the body can cause more serious medical conditions.

After every dive, clean and disinfect any wounds, no matter how small. Larger wounds will often refuse to heal unless you stay out of seawater for a couple of days. Surgeonfish have sharp fins on each side of the caudal peduncle; they use these when lashing out at other fish with a sweep of the tail, and they occasionally use them to defend their territory against a trespassing diver. Their 'scalpels' may be covered in toxic mucus, so wounds must be cleaned and treated with antibiotic cream.

As a preventive measure against cuts in general, the golden rule is: do not touch. Be sure to learn good buoyancy control so that you can avoid touching anything unnecessarily – never forget for an instant that every area of the coral you touch will inevitably be killed.

Bibliography

Amin, M, Willetts, D, and Marshall, P:
Spectrum Guide to the Maldives (1993),
Camerapix, Nairobi, Kenya

Anderson, Dr Charles: *Diver's Guide to Sharks of
the Maldives*, Novelty Press, Malé

Anderson, Dr Charles: *Living Reefs of the Maldives*,
Novelty Press, Malé

Anderson, Dr Charles: *Maldives, the Diver's
Paradise*, Novelty Press, Malé

Anderson, Dr C, and Hafiz, A: *Common Reef Fishes
of the Maldives*, Novelty Press, Malé

Battuta, Ibn: *Travels in Asia and Africa 1325–54*
(1983), Routledge & Kegan Paul

Bell, H C P: *The Maldive Islands: Monograph on
the History, Archaeology and Epigraphy* (1940),
Ceylon Government Press, Sri Lanka

Farook, Mohamed: *The Fascinating Maldives*
(1985), Novelty Press, Malé

Heyerdahl, Thor: *The Maldive Mystery* (1986),
George Allen & Unwin, London

Lamberti, Stefania: *Globetrotter Travel Guide to the
Maldives* (1997), New Holland Publishers, London

Lyon, James: *Maldives* (1997), Lonely Planet,
Hawthorn, Australia

Maldives: A Nation of Islands (1983), Department
of Tourism, Malé, Maldives

Malways: Maldives Island Directory, Atoll Editions,
Richmond, Australia

Maniku, Hassan Ahmed: *The Islands of the
Maldives* (1983), Novelty Press, Malé

Wood, Dr Elizabeth: *Corals of the World* (1983),
T F H Publications, Neptune City, USA

Index

accommodation 17, 23, *23*, 45,
    58-59, 72-73, 85, 97, 116-
    117, 127, 139, 153
Addu Atoll 11, 12, 22, 23, 61,
    92, 93-97
airlines 17, 18
airport 17, 20, 35, 36
Akirifushi 45
Akirifushi Caves 40
alchohol 18
Alifu (see Ari Atoll)
Alifushi 140
Aligau 148
Alimathaa Island Resort 85
Anderson, Chas 86
anemone 102, *103, 120*, 124,
    142, 156, 170
anemonefish 56, 102, *103, 120*,
    124, 128, 156, 159
    Clark's 102
    Maldives 48, 102, *103, 159*
Angaga Island Resort 116
Angaga Thila 112
angelfish 50, 71, 162
Aquarium, The 51
Arabs 12
Ari Atoll *8*, 11, 23, 105-127
Ari Beach Resort 116
Ariadhoo Channel 105
Asdu Kandu 49
Asdu Rock 50
Asdu Sun Island 36, 45
Athafaru Thila 108
Athurugau Island Resort 116
atolls 9, 25, 155-156
Avi Island Resort 127

Baa (see South
    Maalhosmadulu Atoll)
Banana Reef 46
bandiyaa jehun 12, 118, 131
Bandos Island Resort 18, 46,
    50, 58
banks 19
bannerfish 78, *105*, 124, 151
Banyan Tree 59
Baros Holiday Resort 58
Baros Thila 49
barotrauma 166-167
barracuda 27, 39, 54, 84, 94,
    95, 96, 108, 126, 136, 138,
    147, 148, 170
Barracuda Giri 56
batfish 39, 48, 66, 68, 122, 138,
    151, *152*
Bathala Island Resort 53, 127
Bathala Thila 122
Bathalaa Kandu 134
bends, the 166-167
betel nut 14

birdlife 14, 15, *15*
Biyadhoo Island Resort 72
bo feng 18
Bodu Banana Reef 57
bodu beru 12, 75
Bodufinolhu 72
Bodufoludhoo 127
Boduhithi Coral Island 45
Boduhithi Thila 39
Bodumohoraa 75
Boli Mulah 88
Bolifushi Island 72
Bolifushi Thila 70
British 12, 93-4
British Loyalty wreck 94, 97
Broken Rock Thila 108
Buddhism 12
Bulhaalohi Reef 113
Bulhaalohi Thila 113
bullseyefish 54
Bushey Outside Reef 96
butterflyfish 71, 156, 159, 162
    chevroned *159*
    painted 71

Canyon, The 64
Chicken Island 51
Christmas-tree worm 44, *44*
clam, giant 32
clownfish (see anemonefish)
Club Med 46, 58
Club Rannalhi 73
Cocoa Faru 66
Cocoa Island 72
Cocoa Thila 68
Colosseum, The 51
conch 32
cone shell 65, 170
conservation 32, 39, 111,
    157-158
consulates 18
Coral Gardens 64
coral trout 50, 138, 147
coral types 47, 155-158
coral-mining 32, 36, 39, 157
cornetfish 112
cowrie 63
crab *109*, 128, 157
    anemone 49
    hermit *140*
credit cards 19
crown-of-thorns 69, 122, 157, 170
currents 26-27, 28, 32
customs 18
cuttlefish 37, 159, *159*

damselfish 156, 159
decompression illness 166-167
Demon Point 95
Devana Kandu 78

Dhaalu (see South Nilandhoo
    Atoll)
Dhangethi 117
Dhangethi Bodu Thila 108
Dharavandhoo *130*
Dharavandhoo Thila 136
Dhekunu Thila 112
Dhidhdhoo 117, *144*
Dhidhdhoo Faru 149
Dhidhdhoofinolhu 116
Dhiffushi 116
Dhiggaru 88
Dhiggiri Island Resort 85
Dhiggiri Kandu 77
Dhiggiri Kuda Kandu 78
Dhigufinolhu Tourist Resort 66, 72
Dhigurah 117
Dhigurah Thila 110
Dhivehi 20
dhoani 20, *21*, 29, 131
Dhonisu Thila 136
Dhunikolhu Island Resort
    132, 139
dive centres 29
diving emergencies 45, 59, 73,
    85, 97, 117, 127, 139, 153,
    165-171
Doldrums 27
dolphin 32, 109
Dravidians 12
drift diving 28
drinking water 18

ear infections 30
eel 32
    garden 48, 51, 118, 121,
        148, 152
    honeycomb moray 51, *64*, 95
    masked moray 70
    moray 40, 54, 57, 66, 70, 78,
        96, 118, 122, 124, 126,
        160, 170
    ribbon 57, 69, *75*
    yellow-margined moray 70, *160*
    zebra moray 121
electricity 22
Ellaidhoo House Reef 124
Ellaidhoo Thila 124
Ellaidhoo Tourist Resort 127
Embudhu Finolhu 72
Embudhu Thila 65
Embudhu Village 72
equipment 30-31, *31*, 111
Eriyadhu Channel 40
Eriyadhu Island Resort 45
Eriyadhu Thila 40
Eydafushi 131, 133

Faadhippolhu Atoll 4, 11, 23, 36,
    132, 145-153, *153*

Faafu (see North Nilandhoo Atoll)
Faimini Bodu Thila 136
Faimini Kuda Thila 136
Fairytale Reef Blue Caves 42
Fairytale Reef Manta Point 44
falhu 26
faro 26, 156
faru 26
Farukolhu Fushi 58
Farukolhu Kandu 77
featherstar 66, 113, 121, 138,
    140, 157
Fehigili 147
Felidhoo 75
Felidhoo Atoll 11, 23, *74*, 75-85
Felidhoo Kandu 79
Felivaru 145, 146
Felivaru Canning Factory 145,
    150, 151
Felivaru Kandu 151
Fenfushi 117
Feridhoo 127
Fesdu Fun Island 127
Fesdu Wreck 126
Fihalhohi Faru 70
Fihalhohi Tourist Resort 63, 72
Filitheyo 101
film processing 162
Finger Point 39
first aid 165-171
Fish Head 124
fishing 13, 59, 61, 75, 150
flatworm 25, 50
flora 14
Fonimagoodhoo Island Resort
    132, 139
Fotteyo 75
Fotteyo East Point 82
Fotteyo Kandu 80
Fotteyo West Channel 80
Friday Mosque 59
frogfish 25, 121, 122
Fulidhoo 75
Full Moon Beach Resort 36, 46, 58
Fun Island Resort 61, 72
Furana Thila 57
Fushi Faru 121
Fushi Kandu 80
Fushifaru Giri 148
Fushifaru Inside Reef 147
Fushifaru Kandu 147
Fushifaru Thila 148
fusilier 40, 47, 56, 65, 70, *81*,
    83, 108, *111*, 124, 125, 156
  dark-banded 63, 79, 149
  yellowfin 50, 138

Gaadhoo 36
Gaafaru 35, 36, 38
Gaafaru Channel 36, 38
Gaafaru Falhu 36
Gaafaru wreck 151
Gan 12, 22, 93
Gangehi Kandu 126
Gangehi Resort 127

Gasfinolhu Island Resort 58
Gayoom, Maumoon Abdul 13
Giraavaru Tourist Resort 58
giri 26, 156
Girifushi Thila 54
glassfish 51, 118, 126, 147
goatfish *34*, 159, *159*
goby 122, 156, 159, *159*
Goidhoo Atoll 131
government 13
Grand Mosque 59
Graveyard, The 151
grouper 32, 40, 50, 66, 70, 82,
    122, 126, 150
grunt 125
Gulda Lamago 95
Gulhi 61, 73
Gulhi Faru 66
Gulhi Kandu 65
Gulhi Shipyard 61
Guraidhoo (Ari Atoll) 116
Guraidhoo (South Malé Atoll) *19*,
    61, 73
Guraidhoo Kandu South 69

Hadhdhunmathee Atoll 22
Hakuraahuraa Island Resort
    88, 89
Halaveli Holiday Village 127
Halaveli Wreck 122
Hamimadhoo 22
Hammerhead Point 119
Hangngaameedhoo Thila 108
Hannas Reef 57
Hans Hass Place 46, 48
Hans Pass 42
Hass, Hans 42
Hathikolhu Kandu East 69
Hathikolhu Kandu West 69
hawkfish 160
  arceye 160
  blackside 160
  long-nosed 48, 67, *160*
  pixy *91*
health and safety 165-171
Helengeli Thila 42
Helengeli Tourist Village 45
helicopter 20, 61
Heyerdahl, Thor 99
Himendhoo 127
Himendhoo Thila 125
Hinduism 99
Hinnavaru 145, 153
Hinnavaru Kandu 151
Hirundhoo House Reef 134
history 12-13
Hithadhoo 93
Holiday Island 116
Horubadhoo Island Resort
    132, 139
Horubadhoo Thila 138
HP Reef 46, 54
Hudhufushi Island Resort
    145, 153
Hudhuveli Beach Resort 58

Hukuruelhi Faru 111
hulhagu 11, 26
Hulhidhoo 75
Hulhule 17, 36
Hummingbird Helicopters 20
Hurasdhoo Reef 113
Huvadhoo Atoll 9, 61
Huvahendhoo 116
hyperthermia 168
hypothermia 168

Ihuru Tourist Resort 46, 58
independent travel 20
Indian Ocean 25
iruvai 11, 27
Islam 12, 13, 99
Islamic Centre 59

jackfish 27, 40, 42, 47, 48, 49,
    65, 70, 78, 80, 82, 84, 108,
    121, 124, 136, 148, 152

Kaadedhdhuvaa 22
Kaafu (see North Malé and
    South Malé atolls)
Kaashidhoo 35, 36, 38
Kaashidhoo East Faru 44
Kaashidhoo West Wall 44
Kadhdhoo 22
Kagi 45
Kakani Thila 135
Kalhuhadhihuraa Faru 114
Kalhuhadhihuraa Thila 114
Kamadhoo 131
Kandholhudhoo House Reef 122
Kandholhudhoo Thila 122
Kandooma Point 68
Kandooma Tourist Resort 72
kandu 26
Kani Corner 54
Kanifinolhu Resort 46, 58
Kanu Huraa Island 59
Kanuhuraa Island Resort
    145, 153
Kanuhuraa Kandu 147
Keyodhoo 75
Keyodhoo Bodu Thila 80
Keyodhoo Kuda Kandu 80
Kihaadhufaru Island Resort
    132, 139
Koattey 95
Kolhuvaariyaafushi 88
Komandhoo Island Resort
    153
Kuda Haa 46, 48
Kuda Huraa Reef Resort 58
Kuda Kandu Beyra 96
Kudahithi Tourist Resort 45
Kudahuvadhoo 99, 101
Kudarah Island Resort 116
Kudarah Thila 110
Kudiboli 75
Kudiboli Thila 84
Kunarvashi Kandu 84
Kunfunadhoo 131, 139

Kunfunadhoo Thila 138
Kuramathi 118, 127
Kuramathi Blue Lagoon 127
Kuramathi Cottage Club 127
Kuramathi Faru 121
Kuramathi Village 127
Kuredu Island Resort 146, 153
Kuredu Ocean Reef 152
Kurendhoo 145, 153
Kurumba Village 11, 46, 59

Laccadives 12
Lady Christina wreck 41
Laguna Beach Resort 72
language 20, 35
Lankanfinolhu 59
Lankanfinolhu Faru 54
leaf fish 25, 47, 48, 49, 57, 70,
  122, 149
learning to dive 30
Lhaviyani (see Faadhippolhu Atoll)
Lhohifushi Island Resort 59
Lhosfushi Kandu 68
lielaa jehun 131
Liffey wreck 101
Lily Beach Resort 8, 116
Lion's Head 46, 48
lionfish 70, 90, 161, 170
live-aboards 12, 17, 20, 22, 28,
  29, 158
lobster 32, 95, 114, 157
Lohifushi 46
Lohifushi Corner 51
Long Reef 50

Maabadhi Faru 50
Maafilaafushi 145, 153
Maafushi 61, 73
Maafushivaru 117
Maafussaru Kandu 83
Maaga Thila 124
Maagiri Caves 57
Maalhos 127
Maalhos Thila 126
Maamigili 117
Maaya Thila 121
Maayafushi Tourist Resort 127
Machchafushi Island Resort
  104, 116
Madhiriguraidhoo Island Resort
  145, 153
Madhu Kandu 78
Madivaru (Ari Atoll) 111, 119
Madivaru (Faadhippolhu Atoll) 145
Madivaru (North Malé Atoll) 45
Madoogali Resort 127
Magoodhoo 99
Mahibadhoo 105, 107, 117
mail 23
Makunudu Island 45
Malabars 12
Maldives Victory wreck 47
Maldivian Air Taxi 20
Malé 12, 13, 17, 19, 20, 34, 35,
  59, 61, 99, 131

Mandhoo 117
Mandhoo Thila 113
Maniyafushi 61
manta (see ray)
Manta Point 54
Mathiveri 127
Marine Protected Area 32, 39,
  46, 48, 54, 57, 65, 78, 110,
  121, 125, 148
Medhu Faru 69
Medhufushi Island Resort 88, 89
medical care 17-18, 165-171
Meedhoo Beyra Miyaru 96
Meedhufushi 101
Meedhupparu Island Resort
  132, 141
Meemu (see Mulaku Atoll)
Meeru Island Resort 46, 59
Meeru Kandu 50
Milaidhoo House Reef 134
Ministry of Fisheries 53
Mirihi Marina Resort 116
Miyaru Kandu 78
money 19
Moofushi Faru 114
Moofushi Island Resort 116
moorish idol 50, 126, 136
moray (see eel)
Moresby Channel 132
Moresby, Robert 12
Mudakan 96
Mulaku Atoll 11, 23, 75, 76,
  88-91
Mulaku Kandu 89
Muli 88
Mulikolhu Faru 96
Mushimasmigili 124

Naifaru 145, 153
Nakatchchafushi Tourist Resort
  45
names 11
Narcola Giri 152
Nassimo Thila 54
National Museum 59
nautilus 96
night diving 23, 112, 121, 128-
  129, 149
Nika Hotel 127
Nilandhoo 99
nitrogen narcosis 168
North Maalhosmadulu 11, 23,
  131, 132, 140-143
North Malé Atoll 11, 18, 22, 23,
  17, 35-59
North Nilandhoo 11, 23, 99-101
nudibranch 25, 47, 50, 61, 96,
  112, 126, 142

Occaboli Thila 56
Ocean Reef Resort 93, 97, 97
octopus 84, 112, 114, 128, 138
Olahali 45
Olahali Blue Caves 40
Old Shark Point 47

Olhukolhu Faru 149
Olhuveli View Hotel 72
Olhuvelifushi 145, 153
Omadhoo 117
Omado Thila 108
Orimas Thila 124

Palm Tree Island 73
Paradise Island Resort 46, 59
Paradise Rock 54
parrotfish 32, 82, 89, 156, 160
  bumphead 51
  daisy 114, 149
pearl oyster 32
people 9, 12-13, 13
perch 151, 156
photography 25, 162
Pineapple Reef 113
pipefish 25, 40, 50, 160
plankton 25, 128
population 12
porcupinefish 160
Portuguese 12
Powell Islands 140
Prisca Head 50
protected marine life 32
pufferfish 32, 160
  black-spotted 160
  map 151
Pyrard, François 131

Raa (see North Maalhosmadulu
  Atoll)
rainbow runner 77, 78, 151, 152
Rakeedhoo 75
Rakeedhoo Kandu East 82
Rakeedhoo Kandu West 82
Ramadan 13
Rangali Hilton 116
Rannalhi 63
Ranveli Beach Resort Island 116
Rasdhoo 118, 127
Rasdhoo Atoll 105, 118
Rasfari 39, 45
ray
  eagle 39, 42, 47, 51, 54, 64,
    65, 66, 69, 70, 77, 78, 80, 84,
    94, 95, 96, 109, 112, 113,
    114, 121, 126, 138, 148, 151
  manta 26, 27, 39, 42, 44, 49,
    51, 52, 52-53, 53, 54, 56, 57,
    66, 68, 70, 76, 83, 84, 94, 95,
    96, 97, 106, 106, 111, 114,
    118, 125, 126, 132, 138, 148,
    149, 162
  stingray 39, 42, 44, 50, 51, 57,
    69, 79, 82, 108, 114, 121,
    122, 128, 170
recompression chamber 18, 50
Reethi Rah Resort 45
resorts 11, 17, 18, 19, 20, 23, 29,
  36, 38, 45, 58-59, 63, 72-73,
  85, 89, 97, 101, 106, 116-117,
  127, 131, 139, 141, 145, 153
Ribudhoo 99

Rihiveli Beach Resort 61, 73
rock cod 68, 136, 147, *148*

scad 32
scorpionfish *37*, 84, *112*,
  138, 161
Seagull wreck 41
seahorse 160
seaplane 20, *21*
seasons 11, 26-27
Seenu (see Addu Atoll)
sergeant major 151
shark 27, 105, 150, 156,
  162, 170
  blacktip 86
  grey reef 25, 26, 39, 40, 42,
    43, 47, 48, 54, 56, 65, 66, 68,
    69, 77, 78, 83, 87, *87*, 94, 96,
    106, 110, 112, 113, 114, 118,
    125, 138, 147, 148, 151
  hammerhead 26, 54, 68, 69,
    70, 77, 82, 87, 119
  nurse 40, 41, 44, 82, 114, 149
  silky 82, 87, 170
  silvertip 39, 82, 148
  tawny nurse 57, 87, 95, 97
  thresher 70
  tiger 75, 87, 170
  variegated 42, 87, 152
  whale 27, 32, 39, 76, 87, 106,
    107, 108, 111, 121, 132
  whitetip 42, 47, 56, 65, 66, 70,
    77, 78, 79, 83, 86, 96, 51,
    108, 109, 110, 112, 114, 118,
    121, 124, 126, 128, 138, 151
shells 32, 158
short eats 59
shrimp 122, 128
  anemone *98*
  banded coral 124
  marbled *91*
Sinhalese 12
skate 32
Skipjack wreck *4*, 151
snapper 40, 56, 70, 80, 83, 110,
  156, 161
  blue-lined 48, 50, 84, 108,
    110, 118, *120*, 125, 128, *161*
  blue-striped 49, 68, 148
  humpback 68, 148
  midnight 65, 70
  red 49, 57, 70, 79, 84
snorkelling *31*, 32
soldierfish 42, 56, 64, *123*, 126,
  128, 147, 161
Sonevafushi Island Resort
  131, 139
South Huvadhoo Atoll 22
South Maalhosmadulu 11, 23,
  131-139
South Malé Atoll 11, 17, *19*, 22,
  23, 35, *60*, 61-73
South Miladhunmadulu 132
South Nilandhoo 11, 23, 99-101
South Thiladhunmathee Atoll 22

souvenirs 32
squirrelfish 50, 64, 113, 128,
  147, 161
  long-jawed *161*
  sabre 136
  tailspot *129*
Sri Lanka 12
Steps, The 51
stonefish 49, 57, 84, 112, 121,
  138, 170
Stonefish Reef 112
Summer Island Resort 45
Sun Island Resort 116
sunburn 169
Sunni Muslims 13
surgeonfish 79, 84, 114, 124,
  156, 162
sweeper *55*, *143*, 150
sweetlips 40, 126
  harlequin 147, 149
  oriental 54, 56, 57, 68, 78,
    113, 136, *137*
  ribbon *93*
symbiosis 102

Table Reef 147
Taj Coral Reef Resort 45
Taj Lagoon Resort 72
tang 71, 147, 148
Tari Village 59
telephone 23
temperature 11, 26
thila 25, 26, 27, 156
Thinadhoo 75
Thinadhoo Faru 79
Thoddoo 9, 118
Thoddoo Atoll 105
Thulaadhoo 131
Thulhaagiri Island Resort 59
Thulusdhoo 35
Thulusdhoo Kandu 51
Thundufushi Island Resort 117
time difference 22
Tinfushi Thila 109
tourism 11-12, 157
training 30
travellers' cheques 19
travelling in the Maldives 17-18,
  20, 45, 58, 72, 85, 97, 116,
  127, 139, 153
trevally 56, 64, 65, 82, 108, 114,
  138, 147, 148
triggerfish 40, 69, 71, 82, 156,
  161, 162, 170
  clown *55*, *161*
  red-toothed 121, 126
  titan 152
triton 32, 69, 157
Trixie's Caves 42
trochus 32
trumpetfish 110, 138
tuna 42, 49, 54, 56, 61, 64, 78,
  80, 83, 94, 95, 108, 118, 121,
  124, 150, 151
  dogtooth 138, 148, 150

tuna (cont.)
  eastern little 150
  frigate 150
  skipjack 150
  yellowfin 148, 150
turtle 32, 40, 54, 57, 64, 77, 78,
  82, 111, 113, 114, 148, 158
  green 78, 95, 97, 121
  hawksbill 48, 66, 50, 78, *79*,
    112, 121, 122, 126
Twin Island 117

Ugoofaaru 140
Ukulhas Thila 118
Utheemu I wreck 101

Vaadhoo Caves 64
Vaadhoo Channel 36, 63
Vaadhoo Diving Paradise 73
Vaagali Thila 70
Vaavu (see Felidhoo Atoll)
Vabbinfaru 46, 59
vaccinations 17
Vakarufalhi Island Resort 117
Vattaru 75
Vattaru Kandu 83
Vattaruhuraa 75
Velassaru 72
Velassaru Faru 70
Velavaru 101
Velidhoo 127
Veligandu Island 127
Veligandu Kandu 118
Veliganduhuraa 73
Veyofushi Bodu Giri 134
video 164
Vilamendhoo Resort 117, *117*
Viligili *34*
Viligili Faru 47
Viligilivaru 116
Vilingilli Corner 51
Villivaru Island Resort 73
visas 18
visibility 26

Wattaru Kandu 48
whale 32
  pilot 27
  sperm 27
wind 26-27
windsurfing *22*
World War II 12, 97
wrasse 156, 161
  cleaner 39, 51, 53, 148, 161
  humphead (see wrasse,
    napoleon)
  napoleon 32, 41, 42, 50, 51, 54,
    56, 69, 70, 77, 82, 95, 109,
    114, 125, 136, 148, 157, *161*
  rockmover 57

Yacht Thila 66
yachts 17, 22

Ziyaaraiyfushi 45